FACING THE RISING SUN

Facing the Rising Sun

*African Americans, Japan, and the
Rise of Afro-Asian Solidarity*

Gerald Horne

NEW YORK UNIVERSITY PRESS

New York

NEW YORK UNIVERSITY PRESS
New York
www.nyupress.org

© 2018 by New York University
All rights reserved

ISBN: 978-1-4798-4859-1

For Library of Congress Cataloging-in-Publication data, please contact the Library of Congress.

New York University Press books are printed on acid-free paper, and their binding materials are chosen for strength and durability. We strive to use environmentally responsible suppliers and materials to the greatest extent possible in publishing our books.

Manufactured in the United States of America

10 9 8 7 6 5 4 3 2 1

Also available as an ebook

CONTENTS

Introduction

The man who would become Malcolm X was dissembling.

He was in Manhattan during World War II and was being interrogated by the authorities about the possibility of being conscripted by the military, a prospect he surely wanted to avoid. He knew that Army intelligence in Harlem was quite sensitive about the possibility of inadvertently drafting pro-Tokyo Negroes. So, he said, "I started noising around that I was frantic to join" the "Japanese Army." Yes, he enthused, "I want to get sent down South. Organize them nigger soldiers, you dig? Steal us some guns, and kill up crackers!" At that point "the psychiatrist's blue pencil dropped and his professional manner fell off in all directions."[1]

His dissembling had to be taken seriously for at least two reasons: in preceding decades, Japan had made aggressive overtures to win over the beleaguered U.S. Negro community and the Japanese military had made startling advances in the Asia-Pacific theater. Moreover, Malcolm Little was hardly singular in his reluctance to join the war-torn military. By late 1943, African Americans accounted for a whopping 35 percent of the nation's delinquent registrants, and between 1941 and 1946, thousands of Black men were imprisoned for not complying with the Selective Service Act.[2]

It may have been asking too much to expect persecuted U.S. Negroes to unquestioningly throw in their lot with the nation that had pulverized them. In short, pro-Tokyo sentiment was perceived as widespread among U.S. Negroes; this perception was propelled by guilty fear that this oppressed group would seize the moment of war for retribution and retaliation. Even the staid NAACP leader Walter White felt constrained to deny the "astounding and disturbing statement" that "actual proof was available to support the fact that the NAACP was receiving considerable subsidy from the Japanese government."[3] If White had been more forthcoming, however, he would have admitted that he had termed Yasuichi Hikida "my very good friend"; this "friend" had attended Columbia University and was widely thought to be one of Tokyo's chief U.S. agents.[4] He lived in Harlem, wrote an unpublished biography of the Negro hero Toussaint L'Ouverture of Haiti, and had one of the finest collections of books on African Americans in private hands.[5]

Walter Karig, who had made the initial inquiry about Tokyo-NAACP ties that White was forced to deny, provided a tepid affirmation: "I have no knowledge that the NAACP is receiving 'substantial' or any other kind of subsidy from the Japanese," he wrote.[6]

Disturbing events in Illinois would have confirmed his most febrile fears. It was on or about 7 December 1941 when Willie "Pretty Stockyard" Cole rushed through the front door of Nelson Sykes's Brass Rail Saloon at 329 East 47th Street in Chicago, yelling frantically, "The colored folks have bombed Pearl Harbor! The colored folks have bombed Pearl Harbor!" In reply an inebriated "Broke" Hunter, standing at the end of the bar, interrupted Willie's screaming with his own, shouting, "I know the white folks are going to give me a steady job now." He was interrupted in turn by "Fat" Clark proclaiming, "Amen. . . . I recall my father tellin' me how much overtime money colored people made during the last big war." The more elevated Dempsey Travis, in assessing these excited responses, calmly declared that "some Blacks experienced a vicarious pleasure from the thought that 'Charlie' was getting his ass kicked by some 'colored' people." He recollected that in South Chicago there was a group "known as 'the Moors' who were actually pro-Japanese"—and they were hardly alone.[7]

The attitude glimpsed by Travis was not unique. In January 1942 a meeting of U.S. Negro leaders voted 36–5, with 15 abstaining, that their community was not 100 percent behind the war against Japan. A 1942 poll found that 18 percent of Black New Yorkers said they would be better off under the Japanese; an additional 31 percent declared that their treatment would be the same; and only 28 percent said it would be worse.[8] An undated U.S. military investigation (that was likely conducted during the height of the Pacific War) found that "between eighty and ninety percent of the American colored population who had any views on the subject, at all, were pro-Japanese."[9]

The young Brooklyn pianist Randy Weston recalled later that after the bombing of Pearl Harbor, "the Americans"—meaning Euro-Americans in the United States—"were so shook up they panicked, and since they needed all the workers they could get for the war effort, for the first time they allowed blacks to work in the defense plants. . . . Before that, all black folks were allowed to do was sweep floors and be servants, they weren't even allowed to drive a truck." Now, however, they could "make some steady money," providing further incentive for African Americans to be thankful to Tokyo. Subsequently, this illustrious keyboardist observed that during the war "my brother-in-law had told me about how the Japanese snipers" in Okinawa "wouldn't mess with the brothers," meaning African Americans like himself.[10]

In Washington, D.C., Elmer Carroll was judged to be a draft dodger after war erupted. Carroll, according to a journalist, said he was a "brother to the Japs and refused to fight against them," despite authorities' efforts to convince him that the "Moslems" (the religious grouping to which he presumably belonged) were a "fighting people and had been so for thousands of years," and thus he should have no hesitation to join the U.S. military.[11] Months later, in Kansas City, a reporter described "a group of turbaned 'Moslems'" who "were jailed" for evading conscription. "All of those arrested gave ages approaching 100, contending this made them immune to draft registration."[12] New Orleans witnessed a "draft evasion riot" in which twenty-one Negroes were arrested. The defendants, said to be members of the International Reassemble of the Church of Freedom League, contended that military service was contrary to their faith. Ethelbert Anself Boraster, age forty, a native of Belize, was depicted as "general messenger" or leader of the group.[13] Numerous Euro-American men were also seeking deferments from military service, all of which was potentially compromising to national security.[14]

* * *

W. E. B. Du Bois, Booker T. Washington, and other Negro leaders may have had conflicts among themselves, but all looked to Tokyo as evidence that modernity was not solely the province of those of European descent and that the very predicates of white supremacy were senseless.[15] However, what was striking about pro-Tokyo sentiment among African Americans was that it cut sharply across class lines: it was prevalent in the intellectual salons of Harlem, the plants of East St. Louis, and the fields of the Missouri boot-heel, stretching south into Arkansas and Mississippi.

Du Bois, the "father of Pan-Africanism," saw the beginning of the end of white supremacy in Japan's defeat of Russia in 1905 since, as he wrote, "The Negro problem in America is but a local phase of a world problem,"[16] and as the world changed, even the staunchest Jim Crow advocate would be compelled to retreat. A few years later, Du Bois argued that "the fight of the Japanese for equal rights is similar to the fight the Negroes are making for their rights."[17]

Booker T. Washington expressed a view shared widely among U.S. Negro leaders when he told a Japanese journalist in 1912,

> Speaking for the masses of my own race in this country I think I am safe in saying that there is no other race outside of America whose fortunes the Negro peoples of this country have followed with greater interest or admiration. . . . In no other part of the world have the Japanese people a larger number of admirers and well-wishers than among the black people of the United States.[18]

Besieged African Americans felt the need to look abroad for succor and support, following the sage advice of Du Bois and Washington alike. On 2 July 1917 gangs of Euro-American men roamed through East St. Louis and systematically beat, shot, hanged, and immolated African Americans.[19] Homes were torched. Some victims were lynched from telephone poles, left to sway in the breeze.[20] However, there was a new dynamic at play not necessarily contemplated by the lynch mobs. Le Roy Bundy, charged with spearheading the defense of the besieged African Americans in this industrial town, later joined Marcus Garvey's organization, quickly becoming "Knight Commander of the Distinguished Order of Ethiopia" and then Garvey's "First Assistant." During the 1917 unrest, Bundy was accused of being "commander" of a well-armed "Negro army."[21] Soon East St. Louis was to become the de facto capital of pro-Tokyo sentiment in the United States, and those with past ties to Garvey served as chief lieutenants.

In short, Tokyo catered to U.S. Negroes, knowing well how Jim Crow had wounded them. Reportedly, it was during the early 1920s that the Foreign Ministry in Tokyo ordered that all captains of oceangoing Japanese passenger ships afford African Americans preference in every way connected with their travel.[22]

The Negro musician Buck Clayton was struck by this preference when he arrived in Japan during the interwar years. The Negroes "were the only ones allowed to disembark. All the white passengers had to remain aboard while the ship was in dock," he marveled, "while we Blacks were allowed to go ashore and have a ball."[23] Of course, even the U.S. authorities knew that in Oregon "Japanese hotels" were sites where "Negroes have been permitted to sleep at the same time being disallowed in white hotels."[24] The Negro journalist Lucius Harper obligingly noted that "the black man" was accorded "equal privileges in many of the cafes and hotels under [Japanese and Japanese American] ownership."[25] Negroes accustomed to Jim Crow penalties, especially and onerously when traveling, were justifiably impressed by this turn of events.

Sensing the direction of political winds, the U.S. military aviation strategist William "Billy" Mitchell wrote in "confidential" terms of the "Pacific Problem." The "policy of the United States and in fact of all the white countries having their shores washed by the waters of the Pacific Ocean, is to keep their soil, their institutions and their manner of living free from the ownership, the domination and the customs of the Orientals." For "eventually in their search for existence the white and yellow races will be brought into armed conflict to determine which shall prevail." Thus, he continued menacingly, "we are faced with a problem much greater than it appears on the surface, that of maintaining not only the political supremacy but also the very existence of the white race." "The rumblings of this coming strife," he concluded, "have ceased to be inaudible whispers but are the loud protests of the Japanese people, the vanguard of the Asiatics, over the exclusion laws, the land laws and their unequal treatment at the hands of our citizens."[26]

Pro-Tokyo sentiment among African Americans represented a severe challenge to U.S. national security as constructed by the likes of Mitchell. As historian John Dower has argued, though Germany is what comes to mind when many in the United States think about racism in World War II, it was Tokyo that "stirred the deepest recesses of white [supremacy] and provoked a response bordering on the apocalyptic."[27]

* * *

The African American dancer T. C. Dunson had achieved a measure of success in Singapore, but was forced to escape when Japanese forces invaded the British colony in 1942. Writing from New Orleans later that year, Dunson recalled that he was playing mah-jong when he heard massive explosions: "[I] thought it was an earthquake," he said, as panic descended on the city. The Japanese military "said they had come to liberate the Asiatics from the 'white devils,'" invoking rhetoric that had become increasingly popular among Black Nationalists, in New Orleans not least. He was agog to see that some of the previously preening European colonizers were so shocked by the "strain" of this abrupt turn of events that they "went insane."

But even this hardly prepared him for what he was to witness next. As he scanned the skies one morning, it seemed as if the heavens were raining men: he saw "bodies of [dead] British soldiers on parachutes. They were nothing but bloody masses of clothes and pulp," tossed from planes by Japanese military men, determined to impress upon one and all in the most shocking fashion that a new order had descended.[28]

Dunson may have known that New Orleans was one of the many centers of pro-Tokyo sentiment among U.S. Negroes. Presumably he described this ghastly sight to his fellow Negroes in New Orleans, serving to undermine further the magic of white supremacy, which ultimately depended upon the notion that the alleged "ruling race" was born to dominate. Beyond the shores of the Crescent City, the ugly sights of Singapore had left an impressive imprint upon Africans.

What was troubling to Washington was that Black Nationalist sentiment could act as a transmission belt propelling pro-Tokyo sentiment more generally, potentially jeopardizing important global alliances. When Marcus Garvey—the Jamaican who came to embody Black Nationalism—died just as world war had descended on Europe, A. J. Maphike, in faraway South Africa, told the left-leaning *Guardian* in Cape Town that this was an "irreparable loss to the African races [*sic*]" and mentioned that his sixteen-year-old son was named after the Jamaican leader.[29] About eighteen months later, when Singapore fell to Japanese invaders, hundreds of Africans met in this same city and, according to the reporter present, were "deluded into believing that the Japanese may bring them freedom from colour bars" and "may even wish for a Japanese victory."[30] Ahmed Kathrada was to become a leader of South African Communists and one of Nelson Mandela's closest comrades. As Japanese troops began their invasion of Singapore, he confessed unashamedly that he "derive[d] great satisfaction from every blow struck by Japanese against the British in Asia."[31]

The Communist leader I. O. Horvitch conceded reluctantly that there was a "fairly widespread . . . belief that Japan will come to South Africa and free the Non-Europeans [sic]."[32] Like their U.S. counterparts, Communists in South Africa strained to undermine the appeal of Japan among those of African descent,[33] suggestive of the magnetic attraction of Tokyo. Understandably, the consensus among the leadership of the racist regime in Pretoria during this fraught time was that their greatest fear was an invasion by Japanese forces accompanied by a hearty welcome from Africans.[34] The shaken South African leader Jan Smuts said that he would consider the theretofore unthinkable—arming Africans—to thwart a Japanese invasion,[35] a monumental decision that potentially could imperil white supremacy, and that was precisely the import of the "threat" from Tokyo.

The threat to white supremacy was felt in the United States as well, as exemplified in the federal charges brought against a supposed front group of Japan. In U.S. v. Pacific Movement of the Eastern World (1943), prosecutors asserted that "at the instigation of the Black Dragon Society of Japan," an organization of Nipponese ultra-patriots, the alleged "front" group had been organized in "chapters or units" in Chicago, East St. Louis, Cleveland, Cincinnati, Pittsburgh, Philadelphia, Phoenix, Detroit, Gary; Shaw and Greenville, Mississippi; Tulsa, Muskogee, and Boynton, Oklahoma, and elsewhere, notably in Dixie. The group had been incorporated as early as 1934, but it was just one of many pro-Tokyo organizations that had sunk roots among U.S. Negroes and were accused of storing weapons in anticipation of a Japanese invasion.[36]

The federal prosecutor recalled a chilling episode from a few years earlier, when "to an alarming extent the colored people [were] accumulating arms and ammunition" in downstate Illinois, not far from Cairo. "The white folks were lined up [on] one side of the road," he recounted, "and the colored folks on the other and they all had high powered rifles." The "darkies in my hometown," he recalled, "picked out the farms they were going to take over when the invasion by Japan occurred." Speaking for the prosecutorial team, H. Grady Vien cautioned, "this is a very secretive matter" that should "not" be "discuss[ed]" with "anyone at all."[37]

Due south, in Grenada, Mississippi, was the headquarters of what was described as a statewide "secret Negro organization formed to 'end white rule over Negro farmers,'" which had led to "the death of two white plantation owners at the hands of Negro sharecroppers." The National Federation of Colored Farmers was blamed, because hundreds of Negroes had attended its convention in Memphis shortly before this bloody episode. It was unclear whether this incident was driven by the rise of pro-Tokyo militancy among Negroes.[38] In October 1942 the FBI office in Memphis stated carefully that there was "no indication of organized sabotage among Negro citizens" and that "Negro leaders were emphatic in their denial of foreign underground activities."[39] Left unsaid was whether there was "sabotage" that was not "organized" or "underground activities" not directly tied to "foreign" sources.

In Evansville, Indiana, not distant from Dixie, a journalist reported that "sinister rumors of race war were circulated throughout the city."[40] In Jackson, Mississippi, there were resonant fears about what one observer termed the "sanctity of white womanhood" when Euro-American men trooped off to war, leaving, it was thought, more Negro men around with unfulfilled fantasies.[41]

In East St. Louis, Illinois, pro-Tokyo Negroes were accused in 1943 of attempting to blow up the Eads Bridge, which connected the city with the larger St. Louis, Missouri. Their "secret password" was said to be "BYB" or "Black, Yellow and Brown" people united against white supremacy. According to one observer, "arrangements would be made for colonization projects," especially to Brazil, which already contained sizeable populations of Japanese and Africans, and "trade treaties" would be forged "between the two races after the Japanese had conquered the United States."[42]

Dixie may have had reason to fret about the proliferation of pro-Tokyo sentiment among Negroes. A presumed "white southern moderate" during the war alleged that "like the natives of Malaya and Burma, . . . American Negroes are sometimes imbued with the notion that a victory for the yellow race over the white race might also be a victory for them." In fact, according to historian John Dower, "in parts of the American South, fears among white people of a Japanese-Negro alliance were apparently fairly commonplace from the 1930s on."[43] The Pacific War involved for the most part an inter-imperialist rivalry, as Japan sought to displace European (and Euro-American) colonial powers in Asia and the Pacific, while Berlin, for the most part, attacked sovereign states. This often forgotten factor undergirded pro-Tokyo sentiment among U.S. Negroes, many of whom saw themselves as colonized too.

Of course, Dixie was not alone in apprehension. As is well known, there were ongoing Japanese efforts during the war to destroy oil installations in Southern California and to ignite forest fires in Oregon. There were plans for Japanese submarines—after Pearl Harbor's devastation—to proceed to the West Coast for similar purposes.[44]

Ironically, Japan's attack on colonialism, along with the racial challenge that it represented, may have inflamed passions even more. Lester Granger of the National Urban League maintained that "we tend to hate the Japanese more than the Nazis"—tellingly ratifying his perception by not referring to "Germans"—"because they are not of our race." That is, it was harder to object to Japan's project of overthrowing colonialism in Asia (as opposed to Germany's project of overturning sovereignty in Europe). It was necessary to direct more anger at Tokyo in order to justify the heavy lift that was war. This was having a paradoxical impact on U.S. Negroes, who often had been conflated with Asians, and some of whom referred to themselves as "Asiatic." Granger sensed that the hysterical racial chauvinism that was mounted against Japanese was creating a simultaneous backlash against Negroes, though there was a contrasting trend that sought to allay bigotry against domestic "minorities" in the United States in the interest of national security. There was a race between these two powerful trends.[45]

The Midwest and the South—and the routes followed by those migrating from the latter to the former—were prime recruiting sites for Negroes inclined to back Japan. Tracing the serpentine course of the Mississippi River from the Gulf heading northward in some ways tracks the violent persecutions inflicted upon Negroes, and sheds light on why so many were ready to throw in their lot with Tokyo. As shall be seen, East St. Louis, Illinois, and Elaine, Arkansas—restive sites of atrocious post–World War I pogroms against Negroes—were also factors helping to explain the growth of pro-Japan movements among African Americans. Mississippi had a well-deserved reputation as a hotbed of racist chauvinism, and as African Americans fled northward, they took their nervous apprehension with them, making them more susceptible to Tokyo's appeals.[46]

It is fair to infer that Negroes looked to Tokyo not least to gain backing in the event of another pogrom. It is also fair to suggest that the Pacific War inscribed another chapter in a long-running story of Negro armed resistance in the United States.[47]

If racist rulers in South Africa and elsewhere had been able to consult with their counterparts in the Philippines, their fears would have been substantiated. Manny Lawson, a proud graduate of Clemson University in Jim Crow South Carolina, was captured by Japanese forces in the Philippines and was subjected to the horrors of the brutal Bataan Death March. As his group of once haughty Euro-Americans marched—defeated—past sullen Filipinos, he wondered about their "sympathy and loyalty. After all," he mused, "we had been overpowered and captured by an enemy generally thought to be inferior. Defeated and humiliated, we had been on display as the inferiors. Had we permanently lost face?"[48] The answer—generally and emphatically—was yes, not just in the Philippines but in countless sites where white supremacy had reigned theretofore.

* * *

This is a book about pro-Tokyo sentiment, particularly among Black Nationalists—for example, the precursor of the Nation of Islam; Marcus Garvey's forces; the Pacific Movement of the Eastern World; the Moorish Science Temple; the Ethiopia Pacific Movement; and those within their orbit (notably the forces that arose in great number during the Italian invasion of Ethiopia in the 1930s, when it seemed that Tokyo would come to the aid of Addis Ababa).[49] Though this book is principally about the response of Black Nationalists, it would be a mistake to view the ideological tendency they have represented as the sole vector of pro-Tokyo sentiment. Instead, they should be viewed as a vanguard force—the leading but not the sole detachment—instead of the exclusive repository of this sentiment. These Black Nationalists were in the forefront. They were the advance guard, the spearhead. They were the trendsetters, the groundbreakers, the opinion molders. However, they were not alone in their fondness for Tokyo. They were able to influence many others.

The fact is, as shall be seen, some of the most fervent pro-Japanese views came from those like the NAACP leader William Pickens, a notorious fan of Tokyo.[50] "Think how these Japanese work!" he enthused to the influential P. L. Prattis of the *Pittsburgh Courier* in 1934. Yasuichi Hikida had come to visit him and "had with him a copy of every editorial I have written on Japan and the Japanese question," all "mounted on paper—evidently from some PERMANENT FILE," he stressed, "perhaps Hikida's own file."[51] Five years later, Pickens was saluting Tokyo's occupation of Manchuria. Using the Japanese name for this territory, he argued that "Manchukuo in near future has a much better chance for practical as well as technical freedom in the near terms, than has Abyssinia," then languishing under Italian rule.[52] Pickens was among those who were not keen on backing another world war in any case; in 1940 he encountered "intelligent" African Americans who purported to be "happy and hopeful 'because those white folk are killing each other off'" in Europe.[53]

Indeed, the ideological tendency in Black America that was most immune to Japan's charms—the Communist Party and those allied with this group—was precisely the tendency that received the most adamant and resolute opposition from U.S. rulers, which in a sense helped to further bolster pro-Tokyo stances. (A similar trend operated in racist South Africa.) This book is only coincidentally about pro-Negro sentiment in Japan. In sum, this is a book about trans-Pacific racism—not "racisms."[54] That is, this book only incidentally concerns the pre-1945 chauvinism that was so prevalent among the Japanese ruling elite.

This is a book about the acceleration of "Afro-Asian solidarity," a tendency that preceded the rise of Japan,[55] but assuredly this trend attained warp speed in the decades leading up to the final surrender on the battleship *Missouri* in 1945. This book is also part of a larger argument that I have made over the years, that because slavery and Jim Crow—and the malignant attitudes both embodied—were so deeply entrenched in U.S. society, it required external forces, global currents, to alter profoundly this tragic state of affairs.[56]

This is a book about the roots of "Afro-Asian solidarity," which manifested most dramatically when anti–Jim Crow forces in Dixie creatively adapted the doctrine of "passive resistance" honed in India.[57] However, the taproot and flowering of this capacious phenomenon can be traced to the tie between Black Nationalists and Tokyo during the interwar years—or, perhaps, even back to the eighteenth century, when settlers in North America feared that Japan, then in self-imposed isolation, was mustering thousands of hard-bitten troops to invade this continent in solidarity with Native Americans.[58]

* * *

The conflation of Negroes and Japanese was aided by the subordination of the latter, notably along the Pacific Coast, in the years leading up to 1941 and the fact that both groups were barred from the hallowed halls of "whiteness." This conflation could also be found in the popular genre of science fiction.[59] The revulsion by Euro-Americans toward Japan was so pervasive that even the "Yellow Peril" character Dr. Fu Manchu, though ostensibly from China—a nation with which Tokyo had warred repeatedly—was often interpreted in the United States as being Japanese.[60]

It remains unclear how many people were enrolled in the PMEW, the Allah Temple of Islam (which became the Nation of Islam, one of the sturdier Black Nationalist formations), and the other pro-Tokyo groups.[61] However, it is fair to suggest (as shall be seen) that they were more popular among U.S. Negroes than their primary ideological competition—those enrolled in the Communist Party.[62]

For example, in December 1942 FBI director J. Edgar Hoover estimated that in Detroit alone "the combined membership at the peak of these movements," referring to the Pacific Movement of the Eastern World (PMEW), the Moorish Science Temple (MST), the Eastern Pacific Movement, the organization of the late Marcus Garvey, and others, "was around 15,000." They were, it was said, "actively engaged in an underground pro-Japanese movement."[63] The membership of the Moorish Science Temple in Detroit alone, according to the FBI in 1943, was "estimated at between four and five thousand."[64] Overall, according to the FBI in 1944, there were 30,000 believers in the MST, "with 11,000 of them in the Chicago area," which was hardly minor given that there was pervasive "Japanese infiltration" of their ranks.[65]

In the early 1940s a St. Louis journalist reported that several thousand had joined the PMEW there and "tens of thousands elsewhere."[66] The Black Dragon Society of Japan, the assumed sponsor of many pro-

Tokyo Negro groups, was said to have "100,000 followers ready to take up arms in support of a Japanese assault upon U.S. shores," according to the FBI.[67] In Detroit, Satokata Takahata, a former officer in the Imperial Japanese Army and member of the Black Dragon Society, had a U.S. Negro spouse, Pearl Sherrod, and they were the motive force behind the group The Development of Our Own, which partially shared roots with the Allah Temple of Islam of the same city: one press account said that "at one time" TDOO "claimed more than 20,000 members."[68] In 1943 a judge in the case of pro-Tokyo defendants in East St. Louis said of the Pacific Movement of the Eastern World that "at its peak" the "membership" was "more than [one] million."[69] Extraordinarily, claimed one observer, "there were about 10,000" members of the ultra-patriotic Black Dragon Society of Japan residing in California "prior to Pearl Harbor."[70]

Of course, it is probably more appropriate to look at these figures as suggestive of the inflamed state of mind of the assessors, afflicted by a guilty fear of retribution. That is, reflected in these assessments is nervous recognition of how atrociously wrongheaded the maltreatment of U.S. Negroes had been and thus how ready they might be to take up arms against the government that had betrayed them and ally with every foreign foe. On the other hand, it would be a mistake to dismiss peremptorily the extent of pro-Tokyo sentiment among U.S. Negroes.

It would be similarly foolhardy to downplay the influence or the ambitions of these groups. First of all, they were taken seriously by Tokyo in that officialdom paid close attention to such important issues as the number of African Americans in the military; the racial breakdown of various states; rates of Negro illiteracy and mortality, as well as lists of "influential Negro leaders" and "important Negro publications."[71]

Robert Jordan, a leader of pro-Tokyo Negro forces, told Tokyo that "we the dark race of the Western Hemisphere through the Ethiopia Pacific Movement . . . are putting our entire confidence in the Japanese people with the hopes that in the very near future, we will desire a very close relationship with the Japanese government." On his stationery a Japanese national was listed as the group's "chief business advisor."[72] Jordan claimed that he had served with Tokyo's maritime fleet and had been an agent of Tokyo since 1922; like others in this movement, his comrade James Thornhill had been a UNIA member, while others had roots in the Caribbean.[73]

One reason for the difference in membership totals between Black
Nationalists and Black Communists is that even during the war, when
Moscow and Washington were allied, certain authorities seemed more
preoccupied with monitoring Communists than pro-Tokyo national-
ists. Certainly this was the case in Alabama, where a "confidential" 1943
report from the State Council of Defense detailed CP activity among
Negroes and had nothing to say about pro-Japan forces, even though
the CP and the Council were presumably sharing the same trench.[74]
This was all the more remarkable given that the local press in Montgomery tried to caution that the main danger came not only from the
"Yellow Peril" but also from a "White Peril," that is, Berlin and Rome.[75]
Perhaps Communists were perceived as presenting more of a systemic
threat than pro-Japanese forces, who at worst threatened mere lives and
did not necessarily threaten the all-important capitalist system. It is
also fair to infer that in the war's aftermath, the concentrated focus on
Black Communists helped to uplift their major competitor for the title
of champion of a radical reworking of the republic: the Nation of Islam
most notably.

Seeing the Pacific War as a "race war" may have helped to motivate
a number of Euro-Americans (and their racial comrades in Africa too)
to make the ultimate sacrifice for their homeland, but it did not seem to
have a similar impact on their "colored" brethren. During the height of
the war the Harlem Bard, Langston Hughes, reminded Black Chicago
that "the same America that for generations has mistreated the Negro,
lynched him, Jim Crowed him physically, humiliated him spiritually,
packed up all the West Coast Japanese citizens (I didn't say aliens—I
said citizens) and put them in concentration camps."[76] Hughes's fellow
writer Richard Wright concurred with the idea that U.S. Negroes and
Japanese Americans were in the same rickety boat.[77] Likewise, Hughes
and U.S. Negroes generally were in the forefront of those raising pointed
questions about the atomic bombing of Hiroshima and Nagasaki.[78]

This concern was not unilateral. Grave concern was expressed at diverse levels in Japan about the sorrowful plight of U.S. Negroes. Among
pro-war factions in Tokyo, this concern was utilitarian in that it was felt
that such expressed sympathy would translate into pro-Japan sentiment
among Negroes with potential far-reaching consequences during war.
But even antiwar activists of the left in Japan also expressed sympathy

for the oppressed of North America, making the cause of the U.S. Negro exceedingly popular across the ideological spectrum in Tokyo. It was claimed in Tokyo that it was routine in Negro homes to see displayed portraits of both Abraham Lincoln and Baron Nobuaki Makino, whose proposal for racial equality in Versailles after World War I was seen as a step forward not only for Japanese but for U.S. Negroes too.[79]

* * *

In some ways this is an abortive history, in that it focuses on the tremendous amount of pro-Tokyo rhetoric among U.S. Negroes, which was translated into meaningful action only intermittently. But this rhetoric had consequences, as the dissembling of Malcolm Little suggested: after all, he was not conscripted, and thus was unavailable to fight U.S. foes. There were other U.S. Negroes who also were Muslims who were indicted as "draft dodgers" during the war, though the precise number is unclear.[80]

Retrospectively, it is not easy to gauge the impact of threats by pro-Tokyo Negroes on those who were not as enamored with the cause. Apparently, Robert Jordan, a premier pro-Tokyo Negro, had assailed Walter White of the NAACP and Congressman Adam Clayton Powell Jr. as "Dumb American Negroes" who were slated to be "beheaded" because of their unwillingness to break with Washington. An FBI agent claimed that he had attended a party in the home of one of Jordan's comrades, where "the guests cheered radio reports of [Tokyo] victories."[81] It was hardly reassuring when the mainstream press published lurid accounts during the war of "weird human sacrifices and strange blood rituals" that were "practiced by fanatical members of the [Tokyo]-directed 'fifth column'" among Negroes.[82]

One scholar has suggested that Tokyo aimed to recruit spies among "American Negroes," a massive force of largely disgruntled citizens, many of whom had a special axe to grind.[83] This was a common view among many Negroes during the war. "The present Pacific movement and the Ethiopian movement," wrote one Negro journalist in 1943 of two of the principal pro-Tokyo groupings, "both are outgrowths of Marcus Garvey's UNIA." In fact, "Japanese spies took full control of the organized mass through their paid Filipino and radical Negro-West Indian henchmen," both driven by anticolonial fervor. Tokyo's main agent among

Negroes, Satokata Takahashi, "photographed and diagrammed many sections of the United States, in company of various Negro women, of whom he was exceptionally fond"; his "lavish gifts of cash with which he was abundantly supplied won for him innumerable naïve, Negro feminine companions. . . . The American Negro has always been the focal race in Japan's bid for alliances with darker races of the world."[84]

After Washington placed inordinate pressure on the Negro press after December 1941, Negro journalists often turned with a vengeance against pro-Tokyo forces that had previously been countenanced. An organ of the Negro press was quite concerned with the alleged "'Yellow Peril' [which] has spread to the black belts of America," describing the discovery in Cleveland of "a network of Japanese spies who during the past ten years have been preying consistently"; ditto for "the Negro populations in . . . Pittsburgh, Youngstown, Baltimore, Canton, Akron, St. Louis and Detroit." The target of concern was the PMEW, which supposedly was designed to "transport Negroes to Japan," where "they would be treated as equals, get better jobs and be permitted to marry Japanese women."[85]

Pro-Tokyo sentiment was subtle, perhaps unintended, suggesting that it was permeating among U.S. Negroes. When the hymn "Lift Every Voice and Sing," described as the "Negro National Anthem," proclaimed, "Facing the rising sun of our new day begun, / Let us march on till victory is won," it is probable that a salute to Japan was not the explicit purpose. Still, lyricist James Weldon Johnson had visited Tokyo and, like other NAACP leaders, was impressed by what he saw.[86] It was Johnson who contended that Japan was "perhaps the greatest hope for the colored races of the world," a line that mirrored Tokyo's precisely.[87] When one of the leading Negro businesses in the nation, North Carolina Mutual Life Insurance Company, used "Facing the Rising Sun" as the title of its report to policyholders, most likely it was a coincidence that this was congruent with prevailing pro-Tokyo sentiment.[88]

Of course, in today's atmosphere, it is less troublesome and simpler to be accused of being a "coincidence theorist" than a "conspiracy theorist." In light of U.S. Negroes' fascination with Japan and their invoking of this island state in order to discredit the essence of white supremacy, it should not be forgotten that African Americans were well aware that the rising sun was Japan's key symbol.

The United States was in a titanic struggle with Japan and its allies, and national unity and singleness of purpose were mandatory; at least, that was the dominant thinking of the era. The widespread pro-Tokyo sentiment among U.S. Negroes, propelled as it was by almost casual brutalization, was corrosive to the war effort and in retrospect could have spelled an outcome different than what occurred in August 1945. Surely, the wiser among us realized that this kind of brutalization must be halted, if only for reasons of national security. Certainly understanding of this complicated process has been hampered by the fact that, reportedly, an estimated 70 percent of wartime records in Japan were destroyed.[89]

The original drafts and memoranda detailing the ouster of Japanese Americans from the West Coast of the United States were destroyed during the war too, which, for purposes here, is even more unfortunate, since they may have been revelatory about this community's ties to U.S. Negroes.[90]

It is easier, as a partial result, to describe these Black Nationalists organizationally, which is the bent in this book. Still, ideologically, it is fair to say that these groups prioritized "race" over class and gender, even when they had a religious orientation. They viewed Euro-Americans with grave skepticism; some even described them as devils. Some privileged Africa, others saw themselves as "Asiatic," and still others thought it would be worthwhile to carve out a homeland in North America. Few foresaw their redemption emerging in the United States as then constituted.

To reiterate, the argument in this book is that just as historians have pointed to the global correlation of forces—the Cold War, for example—in explicating how and why Jim Crow retreated, a similar argument can be made about the Pacific War.[91] Even before the surrender ceremony on the battleship *Missouri*, the United States was moving toward eroding restrictions on voting by African Americans.[92] Generally, the argument about the impact of World War II stresses the sacrifice of Negro soldiers and their reluctance to return to the status quo ante (though this was not the first time such a sacrifice occurred) and the national revulsion after Nazi atrocities were exposed. This is not inaccurate—but the point in these pages is that the Pacific War and Japan's challenge merit more attention in analyses of the war's impact,[93] particularly when one considers what one scholar terms the "new paradigm," which "grants that Japan had a chance to win the Pacific War."[94] A fortiori, this prospect would have been even more likely if pro-Tokyo plotting by African Americans had gained more traction than it did.

The Negro publisher Carl Murphy was aware of the impact of the war on the fate of U.S. Negroes. "I have heard several persons declare that racial antagonisms are increasing," he wrote in April 1942, "but I know what reforms the necessities of war can bring. I am satisfied that this war means nought but good for all of us. Out of the Civil War we got emancipation. During World War I we moved a million colored people out of the South. Out of World War II I predict will evolve a second emancipation."[95] "This war will be of transcendental moment to all darker races," affirmed another important Negro publisher, Claude A. Barnett: "We do not wish to make it a war of color," he wrote, referring to Tokyo's inflamed rhetoric, "but circumstances seem to be doing that for us."[96]

The authorities were well aware of the catalytic role of the Negro press, which they perceived as subversive.[97] In 1943 Barnett complained bitterly to the attorney general about his federal agency "interfering with the mail addressed" to him; perhaps sarcastically, he told Francis Biddle that he didn't mind if his mail was opened, as long as it was delivered on time.[98]

That is, a long-term problem presented by both slavery and Jim Crow is that, in alienating a substantial percentage of the U.S. population, U.S. rulers made those oppressed quite susceptible to the blandishments of real and imagined antagonists of Washington, to the detriment of national security.[99] By August 1945 this long-term trend had arrived at a crucial turning point. Finally, during the Cold War the edifice of oppression began to crumble—but I argue here that the seeds for this epochal trend were watered vigorously during the Pacific War, when so many Negroes expressed solidarity with Japan at a time when it was engaged in a death match with the United States.

* * *

After the defeat of Japan, many of the Black Nationalists who previously had proclaimed from the rooftops that they were "Asiatic" switched seamlessly to declaiming that actually they were not only "African" but more "African" than thou. The pro-Tokyo proclamations of NAACP leaders like William Pickens were also conveniently forgotten. This too was part of the ironic evolution of the man once known as Malcolm Little, but more than this, it was part of the evolution of a people once known as U.S. Negroes who were desperately seeking global leverage to countenance the unfavorable domestic balance of forces they were compelled to confront.

This leads to a final note: Readers should be aware that if I had been alive during the Pacific War, I would probably have clashed ideologically and otherwise with the leading African American characters in this book. This is due in no small measure to the fact that Black Nationalists chose to collaborate with white supremacists to oust African Americans from the United States. In the 1930s Senator Theodore Bilbo of Mississippi sponsored a bill to this effect, which was endorsed by leading Garveyites and other nationalists, who petitioned energetically to ensure that his measure was passed.[100] "I have been instructed by Mr. Marcus Garvey of London," wrote C. C. Edwards, a colleague of the Jamaican from North Carolina, "to petition for the passage of the bill" demanding "repatriation to Africa."[101]

As a result, when Garvey died, Senator Bilbo—who could fairly be called the "prime minister of Jim Crow"—was sorrowful: "I regret more than I am able to say," he told a colleague of the Jamaican activist, "the sad passing of Marcus Garvey."[102] G. E. Harris of the Garvey Club of UNIA in New York City called Senator Bilbo a "good friend."[103] Mittie Maude Lena Gordon, a premier Black Nationalist, hailed the Dixiecrat as "one of the best propagandists we have ever read," embodying the "spirit of Jefferson, Madison, Henry Clay, Lincoln," and others, which she intended as a compliment.[104]

Garvey's widow, Amy Jacques Garvey, who exclaimed that she was a "stern believer in Race Integrity," was also "sincerely interested in the success of the Repatriation Bill," since "tension between the races is growing wors[e]." Like others, she thought that the migration of Jewish people to Palestine then unfolding was to be emulated by U.S. Negroes migrating "from Gambia to Nigeria."[105] "The Whites and Blacks who realize the need of separation," wrote J. R. Stewart, Garvey's Cleveland comrade, "must fight side by side until victory is ours."[106] Stewart was simply echoing the mandate of Garvey himself, who had told Senator Bilbo in 1938 that "we shall do all that is necessary on our part in helping you" with this bill,[107] a measure that he "wholeheartedly support[ed]."[108]

Mittie Maude Lena Gordon of Chicago, a leader in this "resettlement" movement, told Bilbo in late 1939 that "we have held open air meetings throughout the summer," though the "opposition was great. . . . I have made two trips to St. Louis," then a de facto capital of the movement. Certainly, I wholly understand why there was a desire to flee the United States. Gordon said then of her hometown that "there are 109,000 families on relief, underfed, dying in a land of plenty," as "we have suffered seven years in this Depression and it grows worse each year"; thus, "our hearts are broken, our eyes are filled with tears." This eagerness to abandon the United States was heightened by a like wish to "escape the white man's war," then erupting in Europe, since "it is not our war."[109] Because of the "starvation and death we are facing," she asserted, she planned to contact the American Colonization Society—thought to have been a relic of the nineteenth century—for assistance and pledged that "we shall do our best to bring a million people to Washington for the next session" to press for the bill's passage.[110] Carlos Cooks, a New York–based ideological soulmate of Gordon, informed Bilbo that his hearty band was "ready with speakers to swing into action at any moment" on behalf of this bill.[111]

Bilbo had his detractors, of course. J. A. Rogers, the popular columnist for the *Pittsburgh Courier*, captured the sentiment of many Negroes when he hailed those who blocked Bilbo's attempt to speak in Harlem and termed those who "flirt with him" the "lunatic fringe." Garvey's "biggest mistake," he reminded those with short memories, was "his flirting with the Klan" years earlier, and now this gross blunder was being repeated.[112] Rogers was reacting to the invitation extended by Carlos Cooks of the UNIA's Advance Division in New York City, which had invited the Dixiecrat to "come to Harlem and speak to a Negro audience" in order to "commemorate the birthday of that great father of African colonization, the Hon. Marcus Garvey," a gesture driven by the assertion that "thousands of inquiries from interested Negroes" had been expressed in support of repatriation.[113]

The Bilbo supporters in Harlem may not have recognized that some of Bilbo's Jim Crow defenders thought that after momentum for "voluntary" resettlement had gained strength, it should then be made—it was stressed—"OBLIGATORY," which would have meant "DENATION-ALIZATION OF NEGROES, including MULATTOES" and then "in certain cases sterilization" of the remaining population.[114] Writing—appropriately—from the Hotel Robert E. Lee in San Antonio, F. L. Scofield thought that Jim Crow advocates should "start this 'Back to Africa Movement' by the repeal of the 13th, 14th and 15th amendments as the 18th [pro-alcohol prohibition] was repealed when Public Opinion demanded it"; this—along with the "weapon of divine power"—was needed to "offset this minority Negro vote."[115] When Wyatt Dougherty of the Educational and Benevolent Society of People of African Descent requested a "broadening of your Proposed Bill" by "adding a feature of giving fifty-dollars per month pension for life to all persons who accept the [Bilbo] Plan and leave the United States for Africa," the Mississippi senator was curiously quiescent, perhaps surmising that this amendment sounded dangerously close to a reparative measure.[116]

Yet when Senator Bilbo spoke in Congress on his bill, sitting prominently in the Senate gallery was Gordon, described by a journalist as a "portly mulatto from Chicago"; moreover, she had brought "some 300 of her followers who mostly are on relief (as she is)" along with her.[117]

These Harlemites and Chicagoans seemed unaware that, as Washington insider Joseph Alsop observed in 1938, "Germany's race consciousness" was "lauded by Bilbo in [a] harangue to [the] Senate" on his resettlement bill, which did not bode well for U.S. Negroes.[118] By 1944, as the fate of the planet hung in the balance, Bilbo addressed a joint session of the Mississippi legislature, where he seemed to hail Berlin's fighting prowess while—prematurely—denigrating Moscow's.[119] Likewise, though a triumph for the pro-Tokyo Negroes would have unsettled the fate of those like Bilbo, it was this leading Dixiecrat who congratulated the pro-Japan seditionist he called "Captain James Thornhill," telling him to "keep up the good work."[120]

Segregationists had difficulty reconciling their more than latent pro-Berlin sentiments with their lack of sympathy for Germany's ally in Tokyo. "Hitler was guilty when he hooked up with the Japanese," wrote Joseph Edgar of Arlington, Virginia, bitterly; "like the rumblings of a volcano getting ready to spring into activity, the violations of the Divine Law of Race Segregation continue."[121]

Unsurprisingly, the Harlem Communist leader Ben Davis shed no tears when Garvey expired. He proclaimed that "it is to the eternal shame and utter bankruptcy of Marcus Garvey, discredited Negro stooge for the pro-fascist [Neville] Chamberlain government," that the Jamaican "wants the Negro to become partners with a lyncher, a defiler of the Negro people"; in Bilbo's copy of Davis's article, these phrases were all underlined, probably by Bilbo himself, the target of this radical's invective.[122]

More than likely, I would have supported the United Nations—that is, the Moscow-Washington-London alliance. However, that leads to a more profound point: history is not merely a story of "good guys" versus "bad guys." At times—as here—those supportive of the fundamentally flawed cause that was the pro-Tokyo stance during the Pacific War can nonetheless contribute to a more saintly cause: the agonized retreat of Jim Crow. Similarly, after the conclusion of the war, the so-called good guys—the European colonial powers—rushed to reestablish their misguided misrule in Indochina, Indonesia, and other tortured sites, heightening the agony of millions. Likewise, as I suggest in the following pages, many of these Black Nationalists were quite hostile to the sovereign aspirations of China, blinded as they were by the stunning light emitted by the Rising Sun—but by the 1970s, they had reversed field and were in thrall to Mao Zedong. I hope this book contributes to a more complicated reassessment of U.S. history.

Actually, the fraught matter of how race was reworked transcends the Pacific War. As I have argued elsewhere, the formation of the United States in the late eighteenth century marked a formal departure from the European practice that designated religion as a fundamental axis of society.[123] That is the good news. The bad news is that "race" became the axis of society. In the twentieth century, the rise of socialism sought to demark class as the axis of society, and this potent trend helped to erode the more egregious aspects of Jim Crow. However, it needs to be stressed that Tokyo's attempt to batter white supremacy also contributed to a helter-skelter retreat from the more noxious elements of Jim Crow. However, why this retreat was necessary to the global position of U.S. imperialism was not explained adequately, leading to mass uprisings against the new racial order in Little Rock in 1957, Mississippi in the 1960s, Boston in the 1970s, Yonkers almost thirty years ago, and other conflicted sites too numerous to mention. Part of the purpose of this book is to contribute to the discussion of why Jim Crow retreated when it did so as to forestall the recrudescence of even more conflicted sites.

* * *

In 1995 the civil rights icon James Meredith, who was a one-man battering ram against Jim Crow when he enrolled as a student at the University of Mississippi in 1962, returned to Japan, where he had resided in 1957 at Tachikawa Air Force Base.[124] In 1960, he wrote, "I returned to America inspired by my experience in Japan," determined to "break the System of White Supremacy in Mississippi and the South." Like African Americans in previous decades, he too thought that Japan's very existence was a refutation of the rudiments of white supremacy, providing a lesson well worth studying. Yet even in the final decade of the twentieth century, when Tokyo-Washington relations seemed to have normalized, Meredith felt "certain that when World War Three takes place in the future, our enemy will be Japan."[125] I hope he is wrong—about a cataclysmic war with Japan as antagonist—and I trust that the following pages will provide material to forestall such a catastrophe.

1

Japan Rises/Negroes Cheer

Relations between the United States and Japan began effectively in the 1850s, but by the 1860s Japan had undergone one of the most astonishing turnarounds in world history. The Meiji Restoration placed the island state on the road to capitalism, then imperialism, which had become clear at least by the 1890s and Tokyo's military assault on China. The United States, which had grown accustomed to bowling over peoples not defined as "white," beginning with indigenes of the Americas and Africans, found it difficult not to view Japan through a similarly distorted lens. A template was established by the post-U.S. Civil War journey to Japan by former President Ulysses S. Grant, who found it difficult not to view Japan through the prism of the brutal race relations of Dixie.[1] Yet anticipating the journey of the cigar-chomping, whiskey-guzzling politico, U.S. Negroes had preceded him in traveling to Japan and seeking to establish ties there.[2]

* * *

As if he were sending a signal, when Commodore Matthew C. Perry of the United States disembarked on Japanese shores on 14 July 1853, he was "guarded" "by a couple of tall jet-black Negroes, completely armed."[3] Perhaps this was a signal that if formidable Africans could be subjugated by Euro-Americans, Japanese could hardly resist. These connections did not go unnoticed among U.S. Negroes, who carefully watched Japan's attempts to maintain autonomy and independence in a world dominated by those defined as "white." Perhaps the periodical that contained the most information on Japan was the organ of the African Methodist Episcopal faith, the *Christian Recorder*, published in Philadelphia and founded in the pivotal year 1852.[4]

Arriving in Japan near that same time, the U.S. poet, literary critic, translator, and diplomat Bayard Taylor was struck by the "mild, effeminate-featured Japanese" he encountered. Emerging from a society obsessed with color, Taylor was keen to note that those he met had a "complexion" that was "dark olive, but not too dark," with a "ruddy tinge on the lips and cheeks." Anticipating trends that were to emerge full-blown in the twenty-first century, Taylor detected "their dislike to the Chinese" in their midst, and almost immediately was displeased with the "cunning and duplicity of the people with whom we had to deal."[5]

Townsend Harris, one of the first U.S. diplomats to alight in Japan, took a position on miscegenation there that was not dissimilar to mainstream U.S. thinking at home. "The children of Europeans by native women are a queer race—always warmhearted and hospitable," he wrote with undue optimism: "they are never more happy than when showing their hospitality to white persons. They resemble our Negroes in the love of stilted, considering magniloquence and eloquence as synonyms. They always try to secure the hand of a white for their daughters."[6] Equating Japanese with Negroes—a "nonwhite" people who had been subjugated—did not bode well for Tokyo-Washington relations.

Just after the U.S. Civil War concluded in 1865, Secretary of State William Seward purportedly asked for "intelligence" and "advice" concerning a recent dispatch from Japanese diplomats. He referred to the Japanese as "dark complexioned barbarian[s]," linking this rising power with Africans and Native Americans. But even then a difference was slowly emerging, distinguishing these mighty Asians, as it was felt that "you see at once that he is a man you cannot trifle with" or "he will get the better of you."[7]

This sage advice was not followed consistently. As early as 1875, the United States was moving to curb immigration of Japanese nationals to its shores.[8] By 1892 the U.S. high court ruled that Washington could refuse entry to those of Japanese origin.[9] By 1893 Dr. H. Saburo Hayashi was warning prospective Japanese migrants that they would be "hated and mistreated by Americans," explaining that "Japanese are also suffering from racial discrimination," not unlike the Negroes, with whom they were frequently grouped. By 1894 it was adjudged that those of Japanese origin could be barred from naturalization.[10]

All this exacerbated tensions when Washington and Tokyo began to cross swords in late nineteenth-century Hawaii, which culminated in a U.S. takeover of the archipelago and an attempt to relegate those of Japanese origin to second-class status.[11] This clash was part of a larger regional confrontation that included the U.S. overthrow of the doddering Spanish empire in the Philippines. It was here that the conflation of all those not deemed to be "white" accelerated, a process that reached an ironic efflorescence when Tokyo recruited Filipinos to be their primary agents among African Americans. This process was facilitated when almost immediately with the onset of the U.S. war in the Philippines, "Pan-Asianism" began to take root in Japan, and those of this persuasion began to smuggle weapons to islanders fighting the invaders.[12] Tokyo began to back resistance fighters in the Philippines almost to the very day of the first landing of U.S. troops.[13]

When Filipinos were grouped alongside U.S. Negroes, it was a simple step to include Japanese within the same rubric. Unsurprisingly, Thomas Edison, one of the early cineastes, deployed Negroes to play Filipinos in reenactments of the 1898 war.[14] As the United States sought to subdue Filipino resistance, a chord was struck early on that was to resonate in Japan. As early as 1899 an analyst declared that "what takes place in the South concerning the treatment of Negroes is known in the Philippines"; islanders were "told of America's treatment of the black population and are made to feel it is better to die fighting than become subject to a nation where [the] colored man is lynched and burned alive indiscriminately."[15]

The conflation reached new heights—or depths—when Senator John Morgan of Alabama sought to deport a sizeable portion of the U.S. Negro population to the Philippines. The legislator felt that Filipinos accepted U.S. Negroes more readily than did their "white" counterparts in Dixie, which may have been true.[16] Strikingly, the militant Negro journalist T. Thomas Fortune also sought to engineer a mass migration of African Americans to the archipelago.[17] Like so many other plans to oust U.S. Negroes, this one too emerged stillborn.[18]

Nevertheless, given the role that some Filipinos were to play as agents for Tokyo among African Americans, it is worth noting that Fortune was not alone in noticing that Washington frequently dispatched Dixiecrats to Manila to administer its newest colony.[19] Many of these colonial viceroys had served the so-called Confederate States of America faithfully, giving rise to the notion that the United States had exported racial contradictions to Manila and, with the adroit aid of nearby Tokyo, was preparing the ground for a "global race war."[20] Rebels in the islands did not hesitate to play upon these tensions when they made special appeals to Negro soldiers stationed in the Philippines to join the insurgency: they noted specifically the rise of lynching in Dixie.[21] Apparently such appeals swayed the U.S. Negro David Fagen, who was among the soldiers who defected to the side of the rebels.[22]

Fagen is an exemplar; his taking up arms against the United States in the archipelago was a precursor of the Japanese-Filipino-Negro axis that was to emerge full-blown by the 1930s. (Intriguingly, a large group of these Negro soldiers—members of a military band—visited Yokohama in 1900.) He was twenty-four years old when he enlisted in the U.S. military in 1895 and became one of 30,000 U.S. soldiers sent to the Philippines by the end of the century. After defecting, Fagen proudly served as a lieutenant in the Philippine revolutionary army under General Urbano Lucano, then rose to the rank of captain under Brigadier General Jose Alejandrino and fought against his former U.S. regiment at least eight times, causing his former comrades to post a heavy reward for his capture, dead or alive. Fagen was a harbinger of the pro-Tokyo Black Nationalism that emerged: General Alejandrino asserted that Fagen's most outstanding characteristic was his mortal hatred of those defined as "white." The general did not allow Fagen to guard Euro-American prisoners after he felt compelled to kill a number that he was tasked to guard; he claimed that he did so after they attempted an escape, but was investigated by his Filipino comrades because of his reputation for animus toward those who hailed from his erstwhile homeland. Fagen spoke Tagalog, a local language, allowing him to integrate more effectively into the society there. Fagen and his new comrades sought arms and ammunition from Tokyo. His new comrades included other U.S. Negroes, since dozens deserted from U.S. forces between 1899 and 1902 and about twelve joined the insurgency. Of the 6,000 Negro soldiers who served during this brutal conflict, about 1,200 chose not to return home, but instead continued to reside in the Philippines, where they formed businesses and families alike. The Negroes who served there also had the highest desertion rates of African American troops since the formal organization of racially segregated regiments during the 1860s.[23]

In response, during the war in the Philippines, islanders tended to specifically target Euro-American soldiers for attack while exercising restraint when confronting their U.S. Negro counterparts.[24]

Part of the problem for Washington was difficulty in determining who precisely should be expelled from North America. For example, Senator Anselm McLaurin of Mississippi wanted only "mulattoes" to go, while keeping "our genuine black Negroes here."[25] Assuredly, such malevolent intentions did not go unnoticed. In Boston one contemporaneous commentator leapt to the conclusion that was slowly dawning: that the dastardly plight to which U.S. Negroes were consigned would be the destiny of Filipinos and others in the region. "Do our people see no parallel in all this?" asked Winslow Warren.[26]

Strikingly, Frank Erb of Pennsylvania, then embroiled in combat in the islands, referred to his murderous activity as "this nigger-fighting business"; the epithet used to designate U.S. Negroes was applied to Filipinos almost effortlessly.[27] Naturally, the kind of atrocities visited upon Filipino combatants by U.S. soldiers did not leave African American military men unaffected: they were not exempted from attack at the hands of their erstwhile Euro-American comrades. Those assaulted demanded redress, but as one Euro-American officer concluded, if their demands were to be met, "it is likely that the eight guards from the Southern States would resign in a body."[28] Complicating matters further was the assertion in 1906 that "the Negro troops now being sent to the Philippines will be used exclusively in the island of Mindanao against the Moros, as experience has taught the government that [the] presence of colored troops in the other islands of the archipelago has had an undesirable effect on the natives."[29] On the other hand, given the rise in Islamic sentiments among African Americans that was to flourish in the 1930s and form the backbone of pro-Tokyo stances, sending these armed men solely to the southernmost part of the archipelago, where Moros tended to reside (and Muslims were prevalent), may have been unwise.

As the United States moved westward from the North American mainland and encountered peoples not defined as "white," inexorably they began to treat them in the despicable manner that mimicked how "nonwhites" were treated at home. This policy boomeranged and served to drive Negroes, Japanese, and Filipinos closer together.

Other Asians took notice too. The more muscular U.S. presence in the region did not escape alert attention. In 1899 a Korean editorialist, noting that the United States and its European allies had "invaded the African continent, enslaving black people or working them to death and stealing all the land," wondered whether the Asia-Pacific region was next on the list.[30]

A resonant response to this query was sent in 1905. Escalating global tensions had doubtlessly led Fortune, among others, to conclude that there were signs that the battle of the color line was not to be fought by the Negroes alone, a conclusion made portentously as Japan was in the midst of battering its larger Euro-Asian rival, Russia, during their epochal war in 1905.[31]

For it was then that Japan indicated further its entrance onto the stage of world powers by resolutely subduing Russia. A number of African Americans, including W. E. B. Du Bois, welcomed this victory as if Negroes were responsible.[32] "Japan has produced her Oyama [Iwao]," wrote one Negro journalist, referring to the victorious commander, "and Africa has produced her Hannibal. The two are twins." Once more an attempt was being made to conflate Africans and Asians—or Japanese more precisely—in a way that would ultimately produce the classic Black Nationalist trope, the "Asiatic Black Man." "What the Japanese have done," the journalist continued, "the Negro can do." Forget Booker T. Washington, the accommodating Negro leader, and look to the militancy of Tokyo instead, was the advice rendered. "Free Thought, civilized, educated Atheistic Africa, the companion of Free Thought, Atheistic Japan, what a theme!" "Our movement is in line also with the International Socialist Labor Movement and also with the European Revolutionary Movement. As for the United States, the Negro owes it nothing. The debt is the other way."[33]

Apparently, U.S. Negroes were taking such careful notice of the Tokyo-St. Petersburg war that one Negro reporter was moved to assert, "If the Negro paid as much attention to shaping his own destiny as he does the 'Jap' war, he would find less obstacles heaped up against him!"[34]

Rather quickly, U.S. Negroes began to recognize more than ever that white supremacy was unprincipled to the extent that Washington sought to make limited accommodations for Tokyo and those of Japanese origin, though they could hardly be defined as "white." In addition to unveiling the frailties of this racialized ideology of power, U.S. Negroes also began to think that the better part of wisdom was to ally with a rising Japan in order to undermine white supremacy. Months after the Japanese victory over Russia, a Negro journalist in Indiana noticed that

"when a Japanese marries a white girl, there may be a whisper of surprise and all is over." Yet when a "Negro obeys the same call of Cupid,
it is miscegenation and society is up in arms," primed for a lynching,
even though "the Negro . . . case may be whiter than the aforesaid Jap
[*sic*]. Why the difference?"[35] Why indeed? The question of power was
one answer; white supremacy was quite willing to yield in the face of a
well-armed Tokyo. On the other hand, by 1911, news that a "colored girl
and Japanese marry" was not seen as threatening by the white supremacists, though arguably it augured an alliance that could threaten white
supremacy.[36]

That was the conclusion drawn contemporaneously by a Negro writer
in Topeka. "Uncle Sam says he loves the Little Yellow Men and will see
that they get justice" and "we would [pray] to God that he would say
the same things about the Negroes. But [he] has a reason for saying he
loves the Japs, for Japan has a navy and a large standing army." This was
comforting in that "we are glad to know that Japan has called a halt
on Uncle Sam and his great American White God." So intimidated was
Uncle Sam by the sight of a martial Japan that "he will call some of the
states rights law into question," for example, the segregation of students
of Japanese origin in California schools. "We are watching this case carefully," it was reported, "and the results will be either advantageous to the
Negroes and Japanese"—the two disparate communities now yoked—
"or disastrous to the United States," their mutual foe. "This question of
white men dominating will soon come to an end," in any case. "He must
expect to place himself on equal footing with all mankind," a conclusion
that seemed wildly optimistic at the time.[37]

Perhaps this Topeka scribe was an oracle, but this epochal result was
hard to envision without massive bloodletting. Thus, it was not just in
Kansas but in Indiana too that interest in California school desegregation was piqued. A victory for Tokyo in that case "could be construed to
justify federal intervention in states where the Negro is denied the pro-
cesses of law." Thus, if desegregation benefiting those of Japanese ancestry prevailed in San Francisco, it "will have rendered all of us a priceless
service and our millions of Afro-Americans will rise up."[38]

One Negro observer argued that "as California would treat the Japanese she would also treat Negroes." The Negro press repeatedly cautioned readers to resist any inclination to join the anti-Tokyo movement,

for this trend only reinforced the idea of the United States as a "white" nation to the detriment of all who did not fit this exclusive category.[39] The eminent Negro scholar Oliver Cromwell Cox found it curious that

> the politicians in the South, who advocate the interests of a ruling class that has fairly well subdued white labor through the widespread exploitation of black workers, should deem it advisable to take the side of the workingmen of California in their struggle against their employers' desire to exploit [Asian] labor. And yet it is probably the weight of the Southern vote in Congress which made it possible for California to put over the national policy of anti-Orientalism.[40]

Such musings compelled a Negro writer in 1907 to ask starkly, "What may result if the persecution of the Negroes continues" as Japan rises? "Japan is not a nation to be lightly dealt with. . . . She could seize and hold the Philippines and Sandwich Islands and give San Francisco more than an earthquake." Worse for Washington, "in a certain contingency Great Britain is an ally of Japan," not the United States. Thus, if the United States wages war against Japan, conceivably "Britain would arm our southern Negroes as she did the Indians. Who can doubt which side the Negroes would take"—certainly not Washington's—"and who could blame them?" London would say, "Boys, if we win this fight, you shall have Florida, South Carolina, Georgia, Alabama, Mississippi, including Louisiana, Arkansas and maybe Texas and Porto Rico and we will protect you as a British dependency and while we are about it, we may as well take possession of the Panama Canal."[41]

In short, the rise of Tokyo did not just have an impact on Washington, it complicated the global correlation of forces as a whole, opening possibilities theretofore unimaginable. Negro opinion was buoyed by the reality that in Japan itself there was searching concern about the question of immigration exclusion and school segregation. This concern contributed immeasurably to the Pan-Asian discourse, which too was propelled by the victory over Russia.[42]

Of course, concern was also expressed about the possibility of job competition between Japanese workers and those of African origin, notably in Texas. One Indianan wrote, "Japs are fast displacing the laborers of our race as domestic servants, laundrymen, yardboys, stablemen . . . working for half what the Negro laborer has been getting for the same kind of work."[43] This was part of a "Japanese colony in Texas" that comprised "1000 acres"; tellingly, this colony was initiated as war was launched against Russia "and reached its climax in the early part of 1907 when great numbers of Japanese entered Texas."[44]

Ultimately, U.S. rulers would come to see this labor influx as part of a larger strategy on Tokyo's part to place compatriots in sensitive regions, for example, San Antonio, but this was hardly perceived in 1907. By 1909, one Negro journalist was reporting happily that "after taking a careful inventory of his colored citizen material—the Jap, the Chinese, the Indian, the Filipino and the Negro—'Uncle Sam' is reaching the conclusion that the Negro offers the best returns for the labor."[45] This may have been a premature conclusion at best, for a few years later it was reported that "Jap waiters succeed Negroes" in being "employed on the Great Northern Railway dining cars"; indeed, it was said, "there are many more Japs en route from Seattle to take their places."[46]

However, competition between Japanese and Negroes was not the main chord struck in the African American press. More typical was speculation about how "Japan should secretly employ the discharged and disgraced soldiers of the Twenty-Fifth Infantry," Negro military men recently scandalized in South Texas, "to go through our Southern States and quietly organize the alienated Negroes to quietly meet at some place [on] our Pacific coast to join a Japanese army." This, it was said with understatement, "would be a troublesome problem." Anticipating how Japanese leverage was used to alleviate burdens on Negroes, the question was posed: "Could [this potential debacle] not be prevented by getting the Negro cause to be patriotic rather than alien? Only those who have the confidence of the Negroes know how intensely bitter they feel about their treatment. As we have given the Japanese cause to feel the same way, it would not take long for them and our Negroes to fraternize."[47] A few years later one African American intellectual was speculating that "Negroes have a good chance to join in with the Japanese and bring on a bloody war in this country."[48]

By and large, the Negro press was controlled by the middle class; this influential stratum, often involved in bruising confrontations with white supremacy, was often most susceptible to the siren song of Tokyo. In Washington in 1908 the Prudence Crandall Association, named after a leading abolitionist, held a "Japanese tea," to which a "number of Washington's pretty and clever young misses" came "attired in Japanese costumes." A purpose of this venture was raising funds "with which to purchase shoes for needy poor colored school children. With winter coming on there is many a poor barefooted colored boy and girl that must have shoes in order to attend school," and it was felt that the specter of Tokyo would be sufficient for this stratum to donate to the less fortunate.[49] This was becoming a trend. In Louisville, middle-class Negroes acted similarly: "the prettiest young misses and the handsomest young men of this city staged the Japanese opera 'Mikado'" and, stunningly, "everyone looked [like] a real Japanese."[50]

It may not have been accidental that the Negro middle class was seemingly flocking to Japan's banner, for when Booker T. Washington, the reigning symbol of this stratum, journeyed to Seattle, a Negro reporter was struck by a "most unusual incident": the "large and enthusiastic reception given him by four hundred Japanese residents," including the "Japanese Imperial Consul" himself; as a token of their affection, it was decided by the Japanese present to present a scholarship to Tuskegee in their name.[51]

This in turn impressed many Negroes; one of their periodicals proclaimed that "the Japanese have made great advance toward the greater civilization within recent years. Double quick-time has been their gait. They seemingly are being impelled by some hidden force which deserts them neither night nor day." Importantly, "the Japanese are a colored people and as such have felt the sting of discrimination," that is, "they have felt the scalpel of criticism that the Negro race knows so well. Out of the common situation doubtless sympathy grows up," which would be ultimately beneficial to African Americans.[52]

As it seemed that workers of Japanese origin were flooding into Texas, while middle-class Negroes were seeking to emulate their Japanese counterparts, rumors began to circulate of a secret defensive and offensive alliance between Mexico and Japan; Tokyo was purportedly preparing to land 150,000 soldiers on the west coast of Mexico, due south from San Diego. Part of the context were anti-Tokyo bills circulated in the California legislature, including one that barred Japanese employers from employing women defined as "white," while a group called the Japanese and Korean Expulsion League was pushing even more aggressively in this direction, backed by the mayor of San Francisco and various unions. Once more the threat of war hung in the air.[53]

There was concern about Japanese bombardment of San Francisco and seizure of Manila; meanwhile—and not unrelated—a leading U.S. craniologist declared disdainfully that the "Japanese nation" contained a "slight tinge of Negrito from the islands of the Pacific."[54] Unsurprisingly, by 1912 one U.S. national was complaining that "there is no 'scare' which is worked harder or more regularly than the Japanese scare"; the "charge [is] repeatedly made that Japan is trying to bring on war with America at the earliest possible moment."[55]

Suggestive of how the two Pacific nations were moving closer to war is the fact that as the idea of the "Yellow Peril" was taking hold in California, Ryutaro Nagai of Waseda University in Japan was declaiming at length about the "White Peril": "Our American friends, who talk more about Freedom and Equality than most other nations, have nevertheless many hard things said of them by their own citizens in regard to their treatment of the Indians and Negroes." It was difficult, he wrote "to parallel in any country in the East such savagery as the lynching and burning of Negroes. . . . Even the beggar and the outcast with white skin can be better accommodated than the most refined Indian gentleman." Worse, this was not unique to one region; "practically the same attitude prevails in British South Africa, Canada and the United States. Asiatics can enter only with the greatest inconvenience."[56]

As African Americans looked at their Deep South antagonists and then looked at Tokyo, they sensed nervousness among the former about the latter, which was emboldening to Negroes as a whole. For example, the Black journalist Nick Chiles chided the retrograde "Pitchfork" Ben Tillman of South Carolina, a leading politician who rarely passed up an opportunity to assail Negroes. Yet, wrote Chiles, "Japan has made her demand upon this country to prevent outrageous laws being enacted making their race inferior to the white man of this country and you, as United States Senator [are] acquiescing in this matter to such an extent that your mouth is shut and your ears deaf to the pleas of the whites in California." Chiles did not have to say that a well-armed Japan made even the most resolute advocate of white supremacy more kittenish, thereby undermining a doctrine that was thought to be impervious to the sweet reason of militarization.[57]

Senator Tillman's reticence was all the more remarkable since he did not hesitate to reprove Filipinos, who were dismissed as part of the presumably inferior "colored races," while adding, "coming as I do from a State where this race question has been the cause of untold misery and woe," he found that the "paramount issue" was the "race question." It "may be likened to the 'worm that dieth not.'"[58] Yet somehow he found it advisable to be mute when discussing Tokyo, at least as Chiles saw it.

Meanwhile in the Philippines, a Pan-Oriental Society was formed in Manila headed by General Jose Alejandrino, who had distinguished himself in battle against U.S. forces. Reputedly, he spoke and wrote Japanese, was close to Tokyo, and foreshadowed the pre-1945 trend of Filipinos acting as Tokyo agents in U.S. Negro communities.[59]

A few days after Chiles's accusation, Black Cleveland was signaling a renewed militancy that was thought to have emerged only after World War I. "The better class of colored people," a reporter wrote in May 1913, "understand the principles of the Japanese question to be one directly affecting their own interests." This perception was ratified further "at a big meeting of Japanese held last week in Tokio, Japan in which students played a prominent part," at which "speeches were made denouncing the existence of color prejudice in the United States and the lynching of Negroes in the South was severely condemned. All the speakers agreed that the time had arrived when the Japanese must be given equal treatment," while "aggressions of the whites in the world against the Colored races were condemned."[60]

The more perspicacious in Washington may have then recognized that white supremacy had generated a formidable foe abroad that was not adverse to allying with the like-minded—that is, the Negroes—in the United States itself. As a Chicago journalist wrote, "the Jap resents with all his soul, with all of his might every wrong done him because of his race, his color or his conditions." Negroes should do the same, and perhaps ally with Japan to that end.[61] Another editorialist urged readers to stop using the term "Negro," for, "as stated by an eminent Japanese diplomat it has an unquestioned influence in cutting us off from the thought, sympathy and co-operation of the millions of colored Africans, Asiatics and islanders of the Yonder world."[62] Therein one glimpses the seeds of the concept of the "Asiatic Black Man," which was to emerge full-blown more than a decade later.

The advent of World War I in 1914 and the U.S. entry into this global conflict a few years later opened the door for further collaboration between U.S. Negroes and Tokyo, which may have occurred most dramatically on Texas's border with Mexico when, it was reported, Japan may have been involved in the "Plan of San Diego," a far-reaching effort to liquidate Euro-Americans in that region, reclaim territory that had been seized in the war of aggression against Mexico decades earlier, and to establish independent indigenous and African republics in its stead.[63] Of course, as ever when discussing Tokyo plots in North America, guilt and nervous fear about the possibility that pulverized African Americans would align with the republic's antagonists were instrumental in explaining belief in such elaborate conspiracies.

In some ways, World War I was a dress rehearsal indicative of how Washington's adversaries could play upon the wounded feelings of U.S. Negroes to the detriment of U.S. national security. As early as 1914, Berlin paid a Negro dockworker, Ed Felton, almost $200 per week to place cigar bombs on ships carrying supplies to London. In Baltimore, a Felton comrade was paid to circulate packages containing germs. The plan was for Felton and his counterparts to travel to the port cities where horses were corralled before being loaded onto French and British transport ships. They were to journey to Newport News, Norfolk, and New York, poisoning horses all along the way. Then there was the alleged plot for Berlin to conquer the United States with the aid of Japan and Mexico, adumbrating the "Plan of San Diego."[64]

The Jim Crow champion Senator John Sharp Williams of Mississippi had reason to pay close attention to the rise of Japan during this era. Weeks before the Bolshevik Revolution, for reasons that remain unclear, he told Japan's emissary in Washington that he was unable to attend a dinner for "Viscount Ishii and the other members of the Japanese mission" then visiting the republic.[65] Less than two years later, he took to the floor of the Senate and warned ominously about the rise of Japan. He thought that Japan's growing incursion into China had a diabolical purpose: to "invade Europe," as was done "under Genghis Khan." The "whole world had better let China alone, and not teach her warfare," since "Japan may find out that instead of her conquering China she had taught China to organize and wield the power to throw Japan into the Pacific Ocean."[66]

At this juncture, however, there was another focus. As was to occur during World War II, the U.S. authorities believed that the Negro press was complicit, whether wittingly or not, in stirring unrest, making these various plots more likely to succeed. Even before November 1918, Brigadier General Lytle Brown was acerbic in complaining that "a great deal of dissatisfaction was caused among Negro troops during the World War by Negro agitators and newspapers"; of the latter, at least 250 were deemed culpable, which fundamentally meant an indictment of each and every publication.[67] At a conference of Negro editors convened by Emmett J. Scott, once close to Booker T. Washington, "the existence of widespread unrest among colored people" was confirmed. Further, it was said, "this unrest may be due to the interposition of German agents."[68] Of course, the notion that maltreatment of Negroes was the Achilles' heel of U.S. imperialism was not first discovered by Berlin, but assuredly, this phenomenon became painfully obvious in the wake of World War I, setting the path for Tokyo to emulate, which it had been doing in any case.

Fueling Japan's crusade was the bitter disappointment that accompanied the failed attempt at the Versailles peace conference to install a proviso in the postwar dispensation mandating racial equality. There was bitter disappointment in Tokyo afterwards, but as Washington—and Canberra—saw things, domestic imperatives forbade this global initiative. This was a continuation of the long-term trend that conflated Japanese and Negroes, and also exposed the debilitating rigidity of white supremacy, which had difficulty in distinguishing among the powerful and powerless who were not defined as "white."[69] This inflexibility was reflected in the U.S. high court, which too had little difficulty in placing Japanese in a category that included Negroes, even though the martial prowess of the former suggested that this was an unwise course to pursue.[70] Predictably, Marcus Garvey's organization found it newsworthy when the high court chose to bar "the Japanese from American citizenship."[71] Secretary of State Charles Evans Hughes did not assuage Japanese concern when, as one analyst put it, he called for a "conference of the white nations of the Pacific."[72]

Correspondingly, a number of leading Japanese figures were coming to resent and reject as illegitimate what Konoe Fumimaro termed the "Anglo-American–centered peace." That "the white people—and the

Anglo-Saxon race in particular—generally abhor colored people is an apparent fact," he argued, "blatantly observable in the U.S. treatment of the black population," an atrocious maltreatment that could be extended to Japan.[73]

In retrospect, it is not easy to say whether Tokyo's catering to African Americans was simply a deft diplomatic maneuver or a sincere sympathy for the oppressed. Most likely, at the elite level it was the former, while among the Japanese working class it was the latter, but the combination of the two gave the trend a rare power. Thus, in Japan there was a sincere appreciation for jazz, a music that emerged from U.S. Negro communities. As one analyst put it, there was a tendency in Japan to see this music as "asserting the basic affinity of the 'colored races,'" and positing Japanese as the "yellow Negro." Thus, when Fisk University sent a gospel group to Tokyo in 1920, they were received so warmly that one member of the delegation expressed a desire never to return to the United States.[74]

To assume that U.S. Negroes would remain unaware of the potential of suturing their domestic struggle to Japan's global push for racial equality presupposes that those subjected to lynch law still had a sentimental attachment to those who perpetrated or acquiesced to such atrocities. Actually, in 1920 a perceptive Negro writer pointed out that Democratic presidential candidate James Cox said that if elected he would take the Irish question to the League of Nations. "If so," said this commentator, "could we as a nation object to England taking the Negro and the Jap Question to the League?"[75]

William Pickens, who was to go on to play a leading role in the NAACP, was among those who repeatedly linked "the Negro and the Japan Question," a linkage that was hard not to make, given the escalating anti-Asian bias in the Far West of the United States, which mirrored anti-Negro bias in Dixie.[76] In Macon, Georgia, it was stated that "everywhere there is evidence that the people throughout the country are taking a lively interest in comparing colored Americans and Japanese and endeavoring to prophesy the attitude of the colored people should the United States and Japanese engage in war."[77]

When U.S. Negroes heard that outrage was expressed in Japan about lynching, pro-Tokyo sentiments rose accordingly. The Negro press reported on the outrage in Tokyo following the immolation of a Negro man in Arkansas; Japanese observers called the murder an "indelible stain . . . on the name of America." Further, it was said, "Who does not remember how quickly Rustam Bey, the Turkish Ambassador was forced to be recalled a few years ago because he compared the Negro lynchings here with Turkish massacre of the Armenians?" Thus, noted this Negro writer, "the Japanese people must be made to believe that America aims to subjugate them, segregate them, lynch and burn and mob them because they are colored," that is, treat them as if they were Negroes. Hence, "this Japanese eleventh hour concern over Negro lynching in America is a premonition—a symptom of large significance to the student of world politics—a cue fraught with bigness and consequences."[78]

Unsurprisingly, Marcus Garvey's journal found it worthwhile to display a huge article and headline in 1922 trumpeting that "Japan holds mass meeting of protest against injustices to Negroes in America."[79] The formation of Garvey's group, the Universal Negro Improvement Association, proceeding in the wake of Booker T. Washington's premature death, was to signal a new, more concerted stage in pro-Tokyo sentiments among U.S. Negroes and Jamaican migrants to Harlem.

2

Harlem, Addis Ababa—and Tokyo

Among the most pro-Tokyo organizations to arise among U.S. Negroes was the Universal Negro Improvement Association, founded by the Jamaican-born Marcus Garvey. Since the UNIA had formidable outreach in the Western Hemisphere and in Africa, Garveyism may have been the most significant incubator of the pro-Tokyo groupings that emerged before 1945. Ironically, the UNIA was to clash with Ethiopia, one of the few noncolonized African nations, in the 1930s. Still, at least initially, Garvey's group was to serve as a template for the Black Nationalist groupings that were to emerge in the 1930s, with varying levels of devotion to Addis Ababa and Tokyo and skepticism about the presumed beneficence of the leading North Atlantic powers, which included in their ranks the leading colonizers of Africa and the Caribbean. This chapter concerns, inter alia, the distinct possibility of a diplomatic alliance emerging in the 1930s between Ethiopia and Japan, and how this influenced Black Nationalists in the United States, particularly in their fondness toward Tokyo.

* * *

As early as 1920, a small group of Negroes who allegedly styled themselves "Abyssinians" arrived at 209 East 35th Street in Chicago. One of the leaders produced a U.S. flag and deliberately set it afire. He then began to destroy a second flag in the same manner. Two Euro-American police officers remonstrated with the men but were intimidated by threats and a brandishing of pistols. Then a Negro cop and a sailor were shot, at which point a remaining group of Negroes obtained rifles from an automobile and killed a nearby clerk. In all, about twenty-five shots were fired during the fracas. This was a coming-out party for what was described as the "Back to Africa" movement, which had been in existence for at least two years. The group, the Star Order of Ethiopia and Ethiopian Missionaries to Abyssinia, was viewed as "an illegitimate offspring" of the UNIA. Helping to ignite this protest was a recent visit to the United States by an Ethiopian delegation and the presumed lack of satisfaction it obtained.[1] This confrontation was a harbinger of the militancy that was to characterize overlapping pro-Ethiopia and pro-Japan organizations.

When in the succeeding decade it appeared that Japan would come to the aid of Ethiopia in its confrontation with Italy, there was a surge of pro-Tokyo sentiment among Black Nationalists generally. Certainly the UNIA paved the way for this movement; beginning in the early 1920s, it highlighted events in Japan and their impact on U.S. Negroes. "Japan may attack America in 1922" was a typical headline in its journal.[2] Apparently one of the UNIA's members resided in Yokohama, for it was from there that Emanuel McDonald hailed the "great cause" of the UNIA and the "Moses of the race," "our great Hon. Marcus Garvey"; he expressed the hope that "in the near future we may have ships running to and from the Orient."[3] Subsequently, a writer identified as Emanuel McDowell (who may have been the same man who had been corresponding from Yokohama) this time was in Hong Kong, where he hailed the "Japanese people," who "are respected and feared," notably "here in the Orient." As he saw things, "especially in Japan, there is no opposition to the UNIA. Here a man is a man and there is no discrimination"; more to the point, the UNIA's Black Star Line was "met with a hearty welcome."[4]

"Race war threatens world" was yet another blaring headline in the UNIA journal from the early 1920s; in that article, the former secretary to the "late Premier Ito of Japan" was quoted at length from Honolulu, as he reproved the anti-Tokyo bias of California.[5] This was a prelude to lengthy reports on a disarmament conference where Japan's role was spotlighted as being "very sensitive on the color question"—and "justly so too." Again, California was pointed to as problematic "for Uncle Sam," though "there is a possibility that he will [ultimately] convince England, France and Italy that the California idea" of anti-Japan bias "is right and then Hades will break loose." Tellingly—and unlike other Black Nationalists—the UNIA journal did not invoke the example of European colonialism in order to justify Japanese incursions into China. "Japan is in Shantung upon the same principle that Great Britain is in Africa and she should get out on the same principle which should force

Britain out of Africa"; likewise, the UNIA should not "let Great Britain thrive upon that which we deny the Japanese."[6]

This concern about the impact of disarmament was not unique to the UNIA. The Negro press—in this case the *Savannah Tribune*—thought Tokyo was being targeted and, thus, "plainly the white races of the world are deeply concerned" about Japan. "Whites everywhere," it was reported, were considering what "the darker people of the world are up to," a consideration that prompted President Warren Harding to make conciliatory "utterances in Birmingham" on the matter of racism "due to the clear vision of fact that the world cannot go on and oppress darker people."[7] The Negro press recognized earlier than most that the retreat from white supremacy in the United States was propelled in no small measure by global considerations.

The UNIA was alert to the point that as early as the 1920s, Japanese encroachment in China had commenced. This reality also had dawned on a proliferating number of jazz musicians from the United States who began moving to Shanghai particularly during this time. Though this metropolis was wracked with conflict, compared to what these U.S. Negroes had experienced back home, it was paradisiacal. When this reverie was disrupted, typically Euro-Americans were singled out as the culprits, as, it was thought, the harassment of African Americans was part of their birthright.[8]

Still, this evenhandedness toward Japanese and British colonialism did not include any ambiguity on the bedrock point as to who was responsible for the ominous war clouds then gathering. If "anti-Japanese" propaganda did not cease, it was said, Tokyo would have little choice but to "unite the Indians, Chinese, Egyptians, Mohammedans, Negroes and even Bolshevists in a colossal alliance. What then will be the superiority of the white race?"[9] Lest there be any doubt, more praise was heaped upon the "little brown diplomats" of Japan, who were seen as resisting the hegemony of white supremacy.[10] Hubert Harrison, the Negro Socialist who aligned with the UNIA, was among those who as early as 1922 predicted a war between Japan and the United States, with racism lurking as a motive force.[11]

Tokyo was praised by the UNIA, since it "squashes [the] race inferiority complex." The focal point was Umeshiro Suzuki, a parliamentarian in Tokyo, and his "amazingly frank brochure on the relation of the races."

This member of the Diet foresaw the "white race's abandonment of its dream of world control" in the face of stiffening opposition, which was deemed to be an "amazing doctrine."[12] The UNIA made it clear that it was "opposed" to "the white race organizing to dominate the world."[13] Garvey noted that "though not liked, Japanese are respected."[14] Japan's excoriation of the United States was adopted by the UNIA, which agreed when Tokyo "score[d] American morals" and charged that "men and women" in the republic were "depraved."[15]

Numerous Euro-Americans were also concerned about what might well be termed the racial correlation of forces. In the wildly popular novel *The Great Gatsby*, early on a character asserts, "It's up to us, who are the dominant race, to watch out or these other races will have control of things." The rise of the "Coloured Empires" was a pre-eminent concern.[16]

The UNIA appeared to take great pleasure at the idea of worsening bilateral relations between the United States and Japan, auguring, it was thought, a setback for the former and a weakening of white supremacy. As the *Negro World* reported, the attorney general of California found the "Japanese problem more threatening than [the] Negro problem"; he termed the "racial problem on [the] coast more serious than that of [the] Civil War. . . . As the Japanese line advances, we retreat and we do not like to retreat. . . . We have already lost the Philippines. The Japanese dominate there now."[17] The *Los Angeles Examiner* argued that the Golden State was on track to have a larger population of residents of Japanese descent than those defined as "white," signaling an oncoming era of Asian domination.[18]

Unsurprisingly, when a massive earthquake hit Japan in 1923, the *Negro World* was quick to report on the sympathy and financial support offered by African Americans: "$500 [was] subscribed by the members of the UNIA to give aid to the sufferers." At UNIA headquarters in Harlem, "thousands of members of the race came out" in support of this humanitarian venture. A telegram was sent to the emperor of Japan signed by Garvey declaring that "the Negro peoples look . . . to the Japan[ese] as a friend in the cause of racial justice." His Imperial Majesty in reply expressed his "deep gratification for your sympathetic message."[19] So buoyed, the UNIA seemed to broaden its portfolio, taking on the added assignment of defending Japanese abroad, for example, when journalists from the archipelago were "rebuffed and insulted in South Africa."[20]

Upon the passage of the Immigration Act of 1924, which barred immigration from Japan to the United States, the UNIA reported on the response in Japan. The "Japanese people" were "greatly offended" by the exclusion act, and Washington was reminded of what befell Russia in 1905 when it offended Japan.[21] As the *Negro World* reported, the Diet condemned the exclusion law, and "patriotic societies last evening placarded virtually every telephone and telegraph pole" in Tokyo with angry words of protest. Police officers were recruited to guard the U.S. embassy and consulates as well as hotels where U.S. nationals were thought to reside.[22] Washington was warned that Japan was "lining up Asia for coming race conflict," and that "utmost resentment" toward the United States was a driving force. Once more, 1905 was invoked. "We regret that this war of races is coming, but it was promised when the Peace Conference [Versailles] denied Japan's demand for racial equality. Those who sow to the wind reap the whirlwind."[23] Repeatedly, Versailles and California's exclusionary policies were tied together as indicative of a downward (racist) spiral.[24]

While these immigration provisos were being debated, one Slovakian American journalist agreed with the anti-Japanese restrictions, arguing that Japanese "are not assimilable. They are of the yellow race and we are white." In some ways, this legislation was a gift to Tokyo, since it barred not only Japanese immigration but all immigration from Asia, helping to promote nascent ideas of Pan-Asianism and the related idea that Japan was the "champion of the colored races." Tokyo protested vainly that it had not been granted a quota like those of European nations; a Japanese periodical termed the bill "the greatest insult in our history," as a ritualized disemboweling took place outside the U.S. embassy. Domestically, this biased bill gave further impetus for Italians, Poles, Greeks, and the like in the United States to trumpet their "whiteness," distinguishing themselves from Asians—and Japanese particularly—thus intensifying racial polarization.[25]

In 1924 the Japanese intellectual Sugita Teiichi denounced the United States as barely containing "those with the strongest racial consciousness and the strongest sense of the omnipotence of imperialism," as reflected in the "history of the brutal, cruel and inhuman treatment meted out to the black slaves"; "for people easily moved to tears, it is outrageous."[26]

When the celebrated Negro journalist T. Thomas Fortune visited Japan shortly thereafter, like many other African American sojourners he was overwhelmed. It was a "revelation," he informed readers of the *Negro World*. "I seemed to be very much at home in Japan," where "everybody was so polite," wholly unlike his homeland. He raved about Nagasaki and saluted "glorious Japan."[27]

The UNIA maintained a keen interest in a critically important "Pan-Asiatic Congress" that took place in Nagasaki in 1926.[28] Japan returned the favor. Haruji Tawara, of Japanese origin though residing in Brazil, proclaimed that "every young Japanese knows the name and work of Marcus Garvey"; his message was that the twentieth century would witness "the rise of the colored peoples of the world." "American Negroes," he asked beseechingly, "do you know how eagerly your Asian friends are awaiting the success of Garveyism?"[29]

As the 1920s unfolded, continuing sympathy was expressed in Japan toward African Americans and their sorrowful plight. There was a tendency in Tokyo to use the republic's racist conflicts as evidence that the so-called colored races would overcome worldwide bias under Japanese leadership. Others argued that lynching simply demonstrated the "cruelty of white people." There was a tendency to see a connection between exclusionary immigration measures targeting Japan and the concomitant rise of anti-Negro violence. Revealingly, Japanese diplomats in the United States reported to the Foreign Ministry about anti-lynching legislation. Few were shocked when there were attempts in California to lynch Japanese migrants.[30] A number of Japanese intellectuals saw African Americans as a key anti-imperialist constituency. This view tended to come from the left, but what was striking about pre-1945 Japan was the sympathy for U.S. Negroes that spanned the entire ideological spectrum.[31]

Nevertheless, as "Garveyism" was being hailed, it was already declining in the United States, as Garvey himself was indicted, tried, imprisoned, and then deported. However, as so often happens, the ideas that he propounded did not depart with him, for they reflected a deeper malaise then besetting U.S. Negroes. In any case, the popularity of Garvey's ideas preceded his own fame. Garvey had studied in London with Duse Mohamed Ali, who also established a popular journal and who had been backed by Tongo Takebe of Japan. Ali's fictional creations confronted the complex matter of "race war."[32]

As noted, the tentacles of Garvey's influence stretched to Africa. The international import of Garveyism was revealed in 1927, when Arthur Gray of the Oakland, California, branch of the UNIA shared a platform with Edgar Owens of the U.S. Communist Party, along with representatives from movements with ties to India and China; other than the Communists, all there assembled had varying ties to Tokyo, including the representative of the recently deceased Sun Yat-Sen. Later a Japanese diplomat visited this UNIA branch and saluted Garvey as a "prophet" while hailing the determined struggles of the "colored race" throughout Asia and Africa.[33]

Oakland was a harbinger of a national trend. In April 1932 a leader of the Communist-backed League of Struggle for Negro Rights reported on a "very important matter": Garvey's UNIA was "holding mass meetings with Japanese speakers," stressing the "unity that should exist between the colored races against the whites." Chicago and Gary, Indiana, were the primary sites for this seditious propaganda. It was said that there were "250 Japanese students touring the country and everywhere speaking under the auspices of the UNIA."[34] However, by this late date those who held U.S. national security dear were seemingly more concerned with Moscow than Tokyo, which facilitated the flourishing of the latter's acolytes, just as it hampered the ability of the former's supporters to serve as a counterweight to the latter.

* * *

Nonetheless, as pointed as the UNIA might have been in its orientation toward Tokyo, this militant viewpoint did not emerge from whole cloth but instead had roots in a U.S. Negro community deeply skeptical about the nation in which they found themselves and thus susceptible to looking abroad—be it to Japan or Ethiopia or Africa generally—for sustenance. To a degree, Germany during the Great War had created the template in making appeals to U.S. Negroes in order to undermine the United States itself. However, Tokyo—being "colored" itself—was in an even more advantageous position than Berlin from which to pursue this stratagem. Germany, for example, during World War I had sought to make a special appeal to Muslims in pursuit of its larger ambitions.[35] Tokyo acted similarly in the prelude to World War II.[36]

The logic of Pan-Asianism, an ideology avidly pursued by Tokyo, perforce meant making appeals to predominantly Islamic Indonesia, not to mention the sizeable Muslim minorities in British India—to the detriment of the Netherlands and Britain.[37] As Islamic tendencies spread among African Americans, this too provided fertile soil for the rise of pro-Tokyo sentiments.

Religion generally was a card played by Tokyo in its multipronged attempt to destabilize European colonialism. Mohammed Baraktullah, an Indian political activist resisting British control of his homeland, taught in Tokyo as early as 1909 and promoted "Pan-Islamic" ideas that were congruent with Japan's own Pan-Asianism.[38] "What has happened to the descendants of the people who brought Buddha into this world?" asked Seigo Nakano in 1917. "They are the wheels on the road, while the passengers all have fair skin and blue eyes."[39] As Hajime Hosoi of Japan saw things in 1932, "the white countries in fact occupy 87% of the world's land area and rule over 69% of the world's population," which was "like having a person sitting in a crowded train, where there are people unable to get a seat, who stretches his arms and legs over the other seats and who, if anybody tries to sit even on the edge of a seat, immediately starts berating them as an 'invader.'"[40] Inevitably, this potent sympathy between Japan, India, and Islam was echoed among African Americans, not only in terms of the Muslim groupings that arose during this era but also in the writings of W. E. B. Du Bois.[41]

In 1930 Mehmet Ali of Detroit, rapidly becoming the headquarters of Islamic groups among U.S. Negroes, presented Mustapha Kemal Pasha, Turkey's leader, with a petition calling for the founding of a Negro colony there. "In the name of 28,000 Moslems suffering from racial prejudice in America," he petitioned for "land on the shores of the Bosphorus where we may create a Negro city"; most of the petitioners were "born in the South. Recently in both Detroit and Chicago they have had clashes with the police."[42]

The group that came to be known as the Nation of Islam—whose leaders were indicted in 1942 for alleged pro-Tokyo sentiment—helped to popularize the idea of the "Asiatic Black Man." Japan was at the core of its theology and cosmology, notably in the case of the "Mother Plane."[43]

HARLEM, ADDIS ABABA—AND TOKYO | 49

It too had roots in Detroit. It is unclear whether Nation of Islam members were included in the aforementioned petition, though assuredly all emerged from the same militant root. Just as fascist Italy was preparing to invade Ethiopia, "the 'Muslims' in Chicago," wrote a subsequent critic of the NOI,

> attracted momentary attention in 1935 when fifty or sixty of them attended the trial of a female member who was charged with having broken a white woman's glasses in a quarrel. The Faithful disapproved of the court's procedure and accordingly picked up chairs and went to work. A captain of the Chicago police was killed, a bailiff was seriously wounded, and twelve policemen and six bailiffs were injured.

This critic, Revilo Oliver, spoke of an "individual with the euphonious name of Wyxsewixzard S.J. Challouchilcziliczese who claimed to be a special envoy sent by the Emperor of Ethiopia to the 'Black Nation of the West,'" who was said to have allied with the Nation of Islam.[44]

Thus, when the man known variously by the authorities as Elijah Mohamed, alias Elijah Poole, alias Gulan Bogans, alias Mohammed Ressoull, was placed on trial in 1942 because of his reluctance to endorse the war against Japan, he was accused of asserting that "Moslems [i.e., the Negro members of the Allah Temple of Islam] are not citizens" of the United States;

> they have no flag [they] can call their own but the flag of Islam. That the flag of Islam and the flag of Japan are the same because they both offer freedom, justice and equality. . . . The Japanese are the brothers of the Negro and the time will soon come when from the clouds hundreds of Japanese planes with the most poisonous gases will let their bombs fall on the United States and nothing will be left of it.

According to the Allah Temple of Islam, the precursor of what is known today as the Nation of Islam,

> The Asiatic race is made up of all dark-skinned people, including the Japanese and the Negro; therefore members of the Asiatic race must stick together; that the Japanese will win because the white man cannot success-

fully oppose the Asiatics. That the white man is nothing but a devil; that this is the devil's war and let the devil fight it himself. . . . That the black man owes no respect to the American flag because under the American flag the Negro is oppressed, beaten, and lynched; that the only allegiance a Moslem owes is to the flag of Islam. . . . That the Japanese are fighting to free the colored people. . . . The Japanese flag is similar to our flag of Islam and the likeness is because the Japanese are our brothers. . . . By the end of the year Moslems will have 7,000,000 followers and then with the help of their brothers in the Far East the Moslems will control the United States.[45]

A harbinger of the Allah Temple of Islam was another group, known as The Development of Our Own, also rooted in Black Detroit. A Negro woman born Pearl Barnett in Alabama in 1896 and eventually known as Pearl Sherrod married a Japanese national, Satokata Takahashi, and under their leadership, TDOO was said to have amassed a membership of ten thousand, including those of African, Indian, and Filipino descent.[46] Sherrod, unlike the UNIA, was supportive of Japan's military incursions into China and sought to financially support this intervention.[47]

However, her views were hardly singular. The combustible combination of militant Islam, Filipino insurgency, anticolonialism in India, the rise of Japan, and the existence of an independent Ethiopia was becoming an alternative Weltanschauung challenging white supremacy. From Tokyo's perspective, there was a V-shaped formation attacking white supremacy and European and Euro-American colonialism, with Japan at the point of attack.

Thus, it was William Pickens—not a Muslim but a leading Negro intellectual close to the NAACP—who argued in December 1931 that

Secretary [Henry] Stimson has learned that he must use more respectful and circumspect language when talking about the Japanese "army" than [he] uses when talking about Mexican or Nicaraguan "bandits." Of course, Japanese nerves are not a bit more sensitive than Haitian nerves, but Japanese guns are bigger and longer and Japan's warship tonnage is heavy. . . . [Japanese] are in fact just as "colored" as are the people of Liberia, but nobody in Washington is giving "orders" to Japan [despite its intervention in China].[48]

In sum, the idea was emerging that white supremacy was even more fraudulent than first thought; this seemingly inviolably inflexible doctrine seemed to lack rigidity when confronted with a powerful force. This insight carried grave implications for the future viability of white supremacy in the United States.

Pickens's view was that "Japan in Manchuria takes [a] leaf from the book of 'occupation'" developed by the United States in Haiti.[49] Sounding triumphant, Pickens claimed that "'white supremacy' was slain in Manchuria and its funeral celebration is being held in Shanghai" and "the Japanese killed it." The "best fighting man on earth today is the trained Japanese soldier." Pickens was sufficiently perceptive to note that "in the immediate future the resisting Chinese are going to be a far greater threat to white domination in Asia than Japan ever could be." Repeating a commonly held position among U.S. Negroes, Pickens interpreted the Japanese invasion of China as actually an attempt by Tokyo to toughen fellow Asians so they could better confront white supremacy. "China will no longer be helpless," he said, "after they get through this 'training match' against the Japanese."[50] Pickens was not alone in this view. The *Baltimore Afro-American* described China as a "kind of 'Uncle Tom' of Asia" and asserted that Japan was providing backbone by instructing the Chinese to "stand up straight and be a man."[51]

Pickens declared that "if an intelligent American Negro goes to Japan or China, he is lionized," unlike the routine maltreatment endured in the United States. "No visitor," he assured, "gets quite the hearty reception that a black American gets from the Orientals." Pickens wrote about a Negro soldier who had fought in the Philippines and now cowered in "shame and chagrin" at the prospect that a Filipino might ask him, "Why you come here, help white man treat us like you?" Indeed, said Pickens, "When a Moro warrior said that to me, I confess that I felt small." His conclusion? "Hindered races should make common cause, just as the oppressed classes of all races should make common cause."[52] However, this noble assemblage did not include Chinese fleeing Japanese aggression.

Pickens—neither a leftist nor a Black Nationalist, but a centrist with ties to the NAACP—was probably the most articulate pro-Tokyo intellectual among U.S. Negroes. He was bedazzled by Hawaii, marveling that the "Japanese are the largest single racial element here." Importantly, "one likes them: they are intelligent, industrious, friendly. There is nothing more agreeable than to go into a restaurant or other shop where Japanese are rendering the services. 'Can I give you a lift?' a Japanese woman will say to a strange black man who she sees"; he knew that "people cannot be so friendly in New York—they dare not," while in Honolulu, by way of contrast, "criminals and dirt cannot flourish here."[53]

Months after Pickens's endorsement of aggression in China, news reports indicated that U.S. Negroes were seeking to enlist in the Japanese air force. Similarly, a Japanese ship set sail for home from Belgium staffed by a Negro crew. "Give us jobs and we will not go to Japan," was the plea of these prospective pilots. The journalist on the scene saw this as confirmation of the "gradual consolidation of the colored races of the world in opposition to the whites," though "the instance above is the first in which relations between the Nipponese and Negroes have been disclosed."[54]

* * *

What was driving "Nipponese and Negroes" closer together was also an idea that also had arisen in the 1930s: Ethiopia, one of the few independent African nations, would preserve its independence by dint of alliance with Japan. That U.S. Negroes were moved in large numbers to stand in solidarity with Addis Ababa in the face of Italy's invasion is well-established.[55] What is relevant for purposes here is that in 1932 the idea was bruited of a formal alliance—through marriage—of the royal families of Japan and Ethiopia.[56] Of course, to even hint at a merger between elite families in Washington and Addis Ababa might have ignited a lynching—or worse. What this suggests is that as Ethiopia gripped the consciousness of U.S. Negroes, alliance with Ethiopia served to further differentiate Tokyo from its European and Euro-American competitors. Even after it became clear that no such betrothal would occur, the rumor continued to resonate. And even after the formation of the Anti-Comintern alliance that linked Tokyo with Berlin and, yes, Rome, in the eyes of some U.S. Negroes this assumed marriage proposal served to distinguish Japan from other imperialist powers. Predictably, many of the pro-Tokyo forces that arose among Negroes were also in fervent solidarity with Ethiopia.

Thus, in 1942 among the U.S. Negroes indicted as a result of their pro-Tokyo stances were those who led a group called—revealingly—the

Ethiopia Pacific Movement. According to the indictment, the EPM argued that "Japan is going to win the war and the next leading power in the world will be [the] 'Rising Sun.'" Thus, "when they tell you to remember Pearl Harbor, you reply 'Remember Africa.'"[57] Then there was the Peace Movement of Ethiopia, organized in 1932 purportedly for the purpose of migration to Liberia. Its leader, Mittie Maude Lena Gordon, was also indicted in 1943 for alleged pro-Tokyo activity.[58]

The ties of intimacy arising between Ethiopia and U.S. Negroes were indicative of a growing identification with Africa, thus buoying Black Nationalism generally. For example, in 1936 a baby named Haile Selassie Stewart was born in Jackson, Mississippi.[59] The preceding year, Malaku Bayen, a close relative of the emperor and a graduate of the medical school at Howard University, the capstone of U.S. Negro education, married a U.S. Negro, Dorothy Hadley, formerly of Evanston and Chicago.[60] Daniel Alexander, a U.S. Negro, had been in Ethiopia for three decades by 1930. Born in Chicago, he went there as a missionary and married an Ethiopian woman.[61]

In August 1919 a high-level delegation from Ethiopia arrived in Harlem to confer with a number of leading African American entrepreneurs and scholars. The visitors were pleased to "express the satisfaction we have felt on hearing of the wonderful progress the Africans have made in this country," while adding memorably, "we want you to remember us after we have returned to our native country." Eight years later yet another delegation met with the bibliophile Arthur Schomburg and extended an invitation to "American blacks" to come aid this East African nation with their skills as "mechanics, professional men, farmers" and the like.[62]

In sum, there was a broad and diverse coalition of forces backing Addis, which was made abundantly clear when a thousand clergy in New York City pledged a Sunday of Prayer against Italian aggression in August 1935.[63] The popular cleric Daddy Grace urged his 200,000 followers to pray for His Imperial Majesty, Haile Selassie.[64] That same month 20,000 marched through Harlem, one of the largest manifestations in this Negro community in years.[65] The "biggest seller in New York" on that day was the tricolor flag of Ethiopia, according to one observer.[66] William Pickens declared that actually there were "at least 100,000" on the march in Harlem, while "other hundreds of thousands observed"; this was, he stressed, "the greatest PROTEST AGAINST THE ITALIAN ATTACK ON ETHIOPIA" to be held "anywhere in the world." There were "at least five miles" of marchers—the "raw stuff out of which revolutions are made."[67]

Also in August 1935, fifty North Carolinians of African descent were reported to have "enlisted for service" in Addis: "most of the recruits were former members of the regular army units."[68] Ethiopia's consul in Manhattan thanked Winston-Salem, North Carolina, for its energetic fund-raising for Addis's forces.[69] John Robinson, a Negro from Chicago, took his piloting skills to Addis, where he became a leader of Ethiopia's air force. "Scores" more of "American aviators," as reported in the Negro press, wanted to volunteer too.[70] By April 1936 Robinson was touted in the Negro press as the "head of the Imperial Ethiopian Air Force."[71] Robinson's fellow Chicagoans were in the forefront in supplying Ethiopia with medical supplies.[72] The Chicago Society for the Aid of Ethiopia sought to send "10,000 cablegrams" to the League of Nations summit on Ethiopia.[73]

"Sepia Harlem has gone mad," observed the Negro press in May 1936. "The announcement that Italy has annexed Ethiopia" was the reason. "Nearly every corner of Lennox and Seventh Avenue" was filled with "great crowds assembled to listen to the roar and splutter," while "yelling 'Don't buy from the Wops [sic].'" A "monster parade" ensued.[74]

Yet also on the military front, it was reported in the Negro press in 1935 that Japan was to provide "arms" and "ammunition" to Addis: "there are many Japanese in this country," readers were told.[75] In 1933 the Negro press had reported that there was a Japanese "plan" for a "coalition with Abyssinia" and to that end, His Imperial Majesty "has surrounded himself with Japanese agricultural, mineralogical and commercial experts."[76] Also featured in the Negro press was the point that not only "Egyptians" but "Japanese" too were "clamor[ing] to get in [the] Ethiopian army."[77] Similarly highlighted was the assertion that Tokyo was to send Addis "as many airplanes or other necessities as are desired and with no strings attached."[78]

William Pickens rationalized that "to protect itself from the great 'White Peril', Japan has built up a veritable Frankenstein in its Army," which now could be deployed in Africa.[79] The Red Cross unit maintained by Japan in Ethiopia was singled out for praise.[80] To that end, the

Associated Negro Press (ANP), a consortium of Negro periodicals in the United States, opined that the "utter domination" of Ethiopia by London "would mean better control of her Asiatic possessions and another threat to Japanese expansion," while "Japanese control of Ethiopia would menace Britain in India and Africa."[81]

In St. Louis, in some ways a central headquarters of pro-Tokyo sentiment among Negroes, Toyohiko Kagawa, a famed Japanese Christian leader, addressed an assemblage of ten thousand on the Italian conquest of Ethiopia; he included a critique of Communists for good measure.[82]

Just as the 1924 immigration exclusion law in the United States served to polarize relations within the republic between those of Japanese origin on the one hand, and Italians, Greeks, and Poles on the other, the war in Ethiopia exacerbated tensions between Italian Americans and U.S. Negroes.[83] This was particularly the case after the Negro press reported that Italian Americans in New York City raised a hefty $100,000 for the invaders, along with sleek ambulances.[84]

In New Orleans Negroes vigorously protested the sight of Italians marching in favor of the invasion. The protesters included the leading Negro academics St. Clair Drake and L. D. Reddick; reportedly, three thousand gathered alongside them to consider "economic sanctions against local Italian merchants in a sign of protest."[85] Such clashes may have driven Denis Sullivan in London to conclude that an "army of 500,000,000 blacks roused because Italy conquered Ethiopia" now threatens "white civilization." This led him to believe that not the "Yellow Peril" represented by Tokyo but the "Black One"—which included India—was the main danger.[86]

This polarization had a religious tinge too, which simultaneously tended to forge a kind of Black Nationalism or commonality between Ethiopians and U.S. Negroes. Thus, said the Negro press, "Wahib Pasha, Turkish military genius"—and a Muslim—"who directed Ethiopia's defense because he hated Italians" was invaluable. "Abyssinia was not conquered by gas, bombs or other modern weapons but by internal revolution." Thus, said Pasha, "the majority of the chiefs succumbed to Italian bribery and propaganda"; the Negro commentator continued, "If nothing else, this trait of selling out—so often in evidence in America by Negro misleaders—ought to convince skeptics that Ethiopians and Duskyamericans [sic] are members of the same race."[87]

Meanwhile, from Johannesburg the U.S. Negro press reported that "the Italo-Ethiopian conflict" could mean "the coup de grace of white imperialism or the beginning of the revolt of the docile [*sic*] blacks against the encroachment of the land grabbing whites;" this could occur since "pro-Ethiopian feeling [was] pervading all Africans—literate and illiterate," not unlike the United States itself.[88] The war in Ethiopia was the "cause of many attempts at greater cooperation among Africans" in South Africa, according to the U.S. Negro press; "the war has whetted the appetite for reading. It has spurred the quest for information" and was "encouraging the fight against imperialist oppression," forging "greater solidarity." Yes, it was noted with satisfaction, "Black South Africa is becoming one."[89] This polarization tended to place Tokyo alongside Addis, Africans generally, and U.S. Negroes particularly against Italy and its European enablers.

Tellingly, decamping to Ethiopia were—unusually—a number of UNIA members. This was unusual because Garvey himself derided His Imperial Majesty as "misguided."[90] Still, this growing list of migrants included Augustinian Bastian of the U.S. Virgin Islands and Harlem, who had been living in Ethiopia since 1933 and had traveled there in a party that included a number of Virgin Islanders.[91] The chief motor mechanic in Addis, James Alexander Harte, had lived there for five years though he hailed from British Guiana.[92] His presence did not seem to be happenstance when the fact emerged that back in Guiana, plantation workers went on strike in protest against the invasion and were described as "in a tense mood" because of the conflict.[93]

This tenseness also gripped U.S. Negroes generally and did not bode well for the United States as tensions simultaneously gripped Tokyo-Washington bilateral relations.

3

Japan Establishes a Foothold in Black America

As mentioned earlier, in 1943 the federal government brought charges that amounted to sedition against a group whose membership was heavily African American and which seemed to be flourishing in the Midwest and various other U.S. cities. The grand jury and trial transcripts of *U.S. v. Pacific Movement of the Eastern World* and related records provide a fascinating glimpse of ordinary African Americans and their feelings about Japan, world events in general, and life in the United States in the early twentieth century.

* * *

Policarpio Manansala, also known as Mimo De Guzman, Dr. Ashima Takis, Dr. Itake Koo, and Kenesuka, was born in the Philippines—interestingly—on 4 July 1900. He received a high school education, then joined the U.S. Navy, but received a dishonorable discharge. At that juncture, according to the indictment in *U.S. v. PMEW*, he became a Japanese agent; in early 1943 he "undertook to organize among the Negro population of the United States a movement for the purpose of spreading Japanese propaganda" at "the instigation of the Black Dragon Society of Japan," an ultra-patriotic group "working through Satokata Takahashi, a retired major of the Japanese Imperial Army." The organization through which he worked was the Pacific Movement of the Eastern World (PMEW).

Evidently a number of Negroes assumed he was Japanese. George Young of East St. Louis was born in 1895 in Mississippi and served during World War I in France; by the time of his 1942 grand jury interrogation, he worked as a carpenter. He had joined the PMEW in 1933 but confessed, when asked about De Guzman, "I wouldn't know a Jap from a Philipino [*sic*]. All I know is they ain't white."[1] This rough-hewn attitude was not uncommon among U.S. Negroes, nor was it dissimilar to the approach in Washington, which also tended to group under one rubric the "nonwhite"—including Negroes at the bottom rung of society.

De Guzman worked as a dishwasher in New York City, where he "bumped into a colored man" and heard about the PMEW. This was in 1932. Earlier he had attended a UNIA gathering, where he spoke with a "Japanese Consul in San Francisco" named "Takahashi," who told him to "speak pro-Japanese to the colored people and tell them the Japanese people are going to drive every white nation of people away" and then "the dark people will be free"; this man "said he was a member of the Black Dragon Society." Then, said De Guzman, "we went into different sections of Chicago to organize the Pacific Movement" and from there to St. Louis, where informal headquarters were established at a "Japanese restaurant on the corner of Market and Jefferson Street."[2]

As early as 1932, the PMEW had been noticed by the Negro publisher Claude A. Barnett. Though Barnett routinely hired writers, the PMEW audaciously contacted him to see whether he would write for it. Its weekly magazine, *Oriental African Digest*, was headquartered in Chicago; De Guzman and a colleague, Robin Stokes, said their purpose was "establishing a greater friendliness and a deeper understanding among the darker races of mankind at home and abroad."[3] Barnett characterized the PMEW then as "a group of Japanese, Chinese and Filipinos with a following chiefly of Negroes," which was not altogether mistaken.[4]

In 1933 a PMEW-affiliated newsletter in Chicago entitled *Pacific Topics*, edited by Ashima Takis, hailed "the awakening of the East, the origin of the Pacific Movement"; stressed the "influence of Islam"; and asserted that there was "no sense of continental rivalry among Asiatics as there was among Europeans," since "all Asiatic nations rejoiced over the victories of Japan over Russia." For good measure, an editorial lambasted the United States over the Scottsboro case, the nine Black youths facing execution over false allegations of sexual molestation of two white women.[5] The PMEW's motto recalled that of the UNIA: "One God, One Aim and One Destiny." The first article of the organization's constitution stated that "the colors of this organization shall be anyone who possesses Negro blood, despite. . . . straight hair, blue, brown or gray eyes and white skin."[6] This initiative broadened the base for the PMEW and also acknowledged that in the United States, because of the machinations of the "one-drop" rule, there were many defined as "Negro" who were not necessarily dark-skinned.[7] This capacious definition also opened the door for "race traitors" defecting from the otherwise hallowed halls of "whiteness."

General Lee Butler, the man who became the recognized leader of the PMEW in the St. Louis area, attended his first PMEW meeting in 1933. Butler was born in 1902 in Coahoma, Mississippi, and was married with six children. Migrating from the hellhole that was Mississippi to East St. Louis brought no surcease in bigotry, for his new hometown was the site in 1917 of one of the bloodiest and most startling pogroms to be visited upon U.S. Negroes to that point. By the time he joined the PMEW in 1934, he told the FBI, the group had a thousand members in the city; he thought it was an outgrowth of the UNIA, as did many others. He argued that the PMEW became a part of the Ethiopian World Federation in 1937. By 1940 Butler became the leader of a "revived" PMEW after the EWF fell by the wayside; this was ratified at a convention held at 1505 Hoover Street in East St. Louis "attended by about 30 members." By 1942 one of the group's leaders, David D. Erwin, reputedly announced that St. Louis, Detroit, and Chicago "would be bombed" by Tokyo.[8]

Henry Hall, with roots in Arkansas, was a railway worker who had been part of the PMEW since 1933. "What's the button on your coat with the red, black and green stripes?" a prosecutor asked him in 1942. Answer: "UNIA." He had joined in 1924. "I joined the UNIA before the Pacific Movement ever came to East St. Louis," he said. "Which one do you like the best?" asked the prosecutor. "The UNIA," he said—but since it was the PMEW in the crosshairs, this may have been simply a tactical response. He was also a member of the Baptist Church—presumably joining before his other two contested affiliations. The two—UNIA and PMEW—"sure don't mix," said Hall. "They wouldn't meet in the same lodge hall if they had to starve. I tried to rent the hall once and they wouldn't rent it to me"—that is, the PMEW would not rent to the UNIA, perhaps seeing it as competition or not sufficiently pro-Tokyo to be taken seriously.[9]

It may not have been accidental that East St. Louis was the locus of PMEW strength, for the tumult of 1917, when Negroes were slaughtered en masse, left a deep psychological and political scar. William Baker of neighboring Edwardsville and a worker at the Mid West Rubber Reclaiming Company testified that Butler asked him to buy wholesale ammunition to prepare for a "race riot. He said [that during] the last race riot many of his people were killed and he didn't want that same thing to happen again."[10] Lula Livingston, a married PMEW member with two children, was told by Butler that "the white people going to start a riot against the black people. . . . He said an Italian told him the white people throughout the State and throughout the United States was going to jump on the colored people because they was hot with them, they was mad with them" and thus, the Negroes had to organize.[11]

Charles T. Nash was an undertaker in East St. Louis and claimed to be a UNIA not a PMEW member. "I belong to a gun club in Cairo," Illinois, he said in part because in 1917 in East St. Louis "I lost everything I had in that riot." Negroes were "burned and thrown into the streets." This did not seem to concern the prosecutor interrogating him, who instead told him, "The Japanese had in mind that they might cause a revolution in the United States by getting the colored people to rise up against the white people." Thus, Nash was asked, "Do you think you would live in the United States under white rule than any place else under Japanese rule?" He was also asked, "If these is some dissatisfaction on the part of the colored people do you think that would be any reason for the colored people rising up and starting a revolution in these times?"[12]

Unfortunately, many of these Negroes had experienced sorrow and pain as a result of other brutal episodes, antiseptically denoted as "race riots." Thomas Albert Watkins had lived in Memphis, though he was born in San Antonio. This thirty-three-year-old married man and father of two children moved to East St. Louis, where he was queried about "where I could get several rifles" in a prelude to a war that would eventuate with the "British isles [to be ruled] by Germany and America and China was to be ruled by the Japs and this country by the Negroes." Yet what was firing his imagination was the "riot in Elaine, Arkansas some years back," an infamous 1919 massacre.[13] Contrary to Watkins's recollection, prosecutors there argued that the "riot" was actually a devilish plot by Negroes to murder their Euro-American antagonists.[14]

Lula Livingston, who had joined the PMEW in 1934 and had taken Spanish lessons from De Guzman, said she wanted to go to South America permanently. She hailed from Melwood, Arkansas, not far from Elaine.[15] Artie Mays, a steelworker and PMEW member, was born and had resided in Little Rock, Arkansas, before arriving in East St. Louis.

Unsurprisingly, he owned a "45 pistol and a shot gun" of the "pump" variety—and a sign of the "conquering Lion of Judah," Ethiopia. He also owned a book entitled *Japanese Over Asia*.[16]

The Elaine massacre was also on the mind of William Pickens, notably when he condemned the "anti-Japanese feeling" in the U.S. press. The United States was assailing Japan in a one-sided fashion, he thought, while forgetting Arkansas, where a "white mob was chasing Negroes," then "began shooting," after which a mob member was killed and a Negro was charged with murder. Was not this akin to China, where Chinese, he said, were aiming at Japanese, "Americans were killed," and Tokyo was then denounced?[17]

Frank Mart was born in Alabama in 1867 and had been in East St. Louis since 1905 but also had ties to Mississippi, New Orleans, and Jonesboro, Arkansas. Married three times, he said that he had "maybe eighteen or twenty" children, "maybe more." He joined the PMEW in 1933, when its first meetings were at the "UNIA hall." He owned Swiss rifles and was asked by the prosecutor, "Didn't you know those guns were used in riots down in Arkansas?," a possible reference to the notorious 1919 conflagration in Elaine. Another query was, "How about the Negroes ruling North America and the United States?" and "Do you think the white people should rule the United States?"[18] Presumably, the correct answer to the latter rhetorical query was "yes."

Coordination with Japan was viewed as a sure way to blunt the scourge of white supremacy, according to a number of Negroes. E. M. Johnson, a PMEW member who had served as treasurer, had lived in East St. Louis for thirty-three years and worked as a contractor, doing plastering, painting, and carpentry. By the time he testified in 1943 he was seventy-four years old. When asked about the "cloth of black in the windows" placed by the PMEW, Johnson conceded that "if the Japanese came over here," the homes of those with such a banner "would not be destroyed."[19] He was also asked about a regional gathering of the PMEW in his hometown with "400 or 500" present; a Japanese speaker at the meeting "invited the colored people to come to Japan and said if you do come you will . . . receive just as good treatment as the white man," an extraordinarily enticing proposition.[20]

Pink Brown, a PMEW member from East St. Louis who knew De Guzman, was told that "when the Japs bomb St. Louis and come over and invade us for us to put it [black cloth] in the window and they would know if I did that I was a member of the Pacific Movement."[21]

PMEW member Eugene Moore had lived in Unity, Illinois, since 1927, though he was born in Mississippi. He was deemed to be a major general in the PMEW's military unit, which was said to have fifteen or twenty members. They "sometimes drilled every night." He owned a shotgun and pistol. "One Jap lived there in Unity," he testified. "He is farming right across the field on a white man's place. . . . He just moved there from Villa Ridge."[22]

The federal case against the PMEW in the early 1940s was not the first time the organization's members had faced legal repercussions. By September 1934 members of the PMEW were serving jail sentences for unlawful assembly in Caruthersville, Missouri. Their attorney had been attacked while defending them in nearby Steele, Missouri. He had denied that his clients were seeking to "unite the Negro race in one body with the Japanese race and all the dark races of the world." His clients, he cautioned, should also not be confused with "the Original Independent Benevolent Afro-Pacific Movement of the World," which was said to be in conflict with the PMEW.[23]

This attorney had to tread carefully; he had been physically assaulted, as were his clients, who, according to another source, were thought to be part of this Afro-Pacific Movement, a Negro organization with many members in St. Louis, not to mention numerous hamlets in an area often called "Little Dixie." In Blytheville, Arkansas, those who sought to interrupt the gathering of this group were met by armed Negroes. Revealingly, found at their gatherings was correspondence from Liberia, Haiti—and Japan. Apparently, there were scores (if not hundreds) of members in this group. The authorities claimed that they seized a "Communist handbook," perhaps indicating that the left was seeking to influence these Negroes, along with a "call to arms" to "all black, brown and yellow men" as to how to proceed when the time arrived to enforce their "demands." Also, it was reported, "Negro residents were eager to join this movement" and "numerous Negro clergymen" were said to be cooperating.[24]

This region was due south of East St. Louis, the locus of pro-Tokyo sentiment. The well-dressed David Erwin, the PMEW leader in this site of the infamous 1917 pogrom, had global ties, which was of no small concern to prosecutors.[25] In July 1935 he wrote to a correspondent that "I arrive[d] safe in Mexico on . . . important . . . business. . . . will explain details by word of mouth."[26] "I sailed at noon Nov. 16 [1935] and landed in Southampton" for an international meeting. "Japan, China and everybody is here," he wrote, though Harold Moody, a local human rights leader, who "has a white wife," was "not at the meeting. I was in Marcus Garvey's office" too, he noted proudly, while adding cryptically, "I can't say any more."[27]

In late November 1935 Erwin went to England to participate in what was called the Round Table Conference, "which consisted of Dark and Coloured Representatives of the world," where he "made known the conditions of the 15 million scattered sons and daughters of the black race in America." The meeting was at 47 Doughty Street in London, though a Nigerian address was also listed. It was a "grave fact," it was said, "that slavery in its worst form still exists in the United States," not to mention segregation. This statement was signed by "Wham Po Koo," chairman, and W. E. Akaje Macaulay, international secretary.[28]

The Supreme Executive Council of the PMEW met in East St. Louis in September 1938 with delegates from Mississippi and Oklahoma, in addition to the St. Louis metropolitan region. Mississippi boasted of "having the largest membership." There was discussion of "colonization" in South America, apparently a follow-up to ongoing Japanese migration to Brazil. The recently deceased "International President" was listed as W. P. Schiwhangato of Nanking, China, who was succeeded by W. Yicklung, while "Dr. Takeda is International Vice President." Reportedly a "gigantic mass meeting" was held to mark the occasion. "There are units of our great organization in Mexico, Africa, India, Australia, China and Japan," it was said. Japan was singled out as "the 'CHAMPION' of all Dark and Colored Races. Victory of all Dark and Colored peoples started in Japan" (capitals in original).[29]

After this meeting, General Lee Butler, another top PMEW leader, seemed to be energized. "If we must die," he instructed the Reverend F. R. Baker of Okmulgee, Oklahoma, "let us die fighting for our rites [sic]." And, he added, do not stop "until every black man and woman [is] free" and "out from under the white." In fact, he continued, "on my job today" at the "Midwest Rubber Company of East St. Louis, I was question[ed] about the [PMEW]." This "white gentleman is named Ollie McCoy, the

President of the CIO union"; he asked "why you colored peoples have to go and join . . . with the Japanese."[30] Butler's answer has not survived. But one can surmise that the essence of his response would have expressed skepticism about the viability of the class project that the CIO represented, in light of the history of the Euro-American working class, which had not distinguished itself in its penchant for class solidarity, leaving Butler with the option of pursuing a "race" project.

Like most PMEW members in East St. Louis, Butler was a member of the working class. "I farmed and worked on a dairy in Mississippi" before migrating northward, he said, and then worked for the American Rope Factory, Hill-Thomas Lime and Cement, the American Steel Company, and then a rubber company. He worked at the latter from late 1928 to early 1943, but there were repetitive echoes of 1917: "my life was threatened out there" by "the committee on the fourth shift when I entered the plant." This led directly to his joining the PMEW in 1934, which met every Monday and Wednesday evening. "When I joined," he testified, "it was for the betterment of the conditions of the Negroes," that is, "equal rights and justice." His view was that the PMEW was "working for equal opportunities and against lynchings and burning of human[s] . . . alive," as had occurred in 1917. Yes, he was well armed, but the explanation was innocent: he "wanted to shoot wild geese" and "wild game" and hunt for ducks. Yes, the PMEW "was an outgrowth of" and "advocated the same policies and purposes as the UNIA." As for pro-Tokyo statements he made under interrogation, this was all due to duress, he explained. They had passwords; one was "Gaza," another was "good morning" in Amharic, a major language of Ethiopia.[31]

Erwin was in touch with De Guzman, the Filipino who—he said— served as Tokyo's liaison with U.S. Negroes. De Guzman reportedly delivered "about 65" guns to Erwin and he delivered funds to him too. De Guzman also said that his promiscuous use of aliases was a product of his earlier association with the UNIA, designed to "create the impression of different persons from different towns." He confessed to a personal acquaintance with Garvey himself, though his central UNIA contact was "Madam Demena," a "national organizer" of the group. She was "Porto Rican" with "brown skin." It was through the UNIA, he said, that he met "Doctor Takeda," a "Japanese newspaper publisher," in 1925, who proved valuable in his political work. He also knew "Mr. Yicklung," a "Korean, a member of some radical society in Asia." But his prized contact seemed to be Erwin, who was tasked to "organize colored people of every country" in a "secret" fashion.[32]

It was Madam Demena, said De Guzman, who convinced him to pass as Japanese, though Takahashi paid him to be "pro-Japanese." He was told by "Takahashi" that "the Japanese people are going to invade this country and they going to trick the white folks, going to split them." His Japanese interlocutor also said that "we used to have an alliance with Europe," London more specifically, but "we believe that England has lost her influence and we are going to join with the other white nations in Europe because we wouldn't want to let the white people in Europe get together and they will be able to whip us, but as long as we can keep the white people in Europe divided, we can perform there and have one group fighting the other group, then we can accomplish our object in Asia." The aim: "drive the white power in Asia out." At the University of Tokyo there was a "black race of people . . . being trained to go all over the world and preach to all the dark races the gospel of . . . Africa for the Africans." He also said that "there are now many Japanese in every city in the United States who were disguised as priests, lecturers and propagandists, in a prelude to the "fight" against the United States. The 1924 immigration exclusion bill was the casus belli. It was a "national insult and the American people are going to pay for it." He said that Tokyo "had prepared for this war against the white powers ever since the conclusion of the Russo-Japanese war."

In 1933 De Guzman spoke at a UNIA meeting, conveying a similar message as was told to him about Tokyo's ambitious plans for conquest. He got to know Erwin and gained access to Erwin's office, where De Guzman "went through the files" and found "letters from Japanese" where "they congratulated Mr. Erwin for the work he is doing." The letters were in English: "some came from San Francisco" and "some came from Hawaii." Erwin told Negroes to buy guns; "anything Mr. Erwin or Mr. Butler said to the colored people, 99 out of 100" did so. He recalled meetings of "about 700 or 800 people" of the PMEW with "standing room" only. These were "secretive" meetings with the message being clear: "they will die for the Japanese."[33]

There may have been opportunism and folk religion involved in the popularity of the PMEW in East St. Louis. PMEW member William Officer called himself the "funeral director" of the city. Since at that time Negroes were generally consigned to handle the cadavers of other Negroes, a funeral director could build a successful business and become a stalwart of the middle class. "I knew it [the PMEW] was a racket," he confessed, "but I didn't dare raise my voice against it because some of the people told me you couldn't get to heaven if you didn't belong to the Pacific Movement." A related church of the PMEW provided degrees, including one called "Lion of Juda[h]," confirming the tie to Ethiopia: "they gave me a little lion on a black piece of cloth and I threw it away," he told prosecutors. With a nose for business, he conceded that "what I was after was bodies," and a pro-Tokyo movement among Negroes in East St. Louis was guaranteed to produce a treasure trove of cadavers. Anyway, as "National Secretary for the Funeral Directors," he traveled "26,000 miles a year and I am out of town four or five days a week" and could not be expected to be expert on the details of the PMEW, his membership notwithstanding.[34] Of course, his cavalier, almost flippant testimony was likely designed to convince prosecutors that he was no threat—even if he had been collaborating with pro-Tokyo Negroes.

George Floore may have been as opportunistic as Officer seemed to be. "My nickname is Sport," said this hotel worker and PMEW member. "I was selling sausage and I knew the organization [PMEW] had quite a few members and I thought my presence there with my name on it I could get quite a bit of business." Of course, one cannot rule out that this "opportunism" was a ruse to avoid the appearance of being in sympathy with PMEW goals when being interrogated by prosecutors. Even Floore conceded that the group's purpose was to "stop lynchings and burnings and try to get better living conditions," goals to which he did not object.[35]

* * *

An essential element of the agenda of the Peace Movement of Ethiopia (sometimes called the Ethiopian Peace Movement), which also was tied to Tokyo, was the notion of repatriating U.S. Negroes to Africa, with Liberia being the likely site. Mittie Maude Lena Gordon, their leader, was described as a "mulatto woman . . . about 50 years old" as of 1939, who "succeeded in establishing local branches in several parts of the country," mostly from "the old Garvey movement." She was in

close touch with Senator Theodore Bilbo of Mississippi, the reactionary legislator who also backed the idea of deporting Negroes en masse.
Apparently, the Liberian authorities were in favor of "selective" migration but not a "mass" migration.[36] As early as 1931 Gordon was listed as
president of the Peace Movement of Ethiopia and was endorsed not only
by Bilbo but by his ideological comrade, Earnest Sevier Cox.[37] Gordon's
group should be distinguished from the Ethiopian World Federation,
which was broader in membership and not as stridently pro-Tokyo as
the PME.[38]

Senator Bilbo was told that in December 1932, Mittie Maude Lena
Gordon and her pro-resettlement comrades met in Chicago. They discussed the "limitations" endured by Negroes in the United States, and
she asked how many would join a "Back-to-Africa" movement. "Her audience," it was said, "in one voice cried out, 'We would be glad to go.'"
The very next morning thirty-five card tables were brought to the hall
where they had assembled and seventy volunteers were tasked to aid in
the recording of names for a petition to that effect. "The hall was kept
open night and day for three months," it was reported. "Sub-stations
were opened elsewhere in Chicago and in nearby Indiana"; "in eight
months' time, 400,000 names" were recorded, and by 14 November
1933 these were dispatched to the White House. "Within a period of five
years," it was asserted, "approximately 2,350,000 Negro names" were
duly recorded backing resettlement.[39]

Senator Bilbo and those who backed him analogized their deporta-
tion proposal to the settlement of "Jews in Palestine."[40] By August 1941
the legislator was seeking to speak in New York City under the auspices
of the UNIA and the African Patriotic League in "celebration of the an-
niversary of the late Marcus Garvey." Scores of organizations protested,
but a number could be easily scorned as being, supposedly, "Communist fronts."[41] Yet press mogul Claude A. Barnett most likely echoed the
settled opinion of most Negroes when he wrote that Bilbo's plan was
"laughed at here by national legislators and Negroes alike," though some
had been "lured by a former follower of Marcus Garvey."[42]

In any case, reportedly Liberia was involved in discreet negotiations
with Japan. In early 1937 Shimjiro Akimota of Tokyo went to Monrovia
on a "secret diplomatic mission" resulting in a "commercial agreement,"
according to a Negro journalist.[43] Near that same time, Japan was re-

ported to have started a steamship service to the Congo, which would connect this sprawling region with "West and South African ports as well as these places within the Far East."[44]

The Addis regime, cornered by Rome in any case, utilized "racial" appeals to attract U.S. Negroes, which in turn dovetailed with Tokyo's initiatives in the United States. Malaku Bayen, a close relative of His Imperial Majesty of Ethiopia, informed Claude Barnett of the Associated Negro Press, one of the key opinion molders among U.S. Negroes, that "my country will not get very far with the help that is rendered by the white man for the development of the country," but "we could obtain all the help that we need from the United States and the West Indies." He wanted Barnett's aid in "carefully select[ing] young men and women [with] definite training" with the "possibility of obtaining a position in the service of the Ethiopian government." It was true that "our Government is employing white foreigners in various departments and that these white men have gone on year after year, doing as little as they can for us." Thus, he insisted, Addis desired a "superior type of well qualified black men, who are not fortune hunters and who have race consciousness."[45] To that end, he wanted to "acquaint American Negroes with the happenings in Ethiopia through the Negro press."[46]

Barnett required little prompting. A savvy businessman with wide global interests that his news service's press coverage helped to sustain, he also maintained close ties to Tuskegee Institute. Thus, he told a key administrator there that Addis would "welcome Colored Americans," especially "engineers and scientifically trained men," particularly since they were "suspicious of the whites in their country"—but not the Japanese. Addis "offers the grandest opportunities for American Negroes," he thought.[47]

* * *

Part of the propaganda outreach by Tokyo to U.S. Negroes involved feting them in Japan, gaining adherents who could prove useful in times of war. At times, this did not work out well, most famously in the case of Langston Hughes, whose 1930s journey to Japan ended disastrously—for both sides—in mutually bitter recriminations.[48] However, Hughes was firmly in the embrace of the organized left, including close ties to the Communist Party, which had proven immune to Tokyo's charms. This could also be said of Paul Robeson, who excoriated Japanese aggression in China in no uncertain terms. "There is no such thing as an indivisible racial unity," he charged hotly; "the struggle is a class one." This approach, however, was not widely accepted, even among U.S. Negroes, who tended to frame their dilemma in the context of white supremacy. Robeson and his comrades were of the view that "any person and especially a Negro, who can possibly be in favor of the present Japanese attack on China is obviously on the side of fascism."[49]

More typical was the approach to Japan of W. E. B. Du Bois, who echoed Pickens—and a broad swathe of U.S. Negro opinion—in rationalizing Japanese depredations in China.[50] Du Bois was touched by the hospitality heaped upon him during his 1936 journey to Japan.[51] Akin to the ecumenical approach that united left and right in Tokyo against persecution of Negroes, the conservative George Schuyler, like the progressive Du Bois, was also feted on visiting Japan and wrote several pro-Nippon articles upon his return.[52]

Claude A. Barnett, the affluent Negro publisher in Chicago, told the Japanese consul general in Manhattan in 1934 that "we are much interested in the positive evidence of new social and economic conditions, given shape by the Japanese," particularly since the "American Negro" had a "natural interest in other peoples whose color might be a bar to their fullest and freest expression"; thus, "twelve million Negroes in the United States" chose to "demand fair play for the Japanese." Hence, he wrote, "we are suggesting the possibility of an outstanding Negro citizen being invited to Japan," notably their pro-Tokyo correspondent, William Pickens, who "has written for us for 14 years."[53]

Besides headliners like Schuyler, Hughes, and Du Bois, a steady stream of U.S. Negroes were sailing across the Pacific to Japan. Some of these were trumpeting what was thought to be the rise of the "colored" against the "white," as suggested—or at least it was thought—by the invasion of Ethiopia and Japan's presumed support for Addis Ababa. Consider Dr. Willis N. Huggins, born in Selma, Alabama, circa 1886, and who went on to graduate from Columbia and Northwestern, then received a doctorate from Fordham University in 1929. He was fluent in French, German, Italian, and Arabic, but as early as 1911 he planned a career in Addis. To that end he worked with W. H. Ellis, a rare Black Wall Streeter who worked closely with Ethiopian elites. Huggins was slated to become minister of education in Ethiopia, but instead he chose to lecture on African history at the University of Tokyo by 1938.[54] The leading Negro sprinter Eddie Tolan was offered a job as track coach at this same university, at a time when African Americans were barred generally from prestigious U.S. institutions of higher education.[55] His fellow sprinter Ralph Metcalfe was lionized in Japan, particularly after setting a new record for the two-hundred-meter sprint in Manchuria; hundreds of thousands watched him run there and in Japan.[56] Still, during the 1932 Olympics in Los Angeles, Japanese athletes complained that, like Negroes, they were barred from certain restaurants.[57]

Also arriving in Japan in 1935 were three Negro schoolteachers from Simmons Elementary School and Vashon High School in St. Louis, a city that, with its neighbor, East St. Louis, was probably the citadel of pro-Tokyo feelings among Negroes. Expressing the attitude of all three, one of the group wrote, "I found the Japanese the most kindly, courteous people I have ever known. . . . I was utterly unprepared for the profound feeling they showed. . . . I was prepared to find racial prejudice in Japan," an understandable premonition given where she resided. Instead, "if there was any prejudice it was shown against the white man. The Japanese bitterly resent white America's treatment of Japanese," but "they treated us as brothers and sisters."[58] The trio—Alice McGee, Isabel Dickson, and L. M. Turner—were ecstatic about Japan. Such attitudes propelled the wartime notion that U.S. Negroes might not be worse off if Tokyo prevailed. The headline in the Negro press was evocative: "Japanese men, women weep when told of American Negro [and] are kindest, most friendly people."[59]

By way of contrast, Kenso Nushida, of Japanese origin, was signed to play with a semi-professional baseball team in Sacramento, though, as one Negro reporter put it, African Americans "no matter how good are not given a chance in organized baseball."[60]

Tellingly, the widow of Sufi Abdul Hamid, a notorious Black Nationalist in Harlem, was born in Panama, lived in Jamaica, and visited Japan at length, perhaps because her paternal grandfather was said to be Japanese.[61] Dorothy Hamid, also known as Madame Fu Fattam, was known as the "Negro-Chinese seer" and, along with her spouse, formed the Universal Holy Temple of Tranquility, which was Buddhist in conception and looked toward Japan—and Tibet and India—for inspiration.[62]

Retrospectively, it is difficult to discern whether or not this trend was driven by the contemporaneous rise of Japan.[63]

Negro artists and musicians were finding opportunities in Asia—including Japanese-occupied China—at a time when the Great Depression and normalized bigotry were limiting them in the United States. Nora Holt, a famed Negro chanteuse, performed in Shanghai for eight months beginning in August 1932.[64] Teddy Weatherford, a Negro booking agent in Los Angeles, found Holt's experience to be normative and indicative of opportunities in all of Asia.[65]

Euro-Americans were also not unaffected by these tours by U.S. Negroes. Channing Tobias, who was to serve as a leading NAACP official, visited Hong Kong, Shanghai, Nanking, and Soochow near the same time of Du Bois's journey. There he encountered "Southern white friends from America," including "Texas, Virginia and Mississippi," who despite their inured and ossified racist folkways were charmingly amiable. "How sad it was that racial prejudice back home" magically disappeared abroad. This disappearance was particularly noticeable in the "French Concession" in Shanghai, though "all the peoples of the Orient are tremendously interested in the Negro problem in America."[66]

And it could have been added that the reality of a rising Japan—in China not least—sobered otherwise inebriated Euro-Americans drunk on the bile of white supremacy. Tobias, a leading NAACP official by 1954 at the time of Jim Crow's official demise, also spent two weeks in Japan, and like his compatriots Pickens and Du Bois, he too was impressed with this island state. "Another outstanding observation," he wrote with enthusiasm, "was that all of the government and business work of Japan is carried on by Japanese. In other countries of the East, Europeans are usually found in the government offices and leading business houses."[67]

Tobias might also have noticed what struck Bishop Arthur J. Moore of Atlanta upon his return from Japan after flailing and failing as a missionary. "When you try to convert Orientals," he observed, "they ask some embarrassing questions about how we treat the colored races, how we run business, distribute profits, and about our downright selfishness."[68] By May 1937 newspapers in northern China, where Japanese influence was substantial, were carrying details of the "atrocity" of lynching on the front page. The reaction there was that U.S.

missionaries, according to the ANP, "ought to go to Mississippi instead of coming to China."[69]

As for Pickens, he retained his title as chief defender of Tokyo among U.S. Negroes, though admittedly the competition had become stiffer as the 1930s plodded on. "How many of us are willing to help Mr. Roosevelt to oblige the British Empire by pulling its chestnuts out of the Asiatic fire?" Pickens proclaimed that "England is afraid that Japan's success may stir up even India and make the domination of Asia by white Europeans impossible" since "Europeans feel, and truly so, that they could manage China much longer if China is not dominated by Japan." In contrast to the situation in the North Atlantic nations, he said, in Japan "European, Asiatic, African are all just human beings."[70]

"These Japanese," he exclaimed, "are shooting holes in the ancient myth about 'superior races'. For that reason, it may be better for China if Japan should win her objectives."[71] Of course, there were "jitters" in "white nations" about Japan's ascendancy; "Well," he scoffed, "who in the name of the Lord ought to be masters in the Orient if not the Japanese, or some other Oriental race?"[72]

Part of the problem of rebutting Pickens effectively was exposed in 1938 when it appeared that Moscow and Tokyo might clash again. In attacking the Soviet Union, Pickens fit comfortably within the national consensus, making it more difficult to reject his terming the Soviet Union "this fool nation" and "the aggressors"; he returned to the idea that "the whites who have grown to fear the waxing power of Japan, have doubtless fed this Chinese jealousy" of Tokyo.[73] In short, how could Tokyo be effectively blocked by Washington, as long as subduing Moscow seemed to be the top priority? As a result, anticommunism served usefully as a mask for pro-Tokyo sentiment.

Still, pro-Moscow sentiment at times manifested, despite the penalties resulting from such an attitude. After Japan's aid to Ethiopia withered in the face of its anticommunist alliance with Italy, the moderate Negro journalist Gordon Hancock wrote that Moscow had assumed moral leadership in Africa.[74] Paris and London chose to "grovel," which was bad news for U.S. Negroes, since what fascism intended for Jews was a precedent for African Americans. But this kind of analysis, insofar as it highlighted Moscow favorably, did not fit the prevailing zeitgeist, allowing Japan once more to escape censure by U.S. Negroes.[75]

Other than those within the orbit of the Communist Party—and an occasional outlier like Hancock—those who might have rebutted Pickens were handicapped frequently because they often failed to reject colonialism, not to mention white supremacy. Pickens, on the other hand, asserted that "the Japanese in China have never yet placed Chinese in the same sub-human category into which all these European and American whites have put Chinese there: into segregated areas." Somehow Tokyo was "pushing back . . . ten times their number of Chinese, in spite of all the secret and open aid given the Chinese by almost all the white nations" and it was this, he declared, that drove Japan into "alliance and sympathy" with Rome and Berlin.[76] Hancock was one of the few who lamented the double standard that condemned the Japanese role in China but countenanced the colonization of the British in India, the Dutch in Indonesia, or U.S. forces in the Philippines.[77]

Also influencing the likes of Pickens were news items that suggested that China—seeking aid to repel Japan—was interested in allying with the Jim Crow United States. Surely U.S. Negroes looked askance when a noncitizen Chinese merchant in Phoenix, Arizona, helped to fund an effort by less than affluent Euro-Americans who were seeking to evict two Negro families who were renters from a racially restricted tract.[78] Nor were Negroes assuaged when in 1930 they were obliged to sue a Chinese restaurant in Boston for barring them on Jim Crow grounds.[79]

Augusta, Georgia, boasted of a Negro population of about 26,000 and a mere 250 Chinese, who mostly lived and did business among Negroes: somehow they were recognized as "white" and attended this favored group's churches and schools.[80] However, since a statute in North Carolina sought to bar marriages between Chinese and Negroes, it was reasonable to infer that Asians were responding to societal cues when seeking to uphold Jim Crow.[81] Nevertheless, those of Japanese origin—unlike their Chinese counterparts in North America—had developed a well-merited reputation for flouting the dictates of Jim Crow.

Still, U.S. Negroes often were able to distinguish between the plunder of China and the rather frequent adherence of Chinese Americans to Jim Crow norms. Thus, African Americans were reported to have played a key role in backing "Hands Off China" gatherings, designed to forestall imperial plunder.[82] In complementary fashion, the Chinese Students Club of Colorado College informed the NAACP about its staunch opposition to racism.[83]

Still, on balance pro-Japan attitudes predominated over pro-China ones among Negroes during this era. The Associated Negro Press mirrored this attitude when it cited without comment the vitriolic attitude of Admiral Nobumasa Suetsugu of Japan, who spoke angrily of "driving whites from Asia."[84] Also reported without condemnation were the words of Vice Admiral Sankichi Takahashi of Japan, who assailed the "sense of superiority" he saw in U.S. attitudes toward his nation.[85] Muriel Adams, billed by the ANP as "the Jane Addams of London," agreed that "Japan's aggression in China is the result of the refusal of white Occidental nations to accord her racial equality," referring to the abortive racial equality proposal at Versailles and how that empowered "militarists" and discredited "liberals."[86]

Mittie Maude Lena Gordon thought she espied another cleavage in Black America besides pro-Japan and pro-China sentiments. She told Senator Bilbo that there were "two classes of Afro-Americans in this country": "the intelligentsia" (for example, NAACP leaders and members) and the "dissatisfied, race conscious, depressed and heartbroken, humble and law abiding simple minded class," which had "never been satisfied in America" and "always have desired a nation of our own." They were "forced to live in condemned and tumbled down shacks packed in like sardines in a box without any water or other sanitary conditions, . . . infested with bugs, mice and rats." These were the ones clamoring to emigrate to West Africa—though she was sufficiently tactful not to tell the Dixiecrat leader that these were also the ones who, she surmised, were potentially pro-Tokyo.[87]

Repeatedly, Gordon emphasized that economic misery was driving Negroes to consider resettlement. "We are the poorest people in the country," she told Bilbo; "our membership is composed of those on direct relief," a level of desperation that simultaneously may have made them susceptible to Tokyo's blandishments.[88]

However, as Gordon sought to manipulate Bilbo—and vice versa—her opinion of her ability to execute this tricky task may have been shaken if she had been able to read the missives from the legislator's staunchest supporters. Belle Steiner of Spring Hill, Alabama, had contemplated world war as early as September 1939 and counseled Senator

Bilbo that if such a conflict occurred, "please see that the Negroes are called first. The last war they called the white boys & this country has too many Negroes," which explained why "the white men can't get any jobs."[89]

Kathryn Mitchell of Chicago instructed the Mississippi lawmaker that advocating resettlement while tensions with Japan were rising was playing with fire. "Look how many times the Japs [*sic*] have asked your race," she told him, "to leave its country? Have you left, no!" Yet, "we were born here in America and have as much right to remain here as all the other races here who do not belong here"—though she undermined her case by referring to the "Chinese" and "Japanese" as being part of the latter category.[90] Still, the wider point was that if Negroes could be expelled from North America, perhaps that was a precedent for Euro-Americans to be ousted from the Philippines and a good deal of Asia, a feat that seemingly was on the horizon.

* * *

Even before the assault on Pearl Harbor, currying favor among U.S. Negroes was paying dividends for Tokyo. As Japanese textile exporters began to challenge their U.S. competitors, African Americans did not express any particular objection. Earl Constantine of the National Association of Hosiery Manufacturers assailed Japan, alleging that it was displacing his constituency. But a Negro journalist was nonplussed; the challenge "will have little, if any effect, on colored workers, as there is only one factory in the cotton industry which employs Negroes," and that one was in Durham, North Carolina.[91]

How could the United States muster the national cohesion to confront effectively a formidable Japan when Tokyo had established a firm foothold among U.S. Negroes? This was the seemingly insuperable dilemma that the toxic combination of Jim Crow and U.S. imperialism had created.

4

White Supremacy Loses "Face"

In the period preceding the atomic bombing of Hiroshima, pro-Tokyo and anti–white supremacist sentiments were merging. A survey of leading Black Nationalists of this era suggests why.

Before the bombing of Pearl Harbor, William Pickens reprimanded a Los Angeles radio station for referring to Japanese as "Ethiopians." He observed that U.S. Negroes were also "often referred to loosely as 'Ethiopians,'" suggestive of how African Americans, Japanese, and Ethiopians had been conflated, facilitating a de facto alliance among the three.[1]

This was manifested in groups among U.S. Negroes that included "Ethiopia" in their name but were designed, at least in part, to back Tokyo. Congressman John Rankin of Mississippi, a preeminent reactionary, charged that the "Zoot Suit Rapists" (Mexican Americans, Filipino Americans, and others in Los Angeles falsely accused of various offenses and then beaten in the streets, just as the war was raging) were actually Negroes with "cohorts in the Black Dragon Society."[2] All U.S. "minorities" were being conflated with the antagonist in Tokyo; all were viewed as variants of "Ethiopians," nationals of a nation that somehow had for the longest time managed to elude European colonialism before being brought to heel.

Congressman Rankin was reflecting the unassailable point that pro-Tokyo Negroes often included "Ethiopia" in the title of their organizations, a direct legacy of the tumult of the 1930s when, it was thought, Japan and Addis Ababa were yoked in an alliance.

One such organization was the Peace Movement of Ethiopia (PME), whose leaders were later charged with what amounted to sedition in the early 1940s.[3] Mittie Maude Lena Gordon was a leader of the PME, which was organized in 1932 purportedly for the purpose of migration to Liberia (at this juncture, "Ethiopia" was often deployed as a synecdoche for the continent as a whole). In some ways it was the twentieth-century version of the American Colonization Society, which too was intrigued with the idea of dispatching U.S. Negroes en masse to Africa. As noted, they were not above allying with Senator Bilbo's "voluntary resettlement" bill. Gordon was "permanent president," elected on 24 February 1933. Her paternal grandfather, John Merrill, was described as a "white man" and her paternal grandmother, Ann Merrill, was a slave of Merrill's and, reportedly, a "full blooded Cherokee." When freed, she married a man known as Henderson and lived in Webster Parish, Louisiana. Gordon's mother was said to be a "black African woman whose father was brought to this country when four years old and became a slave."

Gordon's spouse and comrade, William Gordon, worked as a farmhand in both cotton and corn, then in the orange groves of Florida, until age eighteen. Then he became a railway worker. By 1927 he had opened a delicatessen in Chicago and a restaurant by 1934.

David James Logan, another PME member, was similarly peripatetic, seeing enough of the republic to be convinced that Jim Crow was not merely regional nor an isolated phenomenon: he was born in Texas and was also a U.S. military veteran, having fought in the Spanish-American War of 1898, where the fate of the Philippines was at stake. Yet another of Gordon's close comrades, Seon Jones, was born in the British Caribbean, then moved to the Canal Zone, then enlisted in the British military by 1917 and served in Europe. Then it was back to Panama, then Cuba and the United States, where he became a naturalized U.S. citizen.

It was in 1930 that Gordon went to a UNIA meeting in Chicago and met De Guzman, whom she knew as Takis. She thought he was Japanese, as did many others. She also met a man known as "Mr. Leong," whom she thought to be a "Chinaman," and Mr. "Lotario," a Filipino. Takis asked her to assist in founding the Peace Movement of Ethiopia, but she told him he was knocking on an open door since she was already moving in that direction after she ascertained that the UNIA seemed unable to accomplish her goal: dispatching Negroes back to Africa. Takis, in turn, also wanted Negroes to leave the United States, but purportedly his words were "we're going to take your people to Manchuria." Gordon said she disagreed. "I never joined the Peace Movement of the Eastern World," she said, but this remark was made in court when she was facing prison time for being affiliated with the PMEW. She also conceded that "Takis was at my home many times" and that she appealed to the Japanese consul in Chicago for aid in returning to Africa. By December

1932 the PME was a going concern and the perception that the group received backing from Japan did not appreciably harm its prospects in Black America.

* * *

George Johnson was born in Cairo, Illinois, a hotbed of pro-Tokyo sentiment among Negroes. His father was R. Johnson-Bey, whose surname was often carried by those with ties to the Moorish Science Temple (MST), which too was pro-Japan. Johnson said he worked with pro-Tokyo forces to seize control of the MST; this included receiving funds from Japan. He also said that Gordon was funded by similar sources. One of these pro-Tokyo agents was reported to have said, "We will have war. . . . We want you to have enough members by 1944 to overthrow the government." Chandler Owen, a former colleague of union leader A. Philip Randolph and no friend of the PME or PMEW, charged that Gordon, Johnson, and the rest thought "the Negroes should stop killing each other and kill the white people."

The U.S. government thought that at its height the Peace Movement of Ethiopia had "membership" that ranged "between 3 and 4 million," though this seems extraordinarily high and might be a better indicator of the hysteria engendered among the authorities at the thought of being in the midst of pro-Tokyo Negroes. Branches were said to sited in Chicago and Galesburg, Illinois; Gary; Baltimore; Phoenix; Long, Mississippi; Gould, Arkansas; Mathersville, Mississippi; Bamboo, Mississippi; Dunleath, Mississippi; St. Louis; Pittsburgh; Pulatka, Florida; and Center, Mississippi. Gordon taught members that an African of slave ancestry cannot become a citizen of the United States, per the infamous *Dred Scott* decision by the high court of 1857 and, thus, resettlement and/or alignment with Tokyo should be pursued.

Though Gordon denied as much after being indicted, in the prelude to the Pacific War, Wellington Chavis, a druggist, said that he attended PME meetings and heard Gordon make fervent pro-Tokyo statements, all of which were greeted by the audience with "vigorous applause." The authorities charged that before the war, Gordon had urged on this conflict, terming it a "god-send" since "through it black folks shall be free all over the world[,] that is why we have worked so hard for these . . . years." Moreover, she was said to have remarked, "Germany is not our enemy, the preacher is our enemy. She is tearing down the western gates in order that we may return to our land."

Gordon did not neglect Tokyo; apparently in her files was an undated letter to General Sadao Araki of the Japanese military from the PME that said, "We wish a secret alliance with the Japanese government. . . . This war is between the white man and the Japanese and we are not included."

According to a press account, Gordon regarded Senator Bilbo as the "'Great White Father' of the Negro," though apparently his anti-Tokyo sentiments did not overly concern her. At the same time, Bilbo's white supremacist constituency should have questioned him more sharply about his upholding their cause in light of his collaboration with Black Nationalists whose sworn mission—ostensibly—was to dismantle their enterprise.

In one example among many, Johnson, the prison convict who testified against Gordon, was said to have voluntarily returned to prison after breaking parole since, according to a journalist, he "feared for his life when he accepted sums of money from a Japanese agent and then refused to aid the movement." Supposedly he got five hundred dollars. Gordon was said to have approached him in 1933 since he was the son of Johnson-Bey, a leader of the Moorish Science Temple. Reportedly, Gordon and her spouse introduced him to De Guzman.[4] Gordon angrily sought to rebut these damaging allegations, as she adopted prematurely the post-1945 line: that she had nothing to do with Japan and everything to do with Africa.[5]

Though the PME was centered in Chicago, there was also a pocket of strength in New York City. In Harlem at 113 Lennox Avenue meetings were held counseling that Negroes should not join the U.S. military, meetings that possibly included a young Malcolm Little. In the audience at one meeting, according to the authorities, was a "colored man wearing the uniform and distinctive insignia of the United States Army."[6] James Thornhill of the PME was said to have uttered seditious remarks at one of these Harlem meetings:

Black Men of America, wake up, you [have] no part in this so-called Democracy. The white man brought you to this country in 1619, not to Christianize you but to enslave you. This thing called Christianity is not

worth a damn. I am not a Christian, we should be Mohammeds or Moslems, not Christians. . . . This so-called white man means you no good.[7]

Thornhill was not unknown to the New York City police. He was arrested for "unlawful entry" in 1921 on the complaint of a friend (supposedly he purloined a coat). Thornhill also said, "I was convicted for
picketing stores in Harlem for jobs," a sacred cause for Negroes of various ideological persuasions in the 1930s.[8] Born in the Virgin Islands,
Thornhill had been an intermittent street speaker in Harlem for some
years, spreading to denizens there his explosive message. Perhaps his
birth in the Caribbean explains his harshness toward Winston Churchill;
one of his principal messages was that he "wouldn't die for a damn
Englishman."[9]

Thornhill's dyspeptically testy view of the British politician was not
peculiar. In part because of the influx of Africans from the colonized
Caribbean, U.S. Negroes had come to look askance at London and wondered why there should be nonchalance about this empire ruling Hong
Kong, Singapore, and India and fierce opposition to Tokyo supplant-
ing this decrepit power. When the Committee to Defend America by
Aiding the British was unveiled in Harlem before the Pacific War, one
Negro commentator was furious. "To the best of my knowledge," said
Sid Thompson, "nothing like this happened when Ethiopia was at war
with Italy. Forgetting the base intolerance of the British for the colored
peoples of their colonies, their segregation laws in South Africa, their
denial of the right of native Africans to own and inherit the land of their
forefathers, these people have the temerity to ask aid from hard pressed
colored people in America."[10]

Again, it would be an error to think that pro-Tokyo sentiment was
centered exclusively among a fringe of Black Nationalists. This supposed
"fringe" had touched a deep and raw sentiment centered among numerous U.S. Negroes. Even the eminent Rayford Logan, one of the premier
intellectuals among U.S. Negroes,[11] admitted that the one epitaph he
envisioned on his tombstone was "The white man's distress is the black
man's gain!" For "the first time in history, during the last world war one
dark race—thank God—the Japanese found opportunity for equality";
this perforce impacted the essential nemesis of African Americans:
white supremacy.[12]

* * *

As indicated by the testimony of George Johnson, the Moorish Science Temple was in some ways the seedbed of both pro-Tokyo sentiment and Black Nationalism generally. The MST preceded the Peace Movement of Ethiopia and the precursor of the Nation of Islam: many Black Nationalist groups and the ideology generally were marked by the MST. One U.S. source asserted that the MST was founded in 1913 and that "Japanese infiltration" commenced "following the mysterious death of Noble Drew Ali," the presumed founder, and the not coincidental arrival of the Japanese operative Satokata Takahashi on these shores.[13]

Another U.S. source said that the Moorish Science Temple was founded in 1915 by the man known variously as Timothy Drew and Noble Drew Ali, who died in Chicago in 1929. According to MST teachings, U.S. Negroes were descended from the Moors and thus were Islamic and "Asiatic," the purported North African roots notwithstanding. At its height, the MST was said to have sixty-nine branches. Its members were said to believe Tokyo's assertion that "there would a war between the United States and Japan" and that when this occurred, the "colored or dark races are to hang together." The authorities thought that "one of the duties" of the MST was "to try to get all colored members not to join the military forces of this country" and that in case war erupted, "and all the white men were in the Army, that there would be enough colored young men left to cause a revolution in this country and take over things here while the soldiers were away in the foreign service."[14]

Like some leaders of the PME, Charles Kirkman-Bey of the MST, who was born in North Dakota, claimed Cherokee ancestry.[15] Another source claimed that Kirkman-Bey was born in South Dakota and that his father was a "full blooded Sioux Indian, while his mother was a 'Moroccan.'" He was said to have studied in Cairo, Egypt, for six years and also attended "Delhi University." Though he was said to be proficient in spoken Arabic, the FBI claimed that he was "unable to hold an intelligent conversation in Arabic when challenged to do so." His comrade, Cash C. Bates-Bey, according to the FBI, was "known to have been a close associate of Major Satokata Takahashi, Japanese organizer among the Negroes." There were "rumors" of Negroes' "promised removal to 'safety zones' when the bombing of the United States begins." This would be necessary since, as one MST believer in Flint, Michigan, asserted, "Japanese are good fighters. . . . I have heard that the sky would be dark with airplanes and it would be at night, that it would be dark with airplanes of our brothers." Naturally, Negroes were urged to "arm themselves." Kirkman-Bey was slated to rule the United States, it was said, after Japan's triumph. "When this occurs, the position of the white man and the Negro will be reversed," which was a mighty incentive for some; this would also mean that the new "millennium will have arrived." The MST was seen as being part of the assumed Islamic onslaught said to be engineered by Tokyo: "agitation of the Mohammedan race was instituted by Japan as early as 1904," said the FBI; there was "no indication that agitation among American Negroes . . . originated in the Middle East"; indeed, "indications are all to the contrary—that infiltration came directly from Japan."[16]

The MST branch in Hartford hosted frequent visits by Japanese business visitors, the last one taking place reputedly in 1939.[17] It was said that "Japanese race propaganda among Negroes" was rife, and the MST was a prime transmission belt. At several meetings, fervent thanks were rendered publicly to the emperor of Japan himself.[18] The authorities believed that the MST was not only "highly anti-Semitic and subversive" but also "claims to be subsidized by the Japanese government [from] whom they received regular funds"; evidently the MST believed that "'the Japs have the U.S. surrounded' and that a large number of Japanese agents are employed here." The reporting FBI agent, however, doubted what he had found: since "the ability to keep a secret is not usually found in the Negro temperament, I presume there is an intelligent leadership back of the movement"; it was hard to believe that some MST members had been able to keep this pro-Tokyo conspiracy under wraps for so long. Signaling the need for affirmative action, it was determined that it would be "necessary to use a Negro investigator for further assignment in checking on this society."[19] After the war, there was a felt need by U.S. elites to integrate Negroes at various levels of society, notably as an incentive to reject foreign powers like Japan.

The Moorish Science Temple, it was thought, was located at the intersection where most of the pro-Tokyo Negroes interacted. Understatedly, the FBI argued that the MST "shows strong traces of Japanese influence" and had held meetings "at the homes of Japanese nationals." The ubiquitous De Guzman was present at times and was thought to be among "instructors of this society," who "have in the past been largely Japanese and Filipinos" and had ties to the PMEW and the "pro-Japanese Temple of Islam in Detroit."[20] Ultimately, a search of the home of Walter Jones Bey, of the MST in Flint, revealed a "large picture" of Tokyo's infamous General "Tojo in uniform," which he supposedly received from a "female member," though he had a "son in the U.S. Army" at a time when war had been declared against Japan.[21] MST members would have agreed with the contemporaneous words of Japan's Okakura Tenshin, who argued that "the spell of white prestige must be completely broken that we may learn our own possibilities and resources."[22]

* * *

The U.S. military thought it worthwhile to investigate this phenomenon and acknowledged that pro-Tokyo attitudes among U.S. Negroes were fueled by "some local law enforcement agents in the South [who] not only welcome the slightest excuse but actually seek the opportunity to shoot down Negroes." Hence, "subversive elements are sponsoring the Ethiopian-Japanese Association and the Negro-Moorish-American organization, their slogan being that Japan is champion of the colored races and why should the colored race fight another for the benefit of the white race?" Also of concern was that "colored associations have a proclivity for building up hidden caches of ball ammunition, in vague anticipation of the time when they will have to defend themselves against interracial abuse"—though others thought that this arming was in gleeful anticipation of a Japanese invasion of the United States.[23]

The U.S. military, which by definition had to be concerned if Tokyo had broad influence among Negroes, asserted that in 1935 Japanese agents were sent to "Arabia and Egypt to prepare themselves as propagandists to work in the Mohammedan countries" and that "the Koran and holy books were printed in Japan." Helping to foment Islam, directed from North Africa and the vicinity, among U.S. Negroes would provide a kind of shield to deflect what was thought to be the interrelated Christianity and white supremacy that undergirded the U.S. and European antagonists alike. Japan got further traction by "using as much as possible front officials of Negro or West Indian extraction"; the latter, with ties to London, were thought to be notably effective. Thus, by 1929 there were said to be over 18,000 "East Indians in Jamaica alone" serving to feed an already extensive anti-London atmosphere. Tellingly, the Jamaica Progressive Alliance had assumed ties to the Ethiopian Pacific Movement. There were even more "East Indians" in Trinidad and British Guiana, colonies that were also sending migrants to Harlem. "Negroes from the British West Indies are at present the most frequent agitators against the whites." One of the leaders of the Ethiopian Pacific Movement had stated auspiciously, echoing the words of the young Malcolm Little, "If they give me a gun and send me to Asia or Africa, I will use my own discretion." Typically, the Communist Party was blamed for propagating presumed sedition that "lends itself very well to exploitation by the Japanese."[24]

There were a slew of "Japanese-Negro Front organizations," it was reported, including the Emmanuel Gospel Mission of San Francisco, with suspected ties to the "Japanese Buddhist Church." As early as 1922 it was said to be preaching to "Negroes, Hawaiians, Mexicans and Hindus the doctrine of the necessity of a union of all colored races against the whites. The Afro-Asiatic League organized in 1919 also advocated a racial war." Then there was the UNIA, an "inspiration and ally to the Pacific Movement of the Eastern World and to the Ethiopian Pacific Movement," the leading forces in the proliferating galaxy of pro-Tokyo forces. The UNIA was said to be seeking to "get jobs for Negroes in national defense industries." EPM leaders argued that after the defeat of the United States, the nation "will be turned over to the Negro." The EPM leader Robert Jordan "claimed membership in the Black Dragon Society" of Japan.[25]

Reputedly, there were "definitely anti-Semitic . . . branches" of these groups in "Detroit and Chicago and a very significant branch in Washington, D.C. which is reported to include numerous Negroes in government service." The Allah Temple of Islam, which had been "started in Detroit in 1928," made a "claim that the origin of the Negro is in Asia, rather than in Africa," bringing it closer to Tokyo. It was "very active," and "one branch of the Islam Movement, called the Nation of Islam is a military organization." The PMEW had as a "parent organization and [was] a probable affiliate of the League of Asiatic Nations organized in Peiping, China about February 1933."[26]

Though the UNIA, the Allah Temple of Islam, the EPM, the MST, and the PMEW were the major organizational forces surveyed, the fact is that in some ways they were simply the tip of a nationalist iceberg. In Buffalo, for example, there was what was described as a "highly race conscious" group that highlighted the "Mohameddan religion and the Arabic language," both of which were taught; and Negroes were "encouraged to discard their 'slave' names and adopt Arabic names." This was the Addynu Allehe-Universal Arabic Association, not the ATOI.[27] In other words, these groups in many ways were capitalizing on a hunger among U.S. Negroes for alternatives to the status quo as much as they were helping to instill this attitude in the marrow of U.S. Negroes.

The prototype of the pro-Tokyo Negro may have been embodied by the man often known as Robert Jordan. A former UNIA member, he left his native Jamaica in 1914 headed to Asia; in 1918 he worked for a company known as the Japan Mail Steamship Company, the largest of its genre on the island. Described as "small but handsome," by 1935 he was a leader of the Ethiopian Pacific Movement, attracting hundreds regularly to his meetings in Harlem.[28]

At times referred to as Leonard Robert Jordan, he was also thought to resemble a Japanese national, perhaps because of his close and binding association with Tokyo. One of his EPM comrades was cited for the proposition that "I will fight for Japan with every drop of my blood and I wouldn't ask for a penny, for I realize that when the war is over I will be rightly paid and looked upon not as an inferior but looked upon as an equal man of the Japanese people and the dark people in the world."[29]

It was not just the U.S. military that worriedly surveyed how and why Tokyo had sunk roots among U.S. Negroes. After an exhaustive survey, the Associated Negro Press, a consortium of Negro journals, noted that "even before the first World War, the Japanese Foreign Office groped for a method of contacting Negroes in the United States." As reported by the ANP, when Du Bois organized a Pan African Congress in 1919, it was opposed by the major powers except for Japan, which greeted it with "fervent satisfaction." In Dixie, it was reported, "these Nipponese agents invariably began with an oily tirade against all white races," then spoke "freely of the eventual rise of darker peoples." These agents were "better versed in discriminatory laws of the southland than most Negroes and

could interject with marvelous accuracy the phobias and ranting of Tillman, Vardaman, Cole Blease, Thomas Dixon and Heflin of Alabama"
(leading Dixiecrats). Then there were "colored agents": "Japan's black allies in large seacoast cities of the black belt" who "established themselves
as fortune-tellers, seers, clairvoyants, spiritualists, voodoists, palmists,
phrenologists, tea-leaf and coffee ground readers. A few turbaned East
Indian mystics have been revealed as well educated Negroes or West
Indians with a knowledge of Arabic or a smattering of some Oriental
dialect," all of which was enhanced by "their 'foreign' hauteur and aloof-
ness." The fact that many of these individuals were affluent—because
of putative Tokyo subsidies—heightened their allure. They became the
"focus of attention and mysterious admiration" as a result. It was not just
Islam that was put forward as an alternative to Christianity and part of
Tokyo's magnetism: "usually the figure of a Buddha occupies a position
of prominence in the parlor or reception room" of these individuals,
many of whom tended to "prey on superstition." Hence, "in the event
of a full and successful invasion of our borders from the southwest, her
illiterate followers in the black belt were expected to rise with such vigor
that a temporary diversion would facilitate more rapid movement of the
invader."[30]

One analyst blamed Marcus Garvey and the UNIA—not the MST—
for the proliferation of pro-Tokyo sentiment among U.S. Negroes. According to Leon Taylor, Garvey "went along with full knowledge and
approval of the Imperial Japanese Government" of these various initiatives. The UNIA was the "controlling body" and at the top of this group
was a "secret oligarchy" of "West Indian[s]" with grievances against London. Then after his "departure Japanese spies took full control of the organized mass through their paid Filipino and radical Negro-West Indian
henchmen," all tied to Satokata Takahashi. This former officer in the Japanese military "himself photographed and diagrammed many sections
of the United States in company of various Negro women, of whom he
was exceptionally fond." He was notably active "along the Canadian border," where he "plotted and mapped extensive approaches . . . around the
Sault Saint Marie locks." He was not above the effort to "lavish gifts of
cash" upon unwitting Negroes, which, said this waspish analyst, "won
for him innumerable naïve, Negro, feminine companions." An unnamed
Negro woman from Cleveland was reported to be a top agent of Tokyo.[31]

Tokyo weighed in during the 1920s when a high-level directive man-
dated that "the captains of all ocean going Japanese passenger ships"
should "afford American Negro tourists preference in every way," a startling contrast with U.S. vessels, which routinely subjected Negroes to a
debilitating Jim Crow. Thus, Taylor concluded, Kansas City, St. Louis,
and Cincinnati remained the "inland strongholds of those secret organizations while New York, Jersey City and Roanoke afford hiding places
for the eastern aggregations."[32]

* * *

This book's emphasis on U.S. Negroes should not obscure the point that
a number of Euro-Americans engaged in espionage on Tokyo's behalf.
Still, a wartime source reported that in Seattle, hotels owned by those
of Japanese ancestry, many of them close to shipyards where African
American workers were arriving in droves from Texas and Louisiana to
toil, were more willing to serve Negro customers than those owned by
Euro-Americans. Apparently, brothels owned by those of Japanese origin, in contrast to those controlled by Euro-Americans, also were more
willing to entertain U.S. Negroes.[33]

In retrospect it is difficult to ascertain whether Jim Crow advocates
were more upset with Japanese and Japanese Americans supposedly
residing or opening businesses close to critical infrastructure or their
overtures to U.S. Negroes. The U.S. military concluded that "by accident
or design virtually always their communities"—meaning those of Japanese origin—"were adjacent to very vital shore installations, war plants,
etc. . . . throughout the Santa Maria Valley" in California. In the county
of Santa Barbara, including "the cities of Santa Maria and Guadalupe,
every facility, air field, bridge, telephone and power line or other facility
of importance was flanked by Japanese. They even surrounded the oil
fields"; this was "more than coincidence." There was no attempt to ponder how bigotry against U.S. Negroes facilitated the latter aligning with
Tokyo, thus making it more likely that the challenge to national security
sketched was actually plausible.[34]

This penetration of the U.S. Negro community by Tokyo helps to
explicate why Congressman Martin Dies asserted before the bombing
of Pearl Harbor that potential Japanese espionage in this country was
"greater than the Germans ever dreamed of having in the Low Coun-

tries." In the San Francisco Bay area, which had a substantial complement of both Negroes and those of Japanese origin, the situation was
"critical," he said.[35] Earlier, President Roosevelt was informed in a secret
message that "for years suspected espionage activities" by Tokyo in the
United States had been occurring.[36]

Congressman Dies may have had in mind a pre–Pearl Harbor incident when Japanese sailors from a tanker in Hawaii reportedly ascended
the tower of a local hotel and were observed taking pictures of the harbor and nearby fortifications. Other sailors supposedly were taking
measurements of the dock at Hilo. The secretary of the navy was then
informed of what were thought to be worrisome statistics:

> On the island of Hawaii, which is ungarrisoned [*sic*], only 10% of the mili-
> tary male citizens are white Americans, that is 887 out of 8287; while there
> are 2774 military male citizens of Japanese [origin]. In addition there are
> 2886 alien Japanese males of military age and 8688 Filipinos. A compari-
> son for white Americans of military age to all other citizens of military
> age reduces the ratio from 10% to 4%.

Tokyo was also monitoring San Francisco closely, as Congressman Dies
suggested. "Many of the visiting Japanese naval personnel have close
relatives among the local Japanese residents" and there were "active
Japanese agents in Hilo."[37] Amidst the hyperventilating, there was not a
pause to consider that if the national security situation were as frightening as suggested, then why exacerbate it by tormenting and terrorizing
U.S. Negroes, making it simpler for them to ally with Tokyo? Admittedly,
however, this concern gained momentum after the war.

It is comprehensible nevertheless why the otherwise jittery Congressman Dies arrived at such a conclusion. In the early 1940s the FBI was
told about a "prominent Negro real estate dealer" in an unnamed city
who recounted how a fellow Negro arrived at his house with a machine
gun and insisted that he take it, telling him bluntly, "You had better take
it because the time is coming that you will need it," in light of Negro
disgust with white racism combined with sympathy for Tokyo's racial
appeals. The real estate dealer also said that he would estimate that 75
percent of the homes of Negroes in Washington had some sort of fire-
arm. In Detroit, along with East St. Louis, the de facto capital of pro-

Tokyo sentiment among Negroes, as some saw it (St. Louis would have dissented), the FBI was told that "racial tension was great as it ever was," with the expectation that "niggers would be shot by the hundreds" in the next "riot." Revealingly, it was reported, "there are some Negroes that were at one time members of the Communist Party in this country and these Negroes spread the propaganda that should Japan win this war the Negroes would fare better under the Japanese than under the American Government."[38] Of course, another way to view this latter comment is as a ham-handed attempt to link the wartime foe with the assumed postwar antagonist.

Whatever the case, the point remained that Tokyo continued to believe that its trump card was the alienation of U.S. Negroes from their homeland and their concomitant attraction to Tokyo. To that end, Richard Wright's trailblazing novel Native Son was translated into Japanese only nine months after it was published in the United States in 1940. The translation was by a leading member of the Communist Party in Japan, indicative of how sympathy for U.S. Negroes crossed ideological borders in Tokyo, making it that much more profound.[39]

* * *

By December 1941 what had been predicted for years was at hand: Japan and the United States were at war. Days later, Walter White of the NAACP uttered what came to be regarded as conventional wisdom in liberal circles, wisdom that would animate and propel an ongoing push to erode Jim Crow: "Unless there is a more drastic readjustment of racial attitudes the United Nations [U.S. allies] cannot win this war."[40] "Each day until the Japanese are defeated," White warned, "the white prestige is being lessened in the world." Perhaps it was a "far cry from Abraham Lincoln to Singapore," but nonetheless, "there is a close[r] link to the tragedy of the Pacific than most people think." For just as the United States during the Civil War had to move toward abolishing slavery as a tool of survival, the United States now had to ban Jim Crow for similar reasons. Robert Sproul, president of the University of California–Berkeley, who appeared on the dais with White, concurred and also adopted a rhetorical tack that was to become increasingly more popular: he analogized Jim Crow to Berlin's policies. "Nazism unfortunately is not the exclusive possession of the German people. It exists among people in the United States who think ghettos are all right so long as they are confined to the Negroes."[41] A drumbeat of attack against Jim Crow erupted in a manner rarely seen, underlining how the Pacific War transformed the republic. Herbert Agar, editor of the *Louisville Courier-Journal*, urged action immediately on Jim Crow, since "all over Asia," Tokyo was advancing with the cry, "Look what the Americans are doing to their Negroes"—is this what they intend for you?[42] Tellingly, NAACP leader Walter White, when visiting the Philippines during the war, found that Japanese occupation forces had briefed islanders thoroughly about contemporary racist episodes in Los Angeles.[43]

The moderate Negro leader Gordon Hancock reminded one and all that "the stage for the Pearl Harbor debacle was not set in Tokyo but in Paris in 1918," when Japan's demarche on racial equality was defeated.[44] The linkage between Versailles and Pearl Harbor was made repeatedly by U.S. Negroes as they sought to impress upon Jim Crow advocates that their philosophy was downright dangerous.[45]

Hancock too compared Jim Crow defenders to Nazis, arguing that "American fascists seem more determined to defeat the aspirations of the Negro than the ambitions of the Japanese." Alluding to a spate of racist conflicts, he suggested that "whereas riots and lynchings followed victory in the First World War, they are preceding victory in the second." He warned pointedly, "this nation cannot watch Germans and Japanese and Negroes all at the same time."[46] Hancock argued that the "reign of terror in Europe is mirrored in the south of the United States. The resurgence of Ku Klux Klanism and the recent attempt to organize a League to Preserve White Supremacy" and the "recent outbreak of lynching" were compromising the war effort and playing into the hands of Berlin—and Tokyo.[47] By 1944 the NAACP felt compelled to berate Admiral William Halsey after he referred to Japanese as "yellow monkeys," a descriptor (albeit with a differing color) often applied to U.S. Negroes and seemingly designed to allow them to sympathize with Tokyo.[48]

Other anti–Jim Crow advocates took another tack, as did a commentator for the Associated Negro Press, who thought that "white supremacy" had lost "face in Asia" as a result of the rapid retreat of the United States and Britain in the Asia-Pacific basin by early 1942. "Face," a magical potion, it was said, "is vital anywhere to white supremacy," in order to compel those not defined as "white" to instinctually respond to the racist diktat. This loss of "face" was "more perturbing to its balance than territorial and material losses over there," meaning the Asia-Pacific. "Lost ground can be recaptured, yielded territory may be restored but 'lost face' is lost. What next? Anglo-Americans pulling Japanese in rickshaws?"[49]

Something similarly shocking was then unfolding. "If the Japs [*sic*] seize Madagascar and get a foothold for an attack on South Africa," wrote one Negro journalist, "General Smuts will arm the Negroes," as it might be "necessary to abolish racial discrimination and arm the Africans in the event of a crisis"; this would be a "great achievement, perhaps the greatest for Africans since European colonization."[50] General Smuts "declared that he would see that all colored persons were armed before permitting Japanese conquest of South Africa."[51]

Frank Marshall Davis, who went on to play a leading role in shaping Hawaii and its impact on the United States as a whole, including the mentoring of a future U.S. president,[52] observed in November 1943 that it is a "cockeyed society that grants gains to a racial group only when that society itself is in jeopardy, but that is the fact." Like Hancock and others, he recognized that "the major argument against long drawn out hostilities is the rising tide of American fascism. It is growing stronger daily."[53]

* * *

There was a tendency, particularly among white supremacists, to see the Pacific War specifically as an exemplar of beleaguered "whites" arrayed against all others, with the seemingly eternal "Negro Question" made all the more complex as a result. E. H. Pitts of the Eugenics Society of Sacramento told Senator Bilbo that the ongoing "injection of a Filipino problem, a Hindustani problem," and the like would eventually create a "more complex problem" and "intensify our Negro problem." He was reminded of what occurred a few decades earlier when, he wrote, the Quebecois "practically refused conscription in World War I and cynically boasted that the British Canadians would bleed white on the battlefields and leave Canada to them"; this, he noted, "ought to be a warning."[54] In other words, like other Bilbo correspondents, he fretted that Negroes would escape conscription and thus gain strength, no matter the postwar dispensation. Bilbo replied bluntly, "I am in favor of keeping our Oriental, Mongolian friends in Asia and of sending all that we happen to have in this country home [via] the shortest route."[55] He chose to retain a news report declaiming, "end of world racial barriers urged by Chinese spokesmen."[56]

Joseph Edgar told an editor at the *Pittsburgh Post-Gazette* that "the Chinaman should stay to himself, the Japanese to himself, the black man to himself."[57] Bilbo then told a local union leader, "I am still determined to send the Negroes back to Africa. It is their only chance."[58] Left unsaid was that this latter option was also perceived as a way to strengthen white supremacy.

At times it seemed that Senator Bilbo, Jim Crow's most vigorous defender, was as hostile to Tokyo as he was to Negroes, referring to Japanese as "these little yellow devils,"[59] while his fellow Mississippian Mary Polk referred to them as "yellow varmints."[60] Preparing "the war machine" in order to "exterminate the Japs" was his fondest wish in early 1942.[61] The "damnable, atrocious, hellacious Japs" was his mildest assessment in early 1944.[62] Doubtlessly, Bilbo paid close attention when a soldier just back from the southwest Pacific argued that there was "no such thing as a trustworthy Jap," for "over there we talked to Japanese prisoners who said they'd been educated at schools like the University of Southern California, Stanford, University of California, Hollywood High School"; it was concluded, "We've ceased to regard them as human."[63] Assuredly, this anti-Nipponese bloviating dovetailed neatly with the republic's wartime priorities, though the senator's Negro constituents would have been justified in wondering what this raving portended for themselves, which also could have strengthened preexisting pro-Tokyo proclivities.

Yet neither Senator Bilbo nor his most deranged constituents examined critically how he could be simultaneously so hostile to Tokyo, yet so solicitous of pro-Tokyo Negroes like Mittie Maude Lena Gordon. Moreover, this view of the Japanese as nonhuman meshed easily with a similar view of the Negro. This confluence—with perverse irony—may have made this Asian foe seem even more formidable, as one of Bilbo's constituents argued, when the issue was broached of interning Japanese Americans in the Delta. "They will live on rice," said this resident of Cleveland, Mississippi. "They will work. They will save" and "the next thing you know they will own your land and your neighbor's land. . . . You will have Japanese neighbors but you will not have Japanese cotton pickers, choppers, servants." This constituent did not stop there. "When

the war is over and the hatchet is buried, the Japs who are here will belong to that highly privileged class, 'a strong minority' and you [whites]
are but of the under-privileged majority." There were problems enough
"with the Negroes"; "let the Japanese come in and we will have the eternal triangle," already manifest in the Pacific basin. This would incite a
process that would mean "you and I had [to] pack our grips for we cannot compete much better than they."[64]

Homer Brett, also of Mississippi, warned that Tokyo's diabolical plan
was "to organize, regiment and arm the brown and yellow millions of
Asia under their leadership" in order to "subjugate the white races." Yes,
that could mean an ultimate showdown between Berlin and Tokyo—
but where would that leave Uncle Sam in the meantime? He recalled
that Kaiser Wilhelm himself "pointed out the Yellow Peril years before
it was apparent to statesmen." Japanese, he explained, possessed a "fanatical belief in their racial superiority, a bitter hatred of all whites and
incredible bestiality" besides—most of which Negroes had claimed were
traits of white supremacists. He worried that "the Japanese have a potent
weapon," that is, "the racial aversion of the black and brown to the white
which always exists."[65] He warned that racism should not allow for an
underestimation of Japanese capability. The problem Jim Crow advocates hardly envisioned then was how to contain racism after the war
ended and target solely African Americans while ignoring the lessons
of recent history?

Evidently, anti-Tokyo and anti-Negro sentiments were reinforcing
each other, and those in the vanguard of this trend apparently did not
realize that this was contributing to a devolution of white supremacy
as the more sober-minded came to recognize that "race wars" were not
an optimal mode to preserve the status quo. Even Senator Bilbo found
it difficult to ignore what Thorne Lane of Panama City told him as Singapore was falling: "times have changed since" the legislator formulated
resettlement, and now "the country is at war and until that's over I sup-
pose all attention should be directed toward victory"; in other words,
"segregation of the Negro must be suspended for the duration" of the
war.[66] Few dared to suspect that this "suspension" could be extended
indefinitely, while moderate Negroes likewise had difficulty in realiz-
ing after the war that some envisioned a suspension—not necessarily a
termination—of Jim Crow.

5

Pro-Tokyo Negroes Convicted and Imprisoned

After the bombing of Pearl Harbor, the skittish U.S. authorities began a massive crackdown on Negroes expressing pro-Tokyo sentiment. Certainly it was true that many of those detained had engaged in fire-breathing, flame-throwing verbiage. Surely it is accurate to say that those arrested were pro-Tokyo, though this was hard to disengage from their enervating alienation from the United States itself; many sincerely believed that, given lynching and other horrors, their fate could hardly deteriorate with a Japanese victory. Yes, many of the detained did discourage enlistment in the U.S. armed forces, though this was in the face of previous poorly kept promises that the destiny of Negroes would improve if they would just make another blood sacrifice.

Still, the arrests and convictions did not necessarily squelch the kind of thinking exhibited by these defendants. To a degree, much of this thinking was driven underground and rematerialized in the 1950s in, for example, the Nation of Islam. Black Nationalists were then distant from a now defeated Tokyo, though the profession of "Asiatic" origin lingered like the beard that continues to grow on the face of a corpse. Ironically, a good deal of this "Asian" orientation among U.S. Negroes was to re-appear after the entente between Washington and "Red China" in the 1970s.[1] Oddly, this "Maoist" posture persisted despite the fact that, unlike Tokyo, Beijing then was collaborating with the United States across the globe.[2] It was almost as if African Americans were engaging in wish fulfillment, willing China—despite massive evidence to the contrary—to play the role of pre-1945 Japan, indicative of the powerful hold Tokyo continued to exert on the Black Imagination.

Gordon Hancock argued that this spate of arrests of pro-Tokyo Negroes was indicative of a larger organic problem: "at his best," he wrote, "the Negro is often treated as a seditionist and conspirator"; hence, "it is not surprising then that a few should eventually react as seditionist."[3] In other words, Jim Crow had backfired wildly and badly and some of its victims had chosen to enact the seditionist role U.S. rulers had expected in light of the latter's atrocious malfeasance; as had been the case historically, the beleaguered Negro was once more seeking to embrace the sworn foe of Washington—Tokyo in this case—just as in the nineteenth century they had embraced London.[4]

* * *

In December 1942 at the mouth of the Mississippi River in New Orleans, a massive roundup of Negroes took place. The twenty-one men were accused of being opposed to military service and counseling others likewise. Before Judge A. J. Caillouet the defendants argued that Negroes were actually "Hebrews" and thus barred from waging war abroad. Their leader proclaimed, "Negroes don't have to go to war. You are Jews," while "all those who are masquerading as Jews are not Jews." The leader, Ethelbert A. Boraster, was also known as Frank Anselm, Kid Anselm, and Frankie Anselm.[5]

The NAACP was informed contemporaneously that Boraster "preached that Negroes were the direct descendants of Abraham, Isaac and Jacob" and therefore were ineligible for military service.[6] Interestingly, his stance meant that he and his comrades were analogous to those described as Muslim, who were also being arrested for dodging the draft.

The New Orleans sweep was not an isolated event. In New York City that same month, the press reported that leaders of "the so-called Ethiopia Pacific Movement" were detained. They were said to have "aimed at a coalition of Africa and Japan in planning a 'world empire for the dark races.'" Five leaders were arrested—four Negroes and one defined as "white." They were "indicted on sedition charges," according to the press; those charged were Robert Jordan, listed as president; Lester Holness, secretary; the Reverend Ralph Green; James Thornhill; and the man denoted as "white," Joseph Hartrey.[7] Again, fomenting "insubordination, disloyalty, mutiny" in the "armed forces" was the accusation; they were said to have sought to "obstruct recruiting" and "enlistment" in the U.S. military; their pro-Tokyo statements and, in some cases, actions were the evidence.[8]

On 18 February 1942 Lester Eugene Holness was arrested at his Harlem home at 14 West 119th Street by the FBI. "They searched the premises without a search warrant," he said, dismayed; they were seeking a "short wave and radio set and code book" said to be his way to communicate with his Tokyo supervisors. "Finding none," said Holness, they still arrested him and confiscated "all papers, personal and private they could find."[9]

The indictment of the five defendants charged that they "would willfully cause and attempt to cause insubordination, disloyalty, [and] mutiny" in the U.S. armed forces. They were said to "obtain audiences" to "solicit contributions" for their sedition and "would make speeches designed to mislead and to corrupt the patriotic, loyal and law abiding colored population of Greater New York and particularly the community known as Harlem." There they demanded that "Colored United States soldiers should not fight the Japanese"; instead, they contended that "you should learn Japanese so that you will be able to engage the Japanese in conversation when they come to this country" since "the little brown man from the East in a very short time will rule the world." Their advice to Negro soldiers? "Go back to your outfit and start a whispering campaign" to undermine the U.S. war effort.[10]

By January 1943 a jury of three Negroes and nine defined as "white," after deliberating over three hours, found the defendants guilty of sedition and conspiracy. It appears that the jury was moved particularly by words attributed to Jordan, who purportedly stated that "we are going to knock out Pearl Harbor again and then we are coming into Vera Cruz and then into Arizona." After the prosecutor cited these remarks, Jordan replied wanly, "I speak very broken English." He also denied threatening murder, while Holness denied having given a party in February 1942 celebrating the fall of Singapore to Japanese forces.[11]

Jordan, who may have been the pro-Nippon Negro most conversant with Japan, was at times referred to as the "Harlem Mikado" and supposedly was the advocate of the so-called BB Plan, pursuant to which Negroes who became Buddhists, a faith with deep roots in Japan, would win Japanese citizenship, visit, and presumably reside in Japan and study there too, including the sciences; all of this was known to the FBI.[12]

On 14 January 1943 the New York City defendants were convicted. James Thornhill, for example, was sent to prison for eight years for conspiracy to cause and attempt to cause subordination, disloyalty, and mutiny and to obstruct enlistment and recruiting to the U.S. military.

Pointed to specifically were remarks he was said to have uttered at a PME meeting on 4 July 1942.[13] Holness received a seven-year sentence; Best received four years; Jordan received ten years and a $5,000 fine.[14]

In an unrelated case in the metropolitan area, Carlos Cooks, described as "lean and hatchet faced," and whose roots were in the Caribbean but who went on to become a leading Black Nationalist in Harlem, was sentenced for pro-Tokyo sentiment in August 1942.[15]

The PME was not isolated in lofting the pro-Tokyo banner in New York City. In Brooklyn in 1943 William Briggs-Bey of the Moorish Science Temple declared that "we have been warned by the Japan Government that soon a starvation will take place in Europe" and Europeans will flood the United States taking jobs of Negroes. But Negroes need not fear, since Briggs-Bey assured that "I, myself . . . will leave for Tokyo . . . as soon as I can raise $1000" to confer with the comrades there. The FBI took note of this story too.[16]

In neighboring Newark, New Jersey, seven members of the "House of Israel" were arrested. Their leader—Askew Thomas, alias Brother Reuben Israel, alias "Hot Dogs"—was formerly associated with the PMEW and Takis, and thus had been involved in military drills of his followers for purposes viewed as not necessarily benign.[17]

In early 1943 a federal grand jury in East St. Louis indicted two leaders of the Peace Movement of the Eastern World on charges of sedition (as earlier discussed in chapter 3). David D. Erwin, a cook, and General Lee Butler, a janitor, were the designated culprits. Erwin was also listed as bishop of the allied Triumph Church of the New Age, which could fairly be described as broader in scope and membership than the PMEW, with which it was affiliated and which, in part, was designed as a transmission belt to propel Negroes into the PMEW. (The analogy was to the post–Nation of Islam Malcolm X, and his organizing both a political and religious arm.) They were accused of asserting that the "Pacific Movement should pay $1 a week to help Japanese soldiers" and seeking to "accumulate guns and ammunition to aid the Japanese when they invade the United States." Moreover, they were said to have devised "passwords and signs" in league with the presumed invaders. The PMEW was national in scope and claimed sixteen thousand members.[18] As often happens with conspiratorial groups, the passwords and signals were elaborate.[19]

By early 1942 Negro leaders in St. Louis described as "responsible" were alarmed by what they perceived as the rising popularity of the PMEW among African Americans. The doctrine that Negroes had no stake in the war and that, if anything, might be better off if the United States lost, was hardly a marginal viewpoint. Further south in Cairo and the Missouri boot-heel, large "secret" meetings of pro-PMEW Negroes were being held.[20] William Pickens had heard "Negroes saying that the colored citizens of the United States should emulate the people of India" in boycotting the war effort or otherwise backing Tokyo.[21]

Apparently there was overlap between New Orleans and its upriver companion, East St. Louis, in that Boraster was said to have traveled to the latter city to preach a rigorously antiwar sermon. A police officer from East St. Louis attended a PMEW meeting on 11 July 1941 where he heard Boraster speak. There were twenty men and six women present, and the message was to avoid joining the military. "He said he would prove by his Bible and the Constitution" that "no dark race with 1/10 Negro blood in them would be compelled to serve in the war" and said "eventually the white race was going to devour itself" and "the colored race if they stayed out of the war, they would rule the world." At a meeting two days later, Boraster was said to have "told people to buy guns for their protection in their homes."[22]

Boraster also counseled the Negroes in the Land of Lincoln to "collect arms and ammunition." The Reverend L. V. Huff of Mounds, Illinois, who defected from the PMEW, said that Takis—also known as De Guzman—also advised that Negroes arm themselves and "promised . . . free transportation in Japanese ships to Brazil for anyone who contributed to the movement $10 and a weapon." Another defecting member pointed out that the PMEW had "international" linkages with the "dark and colored peoples of the world."[23]

A contemporary observer concluded that the "spread of pro-Japanese propaganda among Negroes" had "caused quite a stir." A leader of the moderate National Negro Business League asserted that the PMEW had been a "nightmare" for years. "Japanese, German and Italian agents were trying to stir up unrest among Negroes," it was said, though Tokyo was in the forefront in this regard. Its slogan, "Asia for the Asiatics—Africa for the Africans," had struck an anti-colonial chord.[24] The influence of the East St. Louis-St. Louis axis was so pervasive that Mittie Maude Lena

Gordon of Chicago was said to have become attracted to their form of sedition "while under the influence of secret activities in St. Louis."[25]

* * *

Perhaps the most insightful way to comprehend these defendants is as simply the leading edge of a broader phenomenon: alienation among bludgeoned U.S. Negroes combined with catering by Tokyo to this same community to propel an organized body capable of committing sedition, draft dodging, and the rest. Another aspect of alienation was espied in 1944 when three students at Howard University, the historically Black school in Washington, D.C., engaged in a suicide pact in order to protest unfair treatment of Negroes in the armed forces and the maltreatment generally accorded Negroes in the United States. One of these men— twenty-two-year-old Norman Spaulding—was also a champion tennis player.[26] The defendants on trial chose not to pursue the path of suicide, but instead contemplated homicide. That same year there emerged the sad case of the Negro pilot Charles Ashe, who, his skills notwithstanding, could not find work; as had happened in the previous decade, there was apprehension that he would defect to the side of the adversary of the United States.[27]

Tokyo well knew that this lamentable state of affairs was the aching Achilles' heel of Washington. Earl Brown, who went on to become an anticommunist city councilman from Harlem, noticed that in late January 1942 Japan "did a very strange thing. They broadcast through the Far East the story of how . . . in Sikeston, Missouri, an obscure American town," a young "Negro named Cleo Wright had been seized by a mob and burned to death." Tokyo, Brown asserted, knew that "there are millions of colored people, yellow and brown, who have had all the white man's rule they ever want to see." The "record of the white man's relations with the colored man is so bad," he said insightfully, "that it requires no particular skill to exploit it." Coincidentally enough, U.S. observers on the scene reported that as "the British retreat got under way" in Burma, "killings of white people by natives began."[28]

Coincidentally enough, Sikeston was in the vicinity of what had become a citadel of pro-Tokyo sentiment among Negroes: the Missouri boot-heel and the area stretching eastward to Cairo, Illinois, and northward to East St. Louis. The *St. Louis Post-Dispatch* lamented that the

"Sikeston lynching has been widely exploited by enemy agents."[29] "Interracial conflicts have been said to have increased significantly since the war began," complained one reporter, who added, the "Sikeston Lynching has not helped."[30] Publicizing this murder would not only discredit the United States in Asia but also sow discord at home among U.S. Negroes. Curtailing such outrages would improve U.S. national security.

Particularly in the early stages of the Pacific War, it was unclear as to who would emerge triumphant, and it was not unreasonable to suspect that the victor would be Tokyo. In that case, the Negroes tied to Tokyo would not have to worry about unemployment, unlike Ashe, nor fret about opportunities in the military, unlike Spaulding.

* * *

In September 1942 federal authorities took into custody eighty Chicago Negroes, including, according to press accounts, members of the "'Peace Movement for Ethiopia', 'The Brotherhood of Liberty for the Black People of America' and the 'Temple of Islam.'" They were said to be "appealing to the very ordinary element" among Negroes. The PME was reported to be "reminiscent of Marcus Garvey days," while "members of the 'Temple of Islam' sported red fezzes as they stalked about the streets."[31] An editorialist reassured the nervously frazzled that there were "277,731 Negroes in Chicago," whereas the scores who had been arrested were from organizations that contained "no more than 2000 members."[32]

No amount of reassurance could erode the impact of these indictments. A number of the detained declared that they were "not citizens of this country but are Asiatics," and should be grouped with Japanese. A dumbfounded observer noted, "they claim that their race was created first and from them stem the Japanese and therefore they are related to the Nipponese."[33]

Mittie Maude Lena Gordon and her comrades stood trial, accused of seeking to foil enlistment of soldiers; she was said to have remarked on 7 December 1941 that "one billion black people" had just "struck for freedom" and "that the Japanese were going to redeem the Negroes from the white men in this country." She was also said to have asserted that "the spoils of the United States would be equally divided among Hitler and the Japanese." These comments, said prosecutors, were made to a "large number of individuals" assembled at a meeting of the Peace Movement of Ethiopia held at Boulevard Hall, 366 East 47th Street in Chicago. She reportedly told the audience that it was "impossible for America and Britain to win this war" and that the PME "owe[d] no allegiance" to Washington in any case. "When the Japanese bombed Pearl Harbor they wrought vengeance against the United States" and, in any event, there was "nothing worth fighting for here." Thus, "the only hope for the American black is Liberia" and they "were going back to Liberia regardless of whether they had to spill blood to do it." Rather unfortunately, Gordon was reported as stating, "The greater the Japanese victories the less victims for us to deal with." She pleaded not guilty to the charge of "intent to cause insubordination, disloyalty, mutiny."[34]

By then she was residing at 4451 State Street in Chicago and termed herself prosaically as a "housekeeper" and "unemployed for more than three years." She also claimed that her spouse "has no money or property or income . . . except his Old Age Pension,"[35] effectively refuting the notion of lush Japanese subsidies.

Her co-defendants—William Gordon, David James Logan, and Seon Emmanuel Jones—were accused similarly. William Gordon was said to have told Negroes that the PME would show them "how to build planes, tanks, submarines and battleships with which they could fight all white people like hell." His spouse was said to have stated in June 1942 that she "had heard on the radio that half the people of India had joined up with Japan" and that "Seattle had just been bombed." In August Jones reportedly averred, "now is the time for the Negroes to act; because if they wait until after the war, they will be back in slavery again; but if they act wisely, they will free themselves now and they will be free." African Americans, he said, "should not fight the Japs because the Japanese are not fighting us [the Negroes]; that the Negroes should do their fighting here because the white man is their enemy."[36] The prosecutors did not see these words as protected speech under the First Amendment but, instead, dangerously seditious statements worthy of imprisonment.

Seon Jones resided at 3511 Wabash in Chicago and by the time of trial was fifty-one years old and working as a carpenter; however, he had not been employed since his arrest on 20 September 1942 (and even when he was working, his wage was a mere $5.20 per day). However, he had served in the British military, giving added credibility to his and his group's assessment of the military capabilities of Pacific War combat-ants.[37] He too endorsed Senator Theodore Bilbo's legislation to resettle U.S. Negroes in Africa, terming it "wonderful," the "best thing ever pro-posed favoring the black people of America." The Dixiecrat was "not a Pharaoh," he said generously, "but most graciously a Moses."[38]

In the prelude to mass arrests in Chicago, FBI director J. Edgar Hoover was told that "there is considerable activity and unrest among the Negroes in Chicago." It was not just the PMEW and the PME but the UNIA, the MST, the Allah Temple of Islam, and others. There were "several meetings a week" of such groups with "in attendance 50 to 400 Negroes." The gatherings were "very strongly pro-Japanese" and it was "stated that the Japanese are coming to America to free the Negroes" and those "Negroes who do not join their group will be killed by the Japanese when they conquer America," an incentive to join the growing consensus. In fact, "some Japanese" had "been in attendance at some of these meetings held since Pearl Harbor." There were "rumors, not yet verified that Japanese have been active in these groups during the past three months." At a meeting of the precursor to the Nation of Islam, an "unknown Japanese" spoke "for approximately two hours urging the col-ored persons to work for a Japanese victory." The worried FBI informant pointed to the "seriousness of the Negro situation in the Chicago area"; thus "the investigation as outlined above is being vigorously pursued."[39]

The FBI believed that the man who came to be known as Elijah Mu-hammad asserted that "the Japanese will slaughter the white man" and "the Asiatic nation is prepared to destroy the white man." "The Asiatic race is made up of all dark-skinned people," he was reported to have declared, "including the Japanese and the Asiatic black man. Therefore, members of the Asiatic race must stick together. The Japanese will win the war because the white man cannot successfully oppose the Asiat-ics." The authorities also believed that his organization was stockpiling weapons, including carbine rifles, and that such weapons were being "stockpiled in black ghettos in nearly every major American city."[40]

Chicago's Linn Karriem, also known as Linn Freeman, was said to have asserted that "members of the Temple of Islam should not go into the army" and "if a member of the Temple of Islam joins the Army against his instructions, he is sure to be killed." Speaking publicly, he was cited for the proposition that "the devil [the white man] is lying about the number of Japanese ships being sunk" and "the devil . . . cannot defeat the Japanese." Tokyo had "constructed a very powerful bomb which will be used against the devil" and "when the Japanese invade the country the Moslems should fall on the ground as a sign to the Japanese that they are not their enemies."[41]

Ironically, as attempts were made to improve the material conditions faced by Negroes—often as a matter of happenstance, rather than intention—impetus was given to pro-Tokyo forces. For example, Dempsey Travis, who was quite conversant with Black Chicago, noticed during the war that "there now existed a thirst for black laborers" that had not been paralleled since World War I; as Euro-American workers departed for "cleaner jobs in the stockyards and for positions in the defense industry, blacks were pulled in as their replacements at Armour & Company as well as other industries."[42] This led some to think that widespread Euro-American apprehension of Japan buoyed this "reform," thus contributing to pro-Tokyo sentiment among Negroes.

It was a slight step from this perception to the larger proposition that the war was beneficial to Negroes; this combined with the long-held companion notion that Japan was "champion of the darker races" helped to drive the idea that it was desirable that Tokyo should be bolstered so that the war could be prolonged. According to the *Baltimore Afro-American*, it was common wisdom that "colored races as a whole would benefit" from the Pacific War, a position that the FBI considered so outrageous that it considered an Espionage Act indictment in response.[43]

Yet the press was simply reflecting attitudes within the community it covered. Charles Newby, also known as Charles Lubby, was similarly perceived as seditious at a public meeting held in Chicago's Washington Park on behalf of the Colored American National Organization. There assembled, said prosecutors, a "large number of persons" who heard him proclaim, "Negroes would fare better under the Japanese than they have under the white people" and that "the only good white man was a dead white man." In fact, "the more white people [that] were killed in this war, the better chance the colored man would have to come out on top." It was "to the Negroes' advantage to side with the Japanese in its war" and "those Negroes who did not sit with the Japanese should have their heads cut off." Tojo and Hitler were "the light of the world for Negroes" and Negroes "need not worry if Hitler or Tojo" prevailed;

rather, they should "worry" about "Sam" (meaning "Uncle Sam"), for if the latter prevailed, "the Negroes would go back into slavery conditions worse than that which existed before Reconstruction."[44] Newby, who had served a term in prison in Leavenworth for stealing a car, threw caution to the winds—as did others—in tempting the authorities to imprison him again.[45]

As things turned out, Newby was a mistaken prognosticator, as a dynamic was created that was to lead to what was often called the "Second Reconstruction" and a step toward enfranchisement for Negroes. Yet because of the numerous lynchings and murders of Negroes, prosecutors were not able to dismiss Newby's inflammatory words as a mere exercise in free speech, since there was reason for beset Negroes to take him seriously.

Joining with Newby at Washington Park was Stokley Delmar Hart, also known as S. D. Heart. "There is a common bond between the Japanese and the Negroes," were his reported words, "because both are members of the colored race"; indeed, Tokyo "will liberate the Negro from the white man's yoke" and "Tojo will be the savior of the American Negroes." When Japanese forces invaded the United States, he advised aid to them. "Those Negroes who are not in his organization"—the CNO—"will be killed" upon the arrival of Tokyo's forces. Hence, Hart's "prayers to Tojo" were "answered by the bombing of Pearl Harbor." Thus, "the Negroes' only interest in this war" was "to seek a Japanese victory"; indeed, he insisted, "the Negroes' freedom depends upon a Japanese victory."[46]

As U.S. forces became bogged down in the Pacific basin, a "large number" of Negroes, said prosecutors, gathered at Bacon's Casino in Chicago at 49th and Wabash Avenue, where they heard the words "God Bless Hitler." Hart supposedly "did not want the [United States] to win this war" for that would "preserve race hatred and discrimination"; "he would rather wear the uniform of a convict" than a military uniform—a wish the authorities were keen to fulfill.[47] Hart and his comrades exhibited a certain logic. When race hatred of Japanese was combined with that of Negroes during a murderously bloody war, it was easy to extrapolate in the way Hart did. And because he and others did not envision the impact of the alliance with Moscow on U.S. domestic fortunes, it is easier to comprehend why they failed to grasp the fundamental change that was soon to occur.[48]

Of course, Hart was joined in his subversive colloquy by others, including Frederick Harold Robb, alias Hammurabi Robb, alias Fidepe Robb.[49] Reputedly born in Africa, Robb had studied at the University of London and earned a law degree from Northwestern.[50] Intriguingly, after he was convicted, Edith Sampson—who became a chief anticommunist spokeswoman for the United States on the global scene after the war—pledged her extensive property on behalf of his bond.[51] In a story replete with ironies, it is striking that a number of leaders in the NAACP orbit who to a greater or lesser degree had boosted Tokyo—Sampson, Pickens, Channing Tobias, Walter White, and others—and apparently saw some domestic value in doing so, after the war concluded proceeded with vigor and élan to savage those who were boosting Moscow because of like domestic considerations.[52]

Robb was lucky to have Sampson in his corner; his many co-defendants were mostly left bereft after their predictable convictions. In contrast, when the man known as Elijah Muhammad appeared in court in Chicago to be sentenced, he was accompanied by a delegation of women garbed in brilliant red and green cloaks and outfits described as "burnooses." They looked on impassively as he and his coreligionists were convicted. Previously when testifying, rather than taking an oath to tell the truth in the usual manner, these defendants stolidly faced Mecca and mumbled quietly, "I do." An observer counted sixty-eight defendants.[53]

After the war and under drastically changed racial conditions, the Allah Temple of Islam was to emerge as a still existent Nation of Islam, while the others—the PME, the PMEW, and the like—either disappeared or had their ideas folded into a larger Black Nationalism of which the NOI was a chief beneficiary.

The man born as Elijah Poole, who came to embody the Nation of Islam, was jailed along with scores of others. However, for reasons relating to her authoritative influence—or simply male chauvinism—the sentencing judge was more expansive in addressing Mittie Maude Lena Gordon. She was a "shrewd, intelligent woman." He complimented her "well composed" letters, since "their diction was as good as most of the people with whom I am acquainted." She had "done an excellent job in self education." But he was remorseless in castigating her for "trying to incite her people against the country of which she is a citizen."

Yet Judge William R. Holly made what was an amazing analysis for that era when he said, "I cannot impose the same punishment on a colored person, whom I have found guilty under the statutes involved in this case that I would inflict upon a white person who is guilty of the same offense." In sum, the judge was conceding that Gordon—and presumably others—might have had reason to join with a foreign foe against white supremacy in a manner that would not apply to a presumed beneficiary of white supremacy. It was only a slight step from that realization to the recognition that, perhaps, eroding Jim Crow could cause even Gordon to shun the Tokyo of the future. She received two years' imprisonment on a conspiracy charge and three years' probation. Her spouse received three years' probation.[54] Charles Newby received a three-year sentence, a term similar to that accorded other Chicago defendants.[55]

* * *

Downstate, in Springfield, the Moorish Science Temple was said to be proclaiming that "when the Japs take over this country, those belonging to this organization will not be molested."[56] Further south, in Jackson, Mississippi—which in its manifest horribleness was in some ways the fountainhead of pro-Tokyo attitudes among U.S. Negroes, spreading ripples northward to Cairo and East St. Louis—the MST was said by the FBI to be "organizing a local chapter among the Negroes and teaching them that the Japanese are fighting a war of liberation for the Asiatic race of which race Negroes are members."[57]

Shockingly, Senator Bilbo was told that in neighboring McComb, Mississippi, in mid-1943, a total of 265 Negroes were "mowed down with machine guns after trying to get swell-headed."[58] Due east, in Richmond, Virginia, a Negro group was said to be "inspired by the Japanese and whose ultimate purpose was the overthrow of the white race."[59]

Yet Jim Crow disciples thought they had reason to jeopardize national security by continuing to repress Negroes in the midst of war. In mid-1943 one correspondent, Charles W. Wade, wrote to Senator Bilbo of the "disgusting acts of Negro soldiers at Centerville [Mississippi]," who "openly stated they were going to clean out" the state, "causing grave concern among the white population here." For "white domination must be protected and vigorously asserted. If the colored people all over the world should be organized by the Japs into a cooperative force," he warned, "the entire white race will be in a hell of a fix." Wade had "spent two years in the Philippines Islands" and knew that every inhabitant there "hates our white skin," as "does every other yellow and black man and no amount of kindness and coddling will make them like us." "The Jap side of [this] war is strictly a race matter," he counseled, and "this Negro Question in the South, is not as local as the government wishes us to believe. It's going to be a worldwide race movement" quite soon, "and you people who call the turns had better get your ears to the ground if you wish to continue to enjoy the advantages of white supremacy. I know that this letter sounds absurd," he acknowledged, "but so should a story like Pearl Harbor two short years ago."[60]

In some ways, white supremacists reacted to this conflict the way their ancestors had reacted 150 years earlier amidst the turmoil unleashed by the Haitian Revolution.[61] In sum, there were those who thought that, as the saying goes, in order for everything to remain the same, everything must change. In other words, to perpetuate white supremacy, the African slave trade should be curtailed; or in order to perpetuate white supremacy and slavery, the harsh edges of Jim Crow should be softened. There were others, in contrast, who felt that advocates of white supremacy should dig in their heels in the face of a revolutionary and/or wartime challenge.

The incarceration of leaders apparently did not squash the sentiment they represented. In late 1944 the NAACP was told that a "combined committee of colored people and Japanese with headquarters in Chicago" was "working to upset things generally." The NAACP was asked pointedly, "What is being done to counteract the harm that this may do to your own people"?[62] The NAACP could have pointed vainly to the convictions in reply.

* * *

As noted earlier, the St. Louis–East St. Louis region was perceived widely as being the bastion of pro-Tokyo attitudes among Negroes. There too leaders were charged with seeking to foment insubordination, disloyalty, mutiny, and refusal to duty among Negro soldiers and sailors. They were accused of asserting that with the United States weakened by war with Japan, Negroes should seize the time and revolt in order to aid Tokyo and liberate themselves. This was expected to unfold during the first half of 1942. Given the attack on Pearl Harbor and the fall of Singapore, the idea that Japan would attack the U.S. mainland was not beyond the realm of possibility. Thus, PMEW members were told to stockpile weapons, among the "overt acts" cited to effectuate the conspiracy.[63]

The judge in the trial of David Erwin and General Lee Butler observed that a "large volume of evidence was admitted" against these defendants, though Butler contended that force and coercion were deployed by the FBI to extract damaging admissions. Nonetheless, the judge found that the defendants' "unvarying purpose" was "to put the interests of the colored races of the earth above the interests" of Washington. Defendant Butler, said the judge, "in particular seemed to be obsessed with the idea of another race riot," though it was unclear if this was a reference to what occurred in East St. Louis in 1917 or what was to come during the war in sites as diverse as Harlem and Detroit.[64] The judge may have sensed the ongoing trend that eventuated in an estimated two hundred wartime racial clashes.[65]

Irrespective of the answer to this inquiry, exhibits in this case included Swiss rifles, hundreds of rounds of ammunition, and "wooden dummy guns."[66] There were also undated photographs of Negro men in uniform drilling with what appeared to be weapons.[67] Harrison Fair of East St. Louis, a PMEW member since 1934, was part of this military unit, also known as the Pacific Movement Legion. He was a major general, he told the court, and confirmed that arms were used in training.[68] There were also brochures touting the virtues of "travel comforts in Japan," including commodious hotels and railways.[69]

K. D. Branch of East St. Louis, a member of the PMEW since 1933, testified that by 1934 the group had a military unit that included five or six women. Though somehow he lost his sight at the beginning of the war, he admitted that the above noted brochures were his. He also owned books on shooting. He knew De Guzman or Takis, who, he said, sought to teach members the Spanish language. Still, the record reveals there was "some laughing" as he testified, given the circumlocution of his testimonial evasions.[70] He was born in Louisiana and had a third grade education. The military unit he joined "used to meet every Friday night"; he had a "black uniform," a "cap that was brown," though he "dyed it black." His unit had almost thirty-five members. The accusatory prosecutor replied, "You know a lot of members of the [PMEW] bought guns a year ago."[71]

FBI agents testified that on 15 September 1942 they detained Butler as he "was beginning to cross the Eads Bridge" carrying "400 rounds of ammunition" that were "laying on the floor in the back of the car." They said that he cursed them.[72] With Butler was PMEW member Finis Williams. The authorities thought they had reason to believe that the men were on their way to blow up the bridge, which crosses the Mississippi River. Henry Bishop of the local police said, "We pulled them into the curb and I put my pistol on them and said, 'police officers', 'put up your hands' and both of them came out with their hands up." He had received an anonymous tip about their intentions.[73]

On 18 December 1941 another local police officer, Edgar Sherrod, went to a PMEW meeting where, he said, a Japanese national spoke; he then trailed the speaker to St. Louis. He was asked how he knew this person was Japanese—as opposed to Korean or Chinese or Thai—but the clear impression was left that days after the bombing of Pearl Harbor, the PMEW was moving toward more active internal subversion.[74]

Frank P. Townsend of St. Louis, who had joined the PMEW in 1934, was then told that the group was "sponsored by the Japanese." He served as both vice president and secretary before leaving in 1939. The peripatetic David Erwin, he said, had been recruiting in Mississippi and Oklahoma—and London. In Europe "he had met many representatives of the different dark countries of the world," for example, "the Japanese, Chinese, Indians." They pledged, he said, to "lend their assistance to straighten out affairs with the colored people in the United States." Erwin also visited California and Mexico to confer with Japanese leaders, Townsend said. There was a local Japanese contact in St. Louis "who operated the Pacific Restaurant on Jefferson Avenue just a few doors north of the National Office Building. This Jap was named Benny." There had been discussions about the PMEW colonizing U.S. Negroes in Brazil. Yes, Townsend said, the PMEW had "passwords and signs" for "protection of the colored people in case the Japanese ever invaded." Though the PMEW had an affiliated religious grouping—the Triumph Church—Townsend was a member of a Baptist church in St. Louis.[75]

L. B. Huff, who joined the PMEW in Charleston, Missouri, and had ties to Cairo, Illinois, met Takis or De Guzman in Mounds, Illinois, in

1939. He too was told that this Filipino leader "was planning a colonization of the colored people in America in South America," Brazil to be
precise. "He said bring all [your] guns and pay $10.00 for transportation
to New York" and "there we would get a Japanese ship and [it] wouldn't
cost anything to South America." As for arms, he confirmed that Negroes were well supplied with "ordinary guns, shotguns and pistols."[76]

A number of PMEW members were passionately interested in self-
determination and self-governance. Sidney Winston of Tamms, Illinois,
who had been a member since 1936, was intrigued after being told by
Takis that "if we got a colony we could trade like other nations, not only
with the Japanese but with the West Indies and France."[77] Winston had
once resided, he said, along the "state line of Missouri and Arkansas,"
though he was born in Jim Crow Alabama. He had fathered eleven children but as of 1942, sadly, there were "nine dead" for reasons that unfortunately were normative in Black America. He recounted a meeting in
the winter of 1940 at Mounds, Illinois, where "something like 150" were
present for a PMEW meeting. Takis/De Guzman was present and "said
the other people had arms and the Negroes should have arms." There
was a PMEW military unit of twenty-five in Mounds and, yes, he had
owned a "Winchester pump gun" since 1917, the year of the racist conflagration in East St. Louis.[78]

Takis or De Guzman confirmed the worst fears of Washington when
he declared that the Immigration Act of 1924 was a "national insult and
the American people are going to pay for it." He said that "Japan had
prepared for this war against the white powers ever since the conclusion
of the Russo-Japanese war." Takis saw the UNIA as an inadequate vessel
for his purposes, necessitating the rise of the PMEW; he felt that playing
on "dissension" between the two was the optimal course. He organized
the PMEW in New York City from the ranks of both the UNIA and
the MST, and "from the different Communist organizations." He also
recruited within the Ahmadiyya, a dissident Islamic sect that had attracted a number of U.S. Negroes too. His contested conclusion was that
this sect was "controlled by Japanese disguised [as] Mohammad movement." Takahashi, he said, was close to the highest levels of the Japanese
Navy and well-positioned to transmit funds and messages from Tokyo.
At every PMEW meeting, it was said, a collection was taken for a contri-
bution to aid the cause of the Japanese military in China. There was also

a "Hindu" named "Mangusta" working with the PMEW, and an African in Mounds, a "tall, skinny man. . . . he is a Captain or Lieutenant."[79]

As the United States fought a determined foe in the Pacific War, concern arose that the home front was not necessarily invulnerable. Given the hellish maltreatment of U.S. Negroes, there was even more reason for concern, which was not allayed when testimony was given in open court about this group conspiring with Tokyo. Ultimately, the far-sighted among the U.S. ruling elite, in an agonizing reappraisal, came to realize that national security demanded and dictated that this maltreatment be at least eased.

6

Japanese Americans Interned, U.S. Negroes Next?

Did the PMEW plan to dynamite the Eads Bridge connecting St. Louis and East St. Louis in September 1942? Certainly the authorities thought so, though what may have been involved was simply militant grousing, a staple even now of African Americans and a frequent trait among oppressed peoples generally. Was the PMEW well-armed? Yes, though members while being grilled by prosecutors declared that the weapons were for hunting. Did the PMEW contain military units engaged in drilling? Yes, without a doubt. Was the PMEW suffused with pro-Tokyo sentiment? Yes, without a doubt. Was the PMEW alienated from the United States and, thus, looked askance at the Pacific War? Yes, without a doubt. Did the PMEW expect a Japanese invasion of the United States on 24 November 1942, two days before the Thanksgiving holiday? Yes, many members expected this. The U.S. authorities looked at these answers and decided that an abundance of caution dictated prison terms for PMEW leaders.

Especially damaging was the press report claiming that PMEW leaders had told their followers that instead of buying U.S. war bonds, Negroes should contribute to a fund for Japanese soldiers, which would be presented to them once they invaded.[1]

Simultaneously, the mass internment of Japanese Americans and the concomitant maltreatment of Negro troops in the United States itself was complicating mightily Washington's war, especially in the early months of 1942, when the conflict's ultimate trajectory appeared unclear.

* * *

Before the trial of Butler and Erwin, on 22 September 1942 a federal grand jury was convened in East St. Louis in Room 238 of the federal building at 7th Street and Missouri Avenue. The prosecutor, Barry Blanton, was from Sikeston, site of an infamous lynching, and events there had helped to drive the initiation of this proceeding. This was not because there was a desire to capture the perpetrators of this heinous misdeed, but because there was concern over the level of "organization" among "colored folks" supposedly initiated by a "couple of gentlemen whose nativity is somewhat in question," one of whom was Takis. There were, said Blanton, "two thousand members" of the PMEW in the Missouri boot-heel and the region ranging east to Cairo and Mounds and north to East St. Louis. "They had quite an organization," he said with seeming admiration. "Organizing the darkies" was their chief priority, but since there were "8000 un-naturalized alien born people in St. Louis," and among them were Japanese, this latter group was seen as their secondary priority. Blanton was especially interested in Tetsu Ueda, "sometimes known as 'Thomas Uyada,'" who had been working at a St. Louis country club, a frequent haunt for Japanese agents seeking to pick up bits of intelligence dropped unknowingly by local elites.

Uyada was "on the pay-roll of the Japanese government," said Blanton; "to show how well he had done his work, when we gave him this hearing, a large number of people including leading individuals" vouched for him, despite the fact that he often spoke to the "darkies," as many as two hundred assembled. "They organized the darkies and built up the proposition that they were not accorded social equality." The PMEW and its backers asserted that "the world was divided into just two classes, the white race and the colored," in dramatic contrast to their ideological opponents, who represented a contrasting potent narrative—with global muscularity—who spoke of the ruling class and the working class or the capitalists and the proletariat. After the war, concessions were made to blunt and blur the former narrative while the latter articulators, who had stood with Washington during the war, were repaid by being battered into submission.

Uyada's Japanese comrades had established a base of support in Sikeston, where "they made their homes" in Negro areas. "Sometimes [they] went around with colored women" and "they usually worked through a colored preacher." Of course, they had "different passwords and hand shakes" for their underground work. Naturally, they "encouraged" the Negroes to "accumulate arms and ammunition."[2]

This grand jury was a necessary precursor to the 1943 trial of Butler and Erwin. At the 1943 trial of PMEW leaders in East St. Louis, other than Erwin and Butler, a chief witness was Finis Williams, because he had been close to both. This railway worker too was from Mississippi and by the time of the trial was thirty-two years old. He was married, had two children, and had not been in the PMEW long before the detention of Erwin and Butler. He claimed that it was after Pearl Harbor that he and Butler began having "secret meetings." The prosecutor asked him whether Erwin said, "It would not be long until the Japanese invaded and conquered the United States and everything the organization has been trying to attain would be accomplished"? The answer: "Yes sir, he said that" after Pearl Harbor. He was asked, did Erwin say, "He wouldn't mind dying if he could carry ten or twenty white men with him?" Answer: "Yes, sir." Did Erwin say, "After the Japanese had fought the United States for awhile and had weakened us then the Negroes in this country should rise up?" Answer: "That's right." And, yes, said Williams, "Butler said what damage he could do if he had about 40 sticks of dynamite to stick under the [Eads] bridge."[3]

According to Williams, Erwin told him in early February 1942 that the Japanese military was set to "bomb Chicago, Detroit and St. Louis." But what was striking was his testimony about his meeting with Butler at the latter's home at 1925 Russell Avenue in East St. Louis. "There was a train loaded with soldiers coming over the highline bridge and Mr. Butler didn't know whether the soldiers [were] black or white and made some remark that if that bridge was knocked out, them soldiers would be wrecked." That is, "if 40 sticks of dynamite was stuck under that bridge that would knock the bridge off." This was the evident plan. However, as the FBI closed in for arrests, minutes of meetings and other documents were burned; as he and Butler were heading frantically to St. Louis in order to hide stockpiled arms, they were stopped by the police. They pulled guns, he said, but were subdued in mid-September 1942.[4]

Butler did not help his case when he spoke of PMEW "members in the army." He had been a member since 1934 and said the group met every Monday and Wednesday evening. "When I joined," he said, "it was for the betterment of the conditions of the Negroes," that is, "equal rights and justice." He downplayed the significance of Japan, not unexpected given the charges against him. His recollection of his 1942 arrest was dramatic. "Butler, get out of that car," was the cry of a police officer who "called me a name" and threatened to shoot him. "They had a gun on me, one was on the side" and "the other at the back." They "began to push me and threaten my life" and said "you are a damned liar, you God damned niggers never know nothing and you all stink" and, besides, "ain't no God damned good." He was told that "if I didn't agree to what he [said]," then "I wouldn't get out of the jail alive." The fact that his adversary's "hand [was] on the pistol" and "in shooting position" as he barked instructions made his words more persuasive. Butler was gobsmacked, recalling that "my life is just as sweet to me as other human beings and these men was going to kill me if I didn't confess." Still, he denied the dynamite story and the account of burning minutes and documents, but the authorities did not believe him.[5]

The other defendant, David Erwin, also denied the accusations made against him. By 1943, this forty-three-year-old man born in Mississippi (as was Butler), had been in the St. Louis region since 1922, "with the exception of one year I was in Chicago." Yes, he knew Takis and knew about the Brazil venture but knew nothing about guns, he said. Asked "Have you ever been mistaken for a Japanese before," this African American answered promptly, "Yes sir." It had happened in Mounds, Illinois; "the prosecuting attorney himself," he added, "thought I was Japanese."[6] Neither the question nor the answer aided his parlous cause.

But was any of this actually incriminating, particularly the Brazil angle? As early as 1931, when Japan was moving to attack China, the Negro press was reporting rhapsodically that "Japan builds thriving colony in Brazil for all races."[7] Just because U.S. Negroes had a hankering for Brazil, which happened to have a substantial population of Japanese extraction, was not in itself incriminating—though it proved to be damning in this case.

Supposedly Butler said that if China prevailed, then U.S. Negroes too would lose; however, even more harmful to his case was Erwin's alleged statement that "when you talk to the white people, pretend you are for them but never forget the Japanese is our friend."[8]

The grand jury and the trial produced page after page of testimony by Negroes affirming their allegiance to Tokyo, their fondness for firearms, and their alienation from the United States. Wolcie Gray, also known as "Wolsia Gray," was an example. This seventy-five-year-old, married (though separated) East St. Louis resident, the father of eight children, worked as a carpenter. He was from Memphis, bordering Mississippi, with its own unique racist history, which may explicate why he joined the PMEW. "I can't write" or read, he confessed. But as a witness, he bobbed and weaved systematically and deftly, seeking to evade direct prosecutorial queries, while providing adroit "non-denial denials." Asked whether he would "rather join with the Japanese" than the United States in battle, he responded cagily, "I know the United States. All I have ever done in my life is through" the United States, as "that's where I have been living." He ducked and dodged further when he was asked about previous pro-Tokyo statements he was said to have made.[9]

Thomas Albert Watkins, who also had lived in Memphis, said that "after the Japanese invaded us on November 24, 1942, they [U.S. Negroes] were assured of holding some dominating position." "That's the month of the invasion," he said in September. "Everybody will be celebrating." Watkins described himself as a "common laborer," though it was reasonable to speculate that if his apparent dreams materialized, he would receive a decided promotion.[10]

Pauline Verser had lived "all my life" in East St. Louis, excepting time spent in Mounds. Butler was her neighbor and told her that if she joined the PMEW, "you could leave the United States," quite an enticement. "He said the Japanese was giving us the right God and we should serve their God," not least since "all that wasn't affiliated with the movement would be destroyed" by "the Japs." But she was "sanctified" and found this hard to swallow.[11]

The prosecutor, perhaps oversimplifying to better convict the defendants, referred to the PMEW simply as the "Japanese Movement."[12] Yet Forest Stancel, a PMEW member, insisted that "they talked about racial questions and about the white man not giving the colored man equal privileges" and, of course, "lynching," common conversational fare among Negroes and hardly unique to those attracted to Tokyo.[13]

Beatrice Branch, who had lived in Chicago and Brooklyn, Illinois, before arriving in East St. Louis, was born in Alabama. The prosecutor showed her a photograph of her spouse, K. D. Branch, in the full military regalia of the PMEW unit. Also pictured were Henry Hall, Roscoe Standifer, and Russell Clark. Why did Mr. Branch speak of Emperor Hirohito? Why did the couple retain copies of local newspapers with articles focused on Japanese leaders? Why were Japanese pamphlets in their home? She too was a PMEW member, but her terse and exceedingly vague responses did not seem to satisfy the prosecutor.[14]

PMEW member John Bedford was among the well armed. He had known Butler since 1927 and did not hesitate to speak of his "16 gauge pump" shotgun and his "Winchester" repeating rifle—both for "hunting," he assured, though the prosecutor seemed skeptical.[15]

Howard Bayne, an agent with U.S. Naval Intelligence, was not only skeptical of these Negroes' assertions, he was horrified by the sedition he found along the Missouri-Illinois border. There had been a suspicious fire on the "Federal Barge Line" near Cairo, and Bayne believed that the "vicious" PMEW might be responsible. He too had heard of the reputed impending Japanese invasion of 24 November and was outraged. He knew that Frank Mart of the PMEW had been quoted as saying that the "black man would rule the Western Hemisphere" and that he was not only a PMEW but a UNIA officer. He knew that both groups had "very strong organization in East St. Louis." Mart had rifles that he planned to use on 24 November, he said—"45s, 22s, 30-30s and 41 or 43s"—and many bullets too. A "Mexican" had briefed Bayne about the strength of the PMEW, particularly in Cape Girardeau, along the Mississippi River. "I know a Japanese down there who made the statement he had pictures of all the bridges. He was a photographer"—a real shutterbug, suspiciously enough.[16]

Harrison Fair, with roots in Arkansas, epitomized Bayne's nightmare. This railway worker—a track layer—had joined the PMEW at the UNIA hall in East St. Louis at 16th and Wilford. He had served in World War I but had taken his expertise to the PMEW military unit, where he rose to the level of lieutenant colonel. "You know Harrison," said the prosecutor with undue familiarity, "that a lot of the colored people have guns?" His forthright answer: "I reckon they have."[17]

Roscoe Standifer, a resident of East St. Louis with roots in Tupelo, Mississippi, had worked at Aluminum Ore Company since 1919. He was a captain in the PMEW military unit and owned a shotgun—for "hunting," he said.[18] Cuver Vernon Young of Macon, Mississippi, and East St. Louis had spent two years in the U.S. Navy, having joined at the tender age of fourteen. He owned three shotguns and a pistol and was asked pointedly whether Erwin had averred that "the Bible said the world should be ruled by Negroes."[19]

The defendants were convicted and the PMEW was routed, along with the notion that a corps of armed Negroes would assist an invading force from Tokyo. But as so often happens, the underlying motivations—including alienation from the United States, militancy, seeking allies abroad, and the like—did not perish. One reason why was that the bludgeoning of Negroes that had helped to instigate pro-Tokyo attitudes in the first instance did not die with the defendants' imprisonment. In mid-September 1942 as a grand jury in East St. Louis was skewering the PMEW, due south in Alabama the NAACP was told that "one of the Colored Nurses from the Army Air Corps here in Tuskegee was beaten by a white policeman when she attempted to get on a bus to come back to Tuskegee. They not only beat her but fined her and put in jail." The observer concluded disconsolately, "The race question is getting worse than ever down here."[20]

The same could be said of the situation beyond the confines of this college town. A few years later, the dam broke and a Negro woman, Rosa Parks, faced a more civilized fate than her 1942 counterpart, due in no small part to recognition that such maltreatment was harming the republic's global image and undermining national security.

* * *

Another reason why U.S. Negroes were inflamed to the point of attempting sedition was the mass internment of Japanese Americans and Japanese nationals generally with, as they saw it, little outcry from Euro-Americans. This could be their fate too, thought many Negroes, and the sour reaction to this epochal event did little to build national unity or convince many Negroes that attaining first-class citizenship might be possible. In 1944 a Negro journalist summarized the stance of many African Americans: "One of the worst features of mass evacuation was that a particular minority was subjected to unusually harsh measures solely on the ground of race or ancestry," which now meant that a "precedent is established" for already beset Negroes.[21]

When the prominent hunter and author Frank Buck advocated the "complete annihilation" of all Japanese, who should be "slaughtered by poison gas" and other devious means in order to "save [the] 'white' race," Negroes knew that they could well be next on the list for mass murder.[22] The preexisting rhetorical barrage about the presumed commonalities of the "colored races" predisposed U.S. Negroes to sense they were next on the chopping block and, perhaps, they should preempt this potential fiasco by aligning with Tokyo; this was the context for the trial in East St. Louis.

In retrospect, it is not easy to overestimate the hysteria that gripped Washington, notably in early 1942 with the fall of Singapore, when it seemed that the war was being lost and a radical reordering of race relations was in store. This is what propelled many African Americans to rally to Tokyo's banner, while causing those like Buck to draw up ever more dire projections. Even Frank Marshall Davis, the African American intellectual known to be close to the Communist Party and, thus, generally resistant to Japan's appeals, argued in February 1942 that "Japan is capitalizing upon resentment toward white supremacy to pave the way for absolute victory." He thought that "'white supremacy' in the Orient is taking such a terrific drubbing from the little brown men of Japan that the Nazis may forget all about any spring offensive against Russia and instead launch a drive against India to beat their partners to this rich prize." Other than ideological predilection, what restrained him from joining the pro-Tokyo bandwagon was that he "envisage[d] the Nazis turning on their Japanese partner just as Hitler turned on Stalin."[23]

Likewise, near the same time, a correspondent for the Negro press in Stockholm found that in Germany the "'Communist Peril' is being replaced by the 'Yellow Peril'" as Berlin seeks "peace between the 'white nations' to enable them to start a joint crusade against Japan." Citing pro-Nazi sources in Sweden, the commentator ascertained that "there still seems to be a difference of opinion as to whether Russia belongs to the 'White Race' or not."[24]

Closer to home, in Columbus, Ohio, a Negro journalist in February 1942 found a source who declared that the "Japanese inspired [the] free world's darker races" to rebel against "white domination."[25] Ironic confirmation for this remark was found in South Africa, where Jan Smuts charged that Tokyo's successes threatened white supremacy and, said an observer, "threatened the rule of white people in South Africa"; supposedly, "the Axis partners had granted Japan the French island of Madagascar as a jumping-ground against the eastern shores of South Africa."[26] It appeared that the Tokyo threat was impacting what came to be called apartheid in a manner similar to the way it was impacting Jim Crow.[27]

*　*　*

Presumably, this news that was so dispiriting to white supremacy sheds light on why in 1942, the Negro press was forced to mull over federal guidelines proffered by the Office of Censorship.[28]

In other words, the Negro press was a special force shaping Negro attitudes during the war vis-à-vis Tokyo and the related internment. The Swedish social scientist Gunnar Myrdal was among those who felt that the Negro press was a reliable barometer of mass Negro opinion. He stressed that "*the press defines the Negro group to the Negroes themselves. The individual Negro is invited to share in the sufferings, grievances and pretensions of the millions of Negroes outside the narrow community. This creates a feeling of strength and solidarity.*"[29] A number of these journals had subscribers abroad and foreign correspondents as well, and many of these journals were affiliated with the Associated Negro Press, which had a global network of correspondents. By 1940, for example, the circulation of the weekly *Baltimore Afro-American* was reportedly over 100,000.[30]

As we have seen, many Negroes and numerous Negro newspapers were less than enthusiastic about the Pacific War, a sentiment that had not escaped the attention of Washington. In this inflaming context, mass internment was seen by many Negroes as both a desperate countermeasure and viciously angry retaliation against those seen as Tokyo's proxy—a descriptor that could be easily applied to Negroes themselves. Thus, the prominent Negro columnist P. L. Prattis argued persuasively that "if Negroes spurn these Japanese Americans, Negroes will probably be the losers. Many whites do not want Japanese Americans and Negro Americans to be friends." Before the mass incarceration, they would "take Japanese Americans to their homes and give them much more of an American's chance than they give Negroes. Their aim, of course, is to keep all minorities divided with the Negro at the bottom of the horizontal [and vertical] scale." While Euro-Americans often persecuted Japanese Americans, those who "live[d] with Negroes find themselves accepted as human beings and suffer no embarrassments socially or otherwise."[31]

Wallace Lee concurred. "Few Negroes join with what is evidently the majority of white Americans in their bitter hate and fear of the 'Yellow Peril,'" he asserted. "Most Negroes feel that discrimination against the Japanese is based on color, much the same as prejudice against Negroes."

Of those Negroes polled, he wrote, "there was a "definite feeling of sympathy for Japanese Americans who have been victims of racial discrimination much akin to the treatment of Negroes in the South." Indeed, the "majority" heartily disapproved of the internment.[32]

Preexisting Negro sympathy for Japan, which had reached a crescendo during the Ethiopian conflict, merged with resentment against white supremacy that ensnared Tokyo and African Americans alike, then combined with overestimation of Japanese victories early in the war and horror at the internment, to create a hailstorm of pessimism by early 1942 about U.S. prospects for triumph. With coruscating sarcasm, Gordon Hancock rued how "we have heard little except contempt for the Japanese and their military ability" and how "the press of the nation had nothing but contempt for the 'little yellow perils.'"[33] Hancock recalled speaking to Euro-Americans who expressed "unmitigated, bitter and unrestrained hatred" for Japanese, which was now backfiring erratically; "only the far-sightedness of Stalin," said this Negro moderate, "whom we have abused and accused, has saved the critical situation."[34] Within a few years such an opinion would be virtually forbidden, even about the war that had saved civilization, making even more incomprehensible wartime alliances and their result, which, ironically, served to benefit those Negroes who had been pro-Tokyo.

But it was the mass internment, more than other factors, that soured Negroes further about the motives and designs of those once referred to as the "ruling race." Reflecting on past anti-Chinese immigration laws, then the valorization of these Asians during the war, another journalist opined that

Negroes are not surprised at these turnabouts employed by the white Americans in evaluating and devaluating the Chinese and Japanese. . . . [Negroes] know that anytime white Americans praise colored people it is only a temporary move at best and furthermore, from actual experience Negroes know that the average white man is out to [feather] his own nest.[35]

That is, Chinese were now being hailed as allies and Japanese denigrated—but it would not take long, it was thought, for a reversal of fortune to occur. There was little surprise when during the war, Chinese students were allowed to study aviation at a Georgia university while Negroes were barred.[36] While think tanks in Virginia were conferring with Chinese, Thais, Indians, and other Asians about Tokyo's attempt to "promote racial friction between the white race and Asiatics," Negroes, per usual, were being segregated invidiously.[37] Such stances did not enhance patriotic cohesiveness during the war.

* * *

In July 1942, as pro-Tokyo Negroes were under surveillance and under arrest, C. L. Dellums, chair of the NAACP Legal Committee and a trade union activist, felt compelled to address Walter White, the group's leader. "Early last month," he began, "several Day Coaches were filled to capacity with Japanese, most of whom were Americans and sent to San Antonio"; the cars were "not air-conditioned" and the detainees were "not . . . allowed to have any windows raised" as they "suffered terribly" for "four full days" before arriving at their destination. Yet "the guards, soldiers who went along with this trip, had a Pullman with every comfort. Even white people now are talking, [since] all restrictions were removed from not only the Italian and German Americans but Italian and German aliens."[38]

Moving promptly, White told U.S. Attorney General Francis Biddle, "I greatly fear that stories" such as that recounted by Dellums "could and would be used by the Japanese" to "create bitterness against the United Nations."[39] But this intervention had little impact on U.S. policy. Congressman Adam Clayton Powell Jr. of Harlem warned that "race haters" were "fomenting dissension not only against Japanese Americans but against Negroes" too on the Pacific Coast with the aim of seeking to create a "white" coast cleansed of both stigmatized groups.[40]

Herbert Hill, a leading NAACP official, collected documents on the internment, perhaps alert to the precedent that it created for his constituency. His collection included a May 1943 "confidential" memorandum from the U.S. military on the Pacific Coast that conceded that "some suspension of the civil rights of the United States born Japanese" was occurring, but since it "was an *orderly* suspension," it was presumably acceptable. The memorandum's author asserted that "Axis propaganda was now wholly ineffective on this count," an overstatement at best; thus, "if Japanese were returned to the coast there would doubtless be rioting and bloodshed with a consequent *disorderly* suspension of civil rights having the flavor of a race war" (emphasis in the original).[41] In the language of the law, this was not only handing a "heckler's veto" to those opposed to civil liberties but a murderer's veto as well. Given this precedent, could Negroes be forced to evacuate from areas where certain Euro-Americans found their presence repulsive or even discomfiting?

The U.S. authorities argued that "because of their physical charac-teristics," Japanese Americans "would be most easily observed, [far] easier than doubtful citizens of the Caucasian race, such as naturalized Germans, Italians or native-born Communists." Left unsaid was that German Americans, for example, could operate more effectively by sub-terfuge precisely because of their "physical characteristics." Again, Euro-American marauders were given a veto that carried ominous import for U.S. Negroes in that "violent anti-Japanese feeling among Caucasians of all classes" and "anti-Japanese agitation by the Yugo-Slav fishermen who frankly desire to eliminate competition in the fishing industry" were al-lowed to prevail.[42]

Not all U.S. conservatives backed the internment. Tellingly, George Schuyler, the doyen of Black Conservatism, viewed this abuse of civil liberties with skepticism and disgust, averring at one juncture that the internment was a "scheme to grab [Japanese American] holdings and hand them over to white people," which was "shown by the efforts to prevent Negroes from taking them over." Like Hill, he too thought that "this may be a prelude to our own fate. Who knows? . . . Once the prec-edent is established with 70,000 Japanese Americans," it would be "easy to denationalize millions of Afro-American citizens."[43]

Decades earlier, the anti-lynching crusader Ida B. Wells had asserted that a motive force for the bloody crime that she fought was the de-sire of some Euro-Americans to eliminate business competition from African Americans.[44] If this outrage against Japanese Americans were to hold, would not this jeopardize African Americans? Thus, in 1942—again, as Negro witnesses were being interrogated by a East St. Louis grand jury—a carpenters' union in Long Beach sought to "amend" the U.S. Constitution so that "citizenship" of Japanese Americans could be revoked, that they "be forever barred from again becoming citizens and owning property" in the United States, and that "all such persons" be "deported to their Mother Country" at war's end.[45] Moving picture projectionists in San Diego made a similar initiative, except that, less delicately, it referred to "every Jap."[46] The applicability of such draconian measures to Negroes may have occurred to Herbert Hill, who retained this remarkable document.

In 1944 the Negro trade unionist Willard Townsend sought to save the jobs of fifty-nine Japanese American employees at the Illinois Central Railroad, their proposed sacking spearheaded by the segregationist Brotherhood of Maintenance of Way Employees, who maintained a Jim Crow policy against Negro workers too.[47] The crusading Black radical attorney Loren Miller deployed his formidable legal skills on behalf of those slated for internment in Los Angeles.[48]

* * *

Nevertheless, U.S. Negroes' stance of solidarity with Japanese Americans was not as straightforward as it appeared. All along the Pacific Coast, as Japanese Americans were removed, U.S. Negroes from the Texas-Louisiana corridor particularly migrated to take their place; in Los Angeles, for example, "Little Tokyo" quickly became "Bronzeville."[49] A Negro woman took over a café formerly controlled by a now removed Japanese American.[50] By May 1942 Augustus Hawkins, a prominent Negro legislator in Los Angeles, was being importuned to "prevent the importation of Mexicans to California to take the place of the Japanese truck growers who have been interned," since now "the path has been smoothed for Negroes to enter that type of farming." Claude A. Barnett huffed that elites might "prefer Mexicans" since "they can ship them back home when they get troublesome. " He wanted Negroes to "leave the [urban] lights and go to the truck farms—as owners or workers"[51] and expressed little concern for the interned.

As the internment was being launched, the prominent Negro entertainer Etta Moten insisted that "this is our country"; unlike many, she exhibited no sympathy for Tokyo or Japanese Americans: "The competition and rivalry for jobs which always existed with Orientals [sic] occupying many posts that normally would have been colored, neutralized any thought that the Japs belonged to the great area of colored races. In fact, the colored Californian knows the Jap well and intimately and frequently has not held him in the highest regard."[52]

Of course, Moten was one of the more affluent Negroes and—as was enunciated as a rationale for eroding Jim Crow after the war—had a stake in the system, making her less susceptible to heeding the appeals of foreign powers, unlike many other Negroes. Moreover, there was a material basis for her view. By April 1942 the Negro press reported that "twenty colored students [per] day" had chosen to "register to replace Jap farmhands."[53]

In mid-1944, when the NAACP branch in Los Angeles launched a campaign on behalf of evacuated Japanese Americans, it was not greeted with unanimous approval.[54] "Negroes may lose most of Little Tokyo if Jap . . . freed" was a typical press account.[55] Yet restraining these more unfortunate anti-Nisei attitudes was the idea peddled by Los Angeles's mayor, who advocated restraining the further influx of Negroes, which reminded those who had forgotten that there might be a larger foe to confront.[56]

Then there was the dilemma of Charles Williams, a Negro photographer in Los Angeles, who chose to be evacuated with his spouse of Japanese origin. He worked with the Negro periodical the *California Eagle*. In the morning of a spring day in 1942 an officer of the FBI knocked on the door of their abode with the aim of providing them orders that they be ready to depart by the evening. "All day Sunday in the colored district where many Japanese have been living for years," according to one observer, "there were scenes of hasty moving."[57] Rather than face internment, the couple fled to Chicago.[58] Williams and his spouse, Yoshi Kuwahara, resided there for years, and the photographer had to relinquish his chosen profession to work in a steel mill to support his family, which included a young daughter.[59]

The case of this couple was not unusual for Los Angeles: in Jefferson High School, where 64 percent of the student body was Negro, many warm relationships had developed between the students and their teachers, many of whom were of Japanese origin. These ties, said one reporter, were "closer than those with whites."[60]

One commentator reprimanded "careless colored persons" in the City of Angels who "are occasionally overheard to praise the Japs, to express regrets for their confinement." Many were "expressing confidence that they would not have harmed colored citizens had they invaded the country," which was a rumored possibility in early 1942. The hand of the Black Dragon Society was detected in shaping these opinions, however. "There were Japanese schools in almost every colored section of the city," it was said, with "one of the largest attended being in a large house at 23rd and Stanford. Just two blocks away there was another. Until a few months ago the big sign still remained," it was reported in October 1943, "across the front in Japanese letters."[61]

By January 1945 one observer in Black Los Angeles was reproving the "anti-Japanese American campaign" he saw unfolding, about which "the press which is generally so rabid and emotional on race issues has been strangely soft-spoken." These "anti-Japanese Negroes," he noted, "contrary to the general belief," were "not ignorant and unlettered" but instead tended to "pack a powerful sentimental argument to justify their position. They point out that the present occupants of Japanese homes are good war workers, their sons are fighting and dying for America." But this observer warned, "there is dynamite in that charge"; proponents "should stop and consider that Japanese sons are also dying for the ideals of democracy as are Negro sons." Stunningly, "many prominent and so-called liberal Negroes have demonstrated anti-Japanese tactics." Fortunes could be reversed once more and Negroes could easily find themselves in the near future imploring Japanese Americans to ride to their rescue. "Loyal Japanese Americans opened their doors to colored people indiscriminately when the best educated whites and Chinese were hanging out 'no colored trade solicited' signs."[62] But this sympathetic view contrasted with the furor that erupted when Negroes were ordered to depart from property owned by those of Japanese ancestry as the civil liberties panic eased.[63]

Seemingly, the influx of Negroes into the Far West was igniting dreams of further expansion. John Larremore of Seattle, who described himself as a "meta-psychologist," pressed Senator Theodore Bilbo to arrange to send Negroes not to Africa but to "Sonora and Baja California" in Mexico, since they had a "desire to remove themselves as speedily as possible from close proximity to white people." Ambitiously, he also desired the "relocation of all white citizens now residing in the state of Arizona as well as California from the Mexican border to a line drawn from San Luis Obispo on the coast to the Nevada line," all of which "would be formed into a Negro Autonomous State known as Afro-America, a protectorate of the United States of America." Though there would be no "exclusion" of Negroes from the United States or Euro-Americans from "Afro-America," this move would "greatly increase the waning prestige of the United States." The plan would be funded by "levying of a one cent tax on tobacco and liquors," which would be "regarded as a belated payment to Negroes for more than two and a half centuries of unrequited toil and eighty years of semi-slavery."[64]

Just as some white supremacists thought the desire for repayment of war debts by London and Paris could be leveraged into land for deported Negroes, Charles Wills of Chattanooga thought deporting Negroes to Mexico could be used as leverage for seizure of that nation's oil interests.[65] These nonstarters were nonetheless indicative of how the war had jumbled the chessboard, causing new and divergent—and not always progressive—thinking.

Still, in Jim Crow Virginia, Governor Colgate Darden was concerned with another kind of evacuation. He denied the existence of "Eleanor Clubs" aiming for the "wholesale evacuation from southern kitchens of Negro servants," at a time when racial skittishness was soaring.[66] This was an ironic complement to the Pacific Coast evacuation, with one feeding upon the other to create a cyclonic racial hysteria. In the short term, this phenomenon contributed to a remarkable spate of apprehension afflicting African Americans; as shall be seen shortly, this was notably the case within the U.S. military, which was not conducive to a military victory over Japan.

* * *

In May 1942 an official report from Alexandria, Louisiana—locale of an important military base—pointed apprehensively to "racial disturbances" and "serious problems." There was "three way friction" in such key sites generally, "between the whites, Southern Negroes and Northern Negroes. Southern Negroes resent the 'high and mighty ways' of the northerners of their race and are jealous of their better financial situation"—and, perhaps, resentful that their frequent reluctance to accept the unique folkways of Dixie complicated life unduly. Then there was unspecified "subversive activity" that "feeds on and is fomented by existing conditions"; this overall problem was "expected to become more dangerous rather than improve."[67]

The U.S. military had been deluged with complaints, it was said, "from various members of Congress and citizens of various cities protesting the stationing of colored troops in their community," which hardly placed these soldiers in the proper mood to head westward to confront Japanese troops.[68] By June 1942, as the Pacific War hung in the balance, Major General George V. Strong reported that "race riots and cases of Negro disaffection have occurred at Fort Bragg, Fort Benning, Camp Davis, Fort Dix, Mitchel Field and in Alexandria, Louisiana which is near Camp Livingston, Claiborne and Beauregard"; worryingly, "most of these disturbances have been between Negro troops and white soldiers or civilians." Inevitably, the Negro press was accused of "carrying numerous articles which might possibly foment discord between the races"; the *Pittsburgh Courier*, "reported to have a large circulation in this camp," was singled out. It remained true that "the Negro press wields a tremendous influence among Negro troops," as "76% of the troops read a paper of the 'Afro-American' chain, while 56% read the 'Pittsburgh Courier.'"

Actual interracial "gun battles" were reported. Though the Communists were on the same side as Washington in the war, they were blamed for these worrisome conflicts while Tokyo, which had been engaged in a concerted campaign for years to influence Negroes, was exonerated. It was as if the latter was much too awesome to consider—or that the authorities realized instinctively and altruistically that while Tokyo merely jeopardized life itself, Moscow threatened something more important: property relations. "No evidence has been found of Japanese responsibility," it was said with relief; anyway, "the 6.5% of the Negroes who favored Japanese rule" (it was unclear from where this figure was plucked) were not formidable, though there was a "fertility of the field in which the Japanese have been working." Moreover, "the violent German racial propaganda of racial superiority has killed its ability to influence the Negroes," it was announced with premature relief.[69]

Major General Strong's words were confirmed by Major Bell Wiley, who went on to become a leading historian. He too stressed the "*subversiveness of the press*" and detailed numerous racial conflicts, particularly between Euro-American and African American soldiers. He focused on the "369th Anti-Aircraft Artillery Regiment originally from New York," composed heavily of Negroes "who had served in Hawaii where they had been well treated by the natives and the nonbelligerent Japanese," and there was "raised the question of whether the Japanese would . . . treat them better than the Georgians"—a query that probably could be answered affirmatively. It was in the Peach State that he found that "for several weeks" during the war "the Negroes surreptitiously collected weapons and ammunition" for a final conflict.[70]

Due south, in Florida, June 1942 found officialdom in Miami Beach reacting angrily to "rumors of possible colored squadrons being sent" there. "This naturally disturbed them," wrote John Duff, president of the Miami Beach Hotel Association. "As you may know," he confided to Major General Walter Weaver, "colored people have never been permitted to sleep on the Beach. To have colored troops occupy a hotel, or a number of them, would almost mean the end of those hotels when the war is over." John McCloy, a member in good standing of the U.S. ruling elite and a principal figure in the internment of Japanese Americans, supposedly had assured that he "would do everything possible to see that colored troops were not sent there," and now this solemn vow seemed to be disintegrating.[71] Miami Beach was joined by Jackson, Mississippi. "We definitely do not want any Negro soldiers stationed in Jackson," sniffed Mayor Walter A. Scott.[72]

In southern Arizona, the military brass reported in a secret July 1942 analysis that "we have the Negro problem definitely in our laps," a reference to the "Negro riot at Tucson." This prompted what could only be described as an "anti-antidote": stricter racial segregation, or "absolutely segregated camps."[73] To prescribe a cure that was arguably worse than the illness and was worsening the underlying malady in a way that Tokyo would find worthy of exploitation was suggestive of the cascading hysteria that was warping sound thinking.

"Brown Americans" Fight "Brown Japanese" in the Pacific War?

As the Pacific War was grinding to a bloody conclusion, Walter White of the NAACP embarked on a four-month journey of 36,000 miles through a central arena of conflict: the Asia-Pacific basin. What stunned him was the "prejudice of some American white soldiers, particularly officers, against Negroes." It was understandable why he would be astounded by the nagging persistence of racial chauvinism; the foe—Japan—had campaigned tirelessly among U.S. Negroes seeking to convince them that their Euro-American counterparts were incorrigible, almost congenitally incapable of diverting from a rigidly racist course. "Everywhere I went," White wrote with disgust, "I was asked how the United States, fighting a war against the racial theories of Hitler and Japan, could send two armies—one white and one Negro—to fight such a war."[1] White was distressed to see the "efforts to plant the racial patterns of Mississippi and Georgia on foreign soil," which, among other things, "has sown the seeds of distrust among our allies in this war," thereby complicating the murderous conflict.[2]

White could not ignore the dysfunctional racial policies that Washington had installed within the military. The publisher Claude A. Barnett was informed in 1942 that "American Indians are not separated in the United States Army. Chinese Americans are likewise taken without restrictions in both the Army and the Navy. There is a separate Philippino [sic] Battalion now being trained in California." The wider point was that the United States had eased the path for Tokyo's propaganda appeals to Negroes by singling them out for a more atrocious mistreatment.[3]

This led to predictable results. After the war, L. D. Reddick, one of the earliest advisors to Dr. Martin Luther King Jr., said that during the conflict, U.S. enemies were once able to batter U.S. cordons at one juncture because the "white American troops and the Negro American troops of our then segregated army were so preoccupied in watching each other that they failed to keep their eyes on the enemy."[4] National security would be perpetually jeopardized unless the more egregious aspects of Jim Crow were somehow softened.

In short, it is evident that Washington had not contemplated all of the manifold consequences of seeking to maintain white supremacy while combating a foe that portrayed itself as "champion of the darker races" and, besides, made a special appeal to U.S. Negroes. Something had to give—and it did. Following the war, there was a concerted effort to erode Jim Crow.

* * *

White supremacy also meant that not only would the Japanese forces be underestimated but Negro troops would be disrespected too. In 1925 a report from the Army War College asserted that the Negro "is by nature subservient and believes himself inferior to the white man"; he was disfigured by "mental inferiority," which supposedly had been displayed by "his failure in the World War." The "lack of honesty" of the Negro was astonishing; that the Negro is "a *rank coward* in the dark" was received wisdom (emphasis in the original).[5]

The question needs to be asked whether such views handicapped the U.S. war effort, prolonging the war, particularly against Japan, which was not above broadcasting widely what Euro-Americans thought of African Americans. And, yes, it is likely that third-class citizenship for Negroes did not predispose them to eagerly make the ultimate sacrifice for the nation responsible for this state of affairs.

In early 1942 a Negro journalist in Kansas City seemed to take grim satisfaction when considering the racial setbacks of his homeland at the hands of Tokyo. "Jim Crow came home to roost in Manila," he chortled, "where the race-conscious Japs ordered all white people off the streets, threatening to shoot them on sight unless they obeyed orders. It is extremely ironical that white Americans as champions of race discrimination and segregation should be the first to squawk when the tables are turned on them." Thus, "Pearl Harbor was the first fell blow against white supremacy as foreseen by [Lothrop] Stoddard" and earlier racial theorists.[6]

If this observer had looked more carefully at Japanese-occupied Manila, he would have noticed that a racial barrage had been unleashed, including hailing Joe Louis—the hero of Black America—as the "dusky champion" of boxing.[7] Benigno Aquino, scion of a leading family that was to play a preeminent role after the war, was among those urging full collaboration with Tokyo, as he chose with a tinge of sarcasm to "ponder the question of why our Supreme Creator in His infinite wisdom made us Malaya-Orientals and not Europeans or Anglo-Saxons."[8] The national hero Jose Rizal was among those "impressed by Japanese life [and] culture,"[9] while Filipinos were informed that the "vicious intolerance" of the Allies was "regretted"—which may have been a premature assessment of Tokyo's opponents.[10] These riveting words and actions were mirrored by certain Filipinos in the United States, then collaborating with African Americans with the goal of implementing Tokyo's aims.

* * *

By March 1945 Tokyo's forces were on the run and Walter White was in Leyte in the Philippines, but it did not appear to him that U.S. forces had learned lessons from their bitter experience under Japanese occupation. One who spoke with him found confirmation of "the old remark about whites treating every dark-skinned person better than the American Negro." White found it hard to fathom why islanders were being treated better by Euro-Americans than their African American counterparts.[11]

Lin Yutang was a celebrated Chinese writer, whose homeland was then being ravaged by rampaging Japanese troops, but he took the time to tell White that "as an Oriental observer of American life, the most shocking thing to me, one that completely surprises me, is not your bathing costumes but the racial discrimination that actually still exists." The hypocrisy was alarmingly distressing since "many people who believe that the white people are superior to the colored people are only accusing themselves when they accuse Hitler."[12] Even as Japan's defeat was assured, Euro-Americans would often enter various sites, then growl in disgust, "What are those niggers doing here?"[13]

This multi-front war unveiled contradictions and snares that Jim Crow found difficult to elude. A Negro soldier, George Watson, found that "one thing stayed in my mind while I was at Camp Patrick Henry, Virginia waiting to go overseas. German prisoners of war served us food every time we went to the mess hall [dining room] to eat."[14] The folkways of Dixie dictated that serving food across racial lines should not unfold in the way that Watson experienced it: the Negro was supposed to be the server.

* * *

It has been estimated that 2.5 million Negroes registered for the military during the war, and for the first time nearly 20,000 of them served as U.S. Marines. This suggested that perhaps the Negro seditionists' appeal to shun the military fell on deaf ears—or their prosecution acted corrosively against those same appeals (or, as Malcolm Little intended, Negroes chose to enlist and protest loudly upon donning the uniform).

These ebony troops provided a target for Japanese propagandists aiming to influence African Americans. One Negro marine recalled the figure known as Tokyo Rose, who "would come on the radio at six o'clock every evening and say, 'We are your friends, not your enemy.' Her show would often be aimed directly at the black troops and would encourage them to turn against their own country." Yet these targeted troops were instrumental in the pivotal battle at Iwo Jima. Arthur Peterson, a Negro who fought there, recalled that "if it had not been for us[,] our situation would have been worse." Yet Negro marine Sam Green recalled sharing foxholes and intimate integration at Iwo Jima—then returning to Jim Crow in Fort Smith, Arkansas.[15] U.S. military officials well knew that Tokyo was engaged in propaganda thrusts, but apparently felt that a Jim Crow army could prevail against this adversary or, alternatively, that preserving Jim Crow was more important than victory.[16]

The 24th Infantry Regiment was the first all-Negro combat unit to face Japanese forces when it landed in the Solomon Islands two days before the pivotal Battle of the Coral Sea; roughly 200,000 Negro soldiers were scattered throughout this vicinity and westward into Asia during the war. They were essential in the defeat of Japan—and knew it—and were loathe to accept Jim Crow as a result, least of all at home upon their return. That Tokyo was making ever more strident racial appeals to them all the while served to stiffen their resolve.[17]

Since there were so many Black soldiers serving in this theater of conflict, Negro reporters flocked there too. Enoch Waters of Chicago was among the latter, though official objections delayed his obtaining credentials. Washington had reason to believe that what these scribes were interested in or might find could be embarrassing—or worse—to the state. "I spent almost three years in the Pacific theatre of war as a war correspondent beginning on June 3, 1943," he declared. "Negro GIs would tell me that they would rather be at home fighting Jim Crow than in the jungle fighting the Japanese." In Papua New Guinea he found that Negro soldiers objected to editorials stating they should be "placed in combat units" rather than "service units." The consensus among these soldiers was "Why should we volunteer to sacrifice our lives for a Jim Crow country?"[18] Waters did not record whether those he interviewed had encountered or known about the New Guinean figure known as Embogi, who supported Japan because of a promise to liberate Pacific Islanders from "white" control.[19]

Australia, which then was pursuing a state-sponsored policy drenched in racialism, was a noticeable object of concern for African American soldiers. White found that "anti-Negro propaganda by many of the Americans who have poured" in there "has had a decidedly harmful effect."[20] Australia was a base from which the U.S. military engaged in hopping from island to island as it tightened the noose around its ultimate target, Japan. Richard Minor Brooks, a PMEW member and avid reader of the Negro press, had a brother in the military in Australia, which was hardly unusual. This presumed seditionist was said to have remarked that, despite Washington's strenuous effort, "The Japanese will take this country [the United States] anyway."[21] It was unclear whether special intelligence from his brother informed this inflammatory opinion.

The importance of the island continent had not eluded the attention of columnist Gordon Hancock, who was struck by this "erstwhile white man's land where the [sign] 'For Whites Only' has become proverbial."[22] Just back from "down under," Los Angeles's Robert Hayes in 1942 recounted how remnants of the 1920s racial bar that banned Negro bands and prize fighters from Melbourne continued to have "influence." What struck him, however, was the mistreatment of the indigenous of Fiji, New Caledonia, and neighboring islands pursuant to the reigning philosophy of white supremacy, an ideology that was undermining the war against Japan.[23]

However, Negroes tended to believe—like White—that Australians were not responsible for whatever difficulties African Americans encountered in the South Seas. As one commentator put it, "Australians want to treat Negroes as equals but Army leaders insist on Dixie Jim Crow and give lectures on race inferiority." This was playing with fire and, it was concluded forebodingly, "unless something is done and done quickly, a war is going to be fought on Australian soil in which no Japanese shall participate."[24]

As U.S. Negro soldiers detected how horribly these indigenes of the South Seas were treated, it often broadened their view of racism, feeding the philosophy that the "darker races," as Tokyo put it, were at odds with Washington itself. Not unlike the war earlier in the century in the Philippines, where commonalities too were found early on, Negro convergences with Pacific Islanders were quickly ascertained and cemented, which helped to convince African Americans returning home that they were not alone and should strive for liberty in the same way that Asians and Pacific Islanders were to do. There were "thousands of Negro soldiers stationed in these islands," it was reported in 1943, and "there is little difference between the Polynesians, Melanesians and Negroes" to the point where "many of the Americans have stated they intend to settle down on these islands after the war and several have married native women."[25] One Negro journalist marveled that "the native of New Guinea and other Pacific islands . . . needs only a haircut and a suit of clothes to make him look like a Harlemite"; thus, "the coming of educated, efficient Negro Americans to this part of the world has stimulated and inspired the native people generally."[26]

Hundreds of miles westward, in India, Negro troops started a "stomp band" that a reporter found to be appealing to "Indian Nagas" who took "to the beat of a boogie-woogie band like a bee takes to honey."[27] The noted historian Thant Myint-U, describing those who built the major military roads leading from Myanmar to India and China, noted that "most of the soldiers involved were African American." This was so evident, he said, that "for a while the local Naga tribesmen assumed that all Americans were black."[28]

Leon S. Bryan, born in Conway, South Carolina, in 1909 and a former student at both the segregationist Citadel and the University of North Carolina–Chapel Hill, was in a unique position to assess the racial dynamics of the Pacific theater. Interracial friction was conspicuous, he said. "Night before last," he wrote in June 1945, "some white sailors were in a café eating & drinking with a bottle of whiskey sitting on the table when a few Negro sailors wearing 45s [pistols] came in & tried to take their spirits. A free-for-all started," one of many during the war: "one Negro was shot thru the abdomen by the shore patrol."[29] He sensed that what was fueling this black-white drama was the overriding racial conflict with Japan. "Our Marines have become just as dirty as the Japs," he said, "when it comes to torture & that a favorite collector's item is Jap teeth and that they are easier to collect if knocked out while the Jap is still alive so he can spit them out. The favorite tool for extraction is a rifle butt."[30] Such deeds did little to assuage the fear expressed by many Negroes that their white peers had less than benign racial convictions and the torturous tactics they used against Japanese could just as easily be applied to them upon their return home.

* * *

By 1945 the Associated Negro Press was reporting that with the war in Europe winding down, "brown Americans will continue to engage brown Japs in the air but in greater numbers."[31] However, the ability of Negro pilots to be trained was made more difficult because of the objection to their presence in various communities.[32] "The location of the majority of air bases in the southern part of the United States, in order to profit by as much good flying weather as possible," was seen by an official Air Force report as being an impediment to training these "brown Americans" so they could engage brown Japanese. As was the case with the armed forces generally, "heightened racial tensions" resulted when "Northern Negroes were assigned in the South" for air training.[33]

Of course, racial chauvinism profoundly hindered the U.S. ability to subdue Japan. The color bar blocked the flying career of James Peck, who had flown for the Loyalists during the Spanish Civil War and thus had more experience than most.[34] Though Negroes had developed a penchant for aviation virtually from the time of the Wright brothers,[35] the Air Corps routinely refused their applications in the prelude to war.[36] "Because I am a Negro," wrote Carl Hurd to President Roosevelt, "I have been barred from the Air Corps."[37] It seemed that it was crucial for white supremacists to keep Negroes away from aviation, which was part and parcel of a larger strategy of consigning them to the bottom rung of society.

The military's use of aviation stretched back at least to the Civil War and the deployment of balloons, used again in 1898. There was official recognition of military aeronautics as a discrete field by 1911, as Congress voted funding specifically for this area; the first military airplane was produced in 1912. The planes were deployed against Mexico by 1916 and by the time of the Pacific War, the plane was seen as a winning weapon.[38] The problem for the United States was that by 1918 Japan was becoming possibly the second air power in the world—second only to France[39]—though by 1920 a U.S. periodical reported that the "next war will be fought in the air."[40] By 1942 this factor, combined with its propaganda edge in the racial realm, was thought to provide Tokyo with the ultimate winning weapon.

Major General H. H. Arnold felt that "it takes from 5 to 7 years to train a good crew chief and 5 to 9 years to train a good line or hangar chief," but the exigency of war meant that this now leisurely pace would have to be sped up tremendously.[41] But there was a problem. William Hastie, the Negro attorney close to the NAACP, demanded an end to racist segregation in aviation units, but the response from on high was blunt: "There must be and will be segregation."[42]

The NAACP protested the establishment of what it termed a "Jim Crow Squadron" in Tuskegee, but other Negroes dissented.[43] In early 1941 Lester Granger of the National Urban League was informed that it was "quite obvious that the facilities for training a Negro Air Corps group at Tuskegee will be inferior to those existing at other Government training fields, such as Kelly Field in Texas and McChord Field in the state of Washington."[44]

* * *

Just before the war started, Brigadier General G. C. Brant was contemplating sending a group of Negroes to a new flying school in San Angelo, Texas. But he worried that the city had "very few Negroes" and that "recreational facilities" were "non-existent for colored soldiers." There was "only one cafeteria system mess" that was "provided for the entire garrison. The messing problem will be considerably complicated unless a separate mess is provided," which required funds better devoted to lethal projectiles for war. Besides, "the City Bus Company operating the bus line to the field will not pick up Negroes unless the buses are almost empty."[45]

Though Houston was more urban and, presumably, more enlightened, this was not exactly the case in the sphere of Jim Crow. Ellington Field was "difficult for both housing and bathroom facilities" for Negroes, said General Brant. "While the city of Houston provides recreational facilities for Negroes," he said, "the trip of eighteen (18) miles from the field to the city is too far." Besides, there was "considerable feeling among the people of the city of Houston against the stationing of colored troops at Ellington Field because of the 1917 race riot," a reference to an uprising of Negro soldiers that proved to be quite troublesome: "it can end only in trouble," so forget this metropolis, he advised.[46]

This was not a minor matter. Jim Crow notwithstanding, by early 1942 in Birmingham, Alabama, a desperate U.S. military was hurriedly training Negro specialists of varying sorts, including 250 airplane mechanics, 4 aircraft machinists, 4 aircraft welders, 6 parachute riggers, 7 teletype operators, 4 weather observers, 20 aircraft armorers, 40 technical and administrative aviation clerks, and 30 radio operators. They were to be trained and graduated no later than 15 September 1942.[47]

Plans were afoot to train other Negroes—for example, 16 radar specialists in Boca Raton; 580 air mechanics at a Negro university; and 12 parachute riggers and 35 propeller specialists at Chanute Air Force Base in Illinois.[48] Though this base was not in Dixie, Major General B. K. Yount expected that "disturbance and possibly riots will probably ensue both at Chanute Field and the nearby communities, if colored troops are sent to Chanute," perhaps because of the relative proximity to the presumed bastions of pro-Tokyo Negroes in East St. Louis and Cairo. As for "establishing a school for colored mechanics," Tuskegee was suggested.[49] Hence, with all the racial roadblocks strewn about, by 1944, according to an official Air Force history, "a very small percentage of Negro airmen received flying training"; in 1944 "there were 1044 Negro flying personnel" in this potent force.[50]

As late as 1941, in the town made famous by Booker T. Washington, an observer described "serious objection to the location of the airport at the East End of Tuskegee," necessary for training, "because of the fact it would partially be in Tuskegee [and] would cut off the expansion of Tuskegee in the only direction for white people to expand." The "objections are so universal" that the writer, William Varner, felt compelled to "join the protest."[51] Attached was a petition from about five dozen eminent "whites" in Tuskegee who expressed "regard for the welfare of the white citizenship of Tuskegee and Macon County" and, therefore, were "protesting . . . against the location of a colored aviation camp on the East or Southeast boundary of Tuskegee," which was "the only outlet of expansion for white citizens."[52]

Fortunately for the United States, the now fabled Tuskegee Airmen were not barred from Macon County, but this did not end the travails of those "brown Americans" who sought to combat "brown" Japanese. Lieutenant Colonel William Maxwell "requested that no colored troops be assigned to Eglin" base in Valparaiso, Florida. "This is a very isolated section which is popular with vacationists during the summer months and there being no recreational facilities for colored people closer than Pensacola," Eglin was out of the question. Anyway, he added, "colored personnel are very unpopular in the immediate vicinity. Very few Negroes have been allowed to remain in this section, and then only as servants living on the premises of their employers." This negative view of Negroes transcended class boundaries in that "the attitude of the lower caste white population is that Negroes will not be permitted to live in this community." This should be taken seriously, Maxwell proclaimed forthrightly, since "intimidation tactics by certain elements of the white population will sooner or later lead to serious conflicts and possible desertion of colored troops." Pleadingly, he cautioned that it was neither "feasible nor practical" to send Negro personnel there because of the cafeteria problem, that is, the "necessity for using a full complement of white personnel for the preparation of food, which is a very undesirable factor."[53] How could white supremacy survive the abruptly unsettling role reversal of those defined as "white" preparing food for those who were Black?

After Pearl Harbor, Dr. Lawrence Kubie, who studied this Jim Crow setup, advised that training all-Negro units—be they pilots or medics or cooks—made overall cohesion of the U.S. military problematic for those not subjected to Jim Crow, who looked skeptically on those who were. This skepticism metastasized and became one of a number of "weak points in the common front, comparable to the weak spots presented to the enemy in the last war at points of juncture between French and British troops." Though "initial problems are lessened by creating separate Negro units"—thus appeasing the racist appetites of countless Euro-Americans—"more important long-run goals may be endangered." Kubie did not mention Japan's incessant propagandizing over the decades and the impact on unit cohesion; instead, he reported that "every Negro aviator and doctor with whom I spoke believes that race riots in the armed forces," which were hardly infrequent, "have been a direct and inevitable consequence of the policy of creating separate Negro units." He concluded that "units built on color lines inevitably breed friction." Yet he had visited Selfridge Field and Oscoda Field; in the latter, there was more intense segregation, and yet the Negroes were happier. When there was "race" mixing in the context of Jim Crow, as opposed to less mixing, there was more pressure on Euro-Americans to conform to Dixie standards, he said, which created a panoply of problems.[54]

An additional salient factor should not be ignored. After the war, the military's highest-ranking Negro, General Benjamin O. Davis, conceded that many Negroes in the military were not eager for integration due to the "relative comfort" of Jim Crow units and the "hostile environment" perpetrated by their white counterparts.[55] General Davis knew of what he spoke in that he was tasked to investigate yet another fracas between Negro and white military men, this time in Bristol, U.K.[56]

Selfridge, though sited in Michigan, was a seething cauldron of racial tension, raising the question as to whether Negro soldiers were more interested in fighting Jim Crow than the Pacific foe. Negro pilots, including those of high rank, had demanded access to the officers' club.[57] A leader of the Negroes was Lieutenant Milton Henry, who went on to become a leader of the "Republic of New Africa," which sought to establish a Black republic on the existing land of what is now the United States and campaigned globally for this goal. At Selfridge Negroes outnumbered those who were white by a four-to-one ratio; thus, in February 1944, Lieutenant Henry and his comrades walked brazenly into the club from which they were barred, leading to his court-martial—and radicalization. He was quoted as saying that he was "not fighting for democracy because this country in its racial attitude was not democratic."[58] Predictably, the Associated Negro Press found that morale among Negro pilots training in South Carolina—sent from Selfridge—was "shot."[59]

The manifest problems of Selfridge seemed to be dwarfed by those in Camp Claiborne, Louisiana. A volcanic eruption there involved numerous Negroes who mutinied, beat their white officers, broke into the arms lockers, and wreaked havoc generally.[60] Lee Archer, one of the Tuskegee pilots—he was part of "169 missions," he recalled—noted subsequently that "after the Civil War, the military became southern. They lost the war. They were planning a big battle which isn't here yet," hence the disproportionate number of bases in Dixie—intentionally sited there, he thought—and the resultant racial confrontations.[61]

* * *

Unfortunately for the United States, these problems did not disappear after troops were posted overseas, particularly in Europe, where African Americans could contrast the racial rigidity at home with the relative fluidity encountered abroad. In a "personal and confidential" report, British allies lamented the "difficult situations owing to the differences of outlook between the white American personnel and the British personnel as to the relationship between black and white people," with the former insisting on strict Jim Crow standards, to the consternation of the latter. This correspondent was baffled and was "try[ing] to understand why it [inter-racialism] is different from the attitude of most people in this country"; he further objected to the notion that "British soldiers and auxiliaries should adopt the American attitude." The British were instructed to—at best—be "friendly and sympathetic towards coloured American troops but remember that they are not accustomed in their own country to close and intimate relationship with white people." Perhaps with an eye cocked to Tokyo, it was stressed that "it is probable that enemy propaganda will make every effort to use the colour question to stir up bad feelings between people in this country and the coloured troops and between American white and coloured troops."[62]

This report was filed as yet another "race riot" was unfolding between Black and white troops—except this was on British soil, which was bound to be worrisome to London, which had its hands full already without having to sort through U.S. problems. U.S. Major General Henry Miller admitted in June 1943 that there had been a "mutiny at Bamber Bridge" in Britain, directed by "colored troops" who "had taken possession of their rifles and ammunition," inflicting casualties. "Southern Negros [tend] to have in general a better attitude than those from the North," it was noted by way of consolation, but this was hardly comforting as the blood began to flow.

As explained by Major General Miller, the bridge in question was strategically located "four (4) miles from the city of Preston, in Lancashire." He conceded that "the race problem was the primary factor in the alleged mutiny," for "instead of there being a ratio of approximately ten whites to one Negro, as in the United States, there is a numerical ratio in this Theater of many times that amount, in favor of the whites. This causes the Negro soldier to 'stand out' . . . far more than in the United States," to his detriment. Again, complicating matters immeasurably was the fact that a "substantial number of the British military and civil population treat the Negro soldier on the basis of social equality," the women not least, which was blindingly infuriating to many Euro-Americans. The gap between the British and Euro-Americans helped to exacerbate interracial tension; it "obviously created conflicts." For "the white American soldier resents seeing a colored soldier with white women in public places," while "colored soldiers have deliberately picked fights with white American soldiers on the streets" and "'take the law into their own hands' on numerous occasions." Typically, the Negro press was fingered as an instigator—the *People's Voice* of Harlem in this instance. Emphasized nervously was that "*no evidence of any enemy subversive effort in any way [was] involved*"—but this episode was no less frightening since "men were seen to be crying, shrieking, and giving vent to their emotions." The "storerooms" containing "arms and ammunition were reasonably safeguarded," but the bold and angry Negroes—the "mutineers"—"gained access by force."[63]

How could "brown Americans" be enlisted to confront "brown Japanese" when they were so busy fighting their "white" counterparts?

The problems faced by Negro forces in Europe were of a different character though no less poisonous than those in Dixie. In Western Europe a repetitive flashpoint seemed to be intimate fraternizing between Negro men and European women, which was unacceptable to many Euro-Americans. In November 1944 the ANP correspondent Rudolph Dunbar was in France "talking to a French man" who said that "when

France was liberated his wife told him that she must kiss an American. He told her that he would agree to her request under one condition: . . . she must kiss an American Negro soldier because he is the only true American."[64]

London had its own problems in this sphere. Dunbar had reported earlier that there was a "parallel between the Royal Air Force in England in comparison with their Colonial subjects and the method . . . employed by the American Air Force," that is, a replica of the "Air Force Unit for Negroes."[65] Dunbar was as close to the action as any war correspondent extant, having sent a note to ANP headquarters on the stationery of Adolf Hitler himself, which he had purloined after the erstwhile chancellor was routed in the Reich Chancellery.[66]

In any case, after Tuskegee leaped hurdles and was established as an aviation center, a British official hastened to assure that "there is no intention of setting up a training school for British cadets in Tuskegee, Alabama."[67] Still, one U.S. military official complained in October 1944 about the unjust and often brutal treatment of the Negro forces there by white police officers in nearby towns.[68]

Retrospectively, it is remarkable how U.S. brass seemed willing to accept setbacks—perhaps even defeat—in the war rather than alter mossback racial practices. This was even more conspicuous and glaring since a principal foe had made it clear that it intended to capitalize upon this very same praxis. It is easy to infer that preserving Jim Crow was deemed more important than unit cohesion, perhaps even victory. Still, the U.S. military was told to avoid "the use of any epithet deemed insult to a racial group"; but the fact that this message was distributed globally leads to the supposition that it was intended more for indigenes overseas in places like Burma rather than internally. Moreover, this communication was distributed as Singapore was falling—a real turning point in terms of the perception of the impact of Japan's racial propaganda—and may have been a reflection of an ephemeral sensitivity more than anything else.[69] What should be considered is this: to what extent did desegregation of the armed forces represent a bending toward attitudes of allies nervous about importing peculiar U.S. folkways to their soil with all the attendant tensions and conflicts?

* * *

"Brown American" pilots did not drop the atomic bombs on Hiroshima and Nagasaki, but Negro opinion molders were hardly quiet as this holocaust was unwinding.[70] In a Sunday sermon in August 1945, the Reverend J. E. Elliot, pastor of St. Luke Chapel in Washington, D.C., excoriated the bombing and claimed that racism was a driving force behind it. "I have seen the course of discrimination throughout the war," he said despondently, "and the fact that Japan is of a darker race is no excuse for resorting to such an atrocity."[71] Langston Hughes agreed.[72] Again, George Schuyler, the leading Negro conservative, was more acerbic than most, proclaiming that "controlling this tremendous power" of nuclear weaponry "for evil are second-rate and small-minded men filled with racial arrogance such as Truman, Tom Connally, Jimmy Byrnes, Stimson, Bilbo and our military officers clique, who believe in racial segregation."[73] If mass murder could be inflicted upon Japanese civilians, what did this portend for U.S. Negroes?

An ironic confirmation of Schuyler's dyspepsia was provided by U.S. General Joseph Stilwell, who ghoulishly said, "When I think of how these bowlegged cockroaches have ruined our calm lives it makes me want to wrap Japan guts around every lamppost in Asia."[74] U.S. serviceman Robert L. Bennett was not as coruscating in his remarks but just as skeptical of Tokyo's seemingly evaporated objectives. Writing from Japan in August 1945 as the embers of war still glowed, he remained "doubtful" of the vanquished foe's intentions because of "the way the Japs are acting!!" "Although the war is over," he added worriedly, "I think our work has just started" in bringing Tokyo to heel.[75]

Viewing the first and only atomic bombing through a racial lens was, in a sense, a lingering legacy among African Americans. In 1949 the moderate Gordon Hancock celebrated Moscow's acquisition of the atom bomb since "it will contribute to the peace of the world," a view unrestrainedly at odds with Washington's view. "The tragic mistake was made," he continued, "when atomic fury was 'practiced' against hapless Nagasaki and Hiroshima. This was the tragedy of tragedies." Worse, he noted, "the fact that the bomb was tried out on a darker people has double significance. If the bomb was to be pressed into service, why was it used on the Japanese instead of the Germans who were in the midst of slaughtering millions of luckless Jews?" The "sordid fact remains that the pouring out of the vial of wrath upon Japan was a part of the white supremacy picture." But contradictions had emerged, he said, since "to all intents and purposes the atomic bomb as an instrument of human destruction for the externalization of white supremacy is working in reverse and herein lies the hope of mankind." What he seemed to be suggesting was that Moscow getting the bomb meant that the "so-called white nations are divided among themselves." That is, "when white threatens white maybe Christ and Peace have a chance."[76]

Hancock found it strategically significant that now it was Moscow that was seen as the primary threat to "white supremacy." "Churchill and Bilbo and Rankin," the latter two being prominent Mississippi lawmakers, "know that the only threat to white supremacy ideology is the Communistic ideology of Russia."[77] Ultimately it would be realized that as one powerful antagonist after another confronted Washington on the mine-laden battlefield of "race," U.S. leaders would have to seriously consider whether this ideology was worth the debility it so clearly wrought.

In 1954 an ANP correspondent observed that "what we are witnessing today is a color war: [the] U.S.A. would never have used the A-bombs on Germany but a colored nation did not count, so they tried them out on Japan. Japanese have never forgiven Americans for that."[78] Also in 1954 the Negro publisher Claude A. Barnett, who previously had viewed the internment as an opportunity for Negroes, now more soberly concluded that "when the Japanese were driven out of California and put in concentration camps, the only people who succored them, or the principal people who did, were colored folk. They visited the camps, took them food and did errands for them."[79] Perhaps he was looking ahead and gathering chits for a day when the roles would be reversed and Negroes would need aid in internment camps.

U.S. Negroes found it hard to forget the racial chauvinism that they had endured, even after it was declared officially verboten in the wake of the 1954 landmark *Brown v. Board of Education* decision. Sharp note was taken of the verbal miscue by Senator Styles Bridges, who on national television said that no "white soldiers" would be used in an invasion of China. "I mean American soldiers would never be used," he clarified, though his initial words betrayed a continuing widespread belief that to be "American" was the equivalent of being "white."[80] Negro apprehension was not assuaged when Sherman Adams, a top White House aide, said on television the next year that the "white race" was going to "hang together" in world affairs.[81]

Yet with the formal declaration that Jim Crow was no longer the law of the land, pro-Tokyo Negroes in disarray and pro-Moscow Negroes under fire, the idea was rapidly disappearing that continued external pressure would be necessary if such retrograde views were to disappear. It was then—once again ironically—that Negroes deeply influenced by M. K. Gandhi and New Delhi arose to fill the resultant vacuum in the person of Dr. Martin Luther King Jr., confirming the still (sadly) contested proposition of the importance of global trends for U.S. Negroes—not to mention opening yet another chapter in the illustrious story of Afro-Asian solidarity.[82]

8

Aftermath

It was February 1965 when the man who had come to be known as Malcolm X was shot in Manhattan. Cradling his head as he expired was the Japanese American activist Yuri Kochiyama.[1] The assassination came in the wake of sharp conflict between the New York–based minister and more traditional forces.

In 1963 Revilo Oliver, a harsh critic of the Nation of Islam, had written disparagingly of Elijah Muhammad's arrest during the war ("the Messenger of Allah was finally discovered hiding under his wife's bed wrapped in a carpet"). After this abrupt dismissal, Oliver pointed out accurately that the group's "spectacular growth did not begin until May 1954," with the juridical attack on Jim Crow and the concomitant attack on activists like Paul Robeson, which created an ideological vacuum that was filled by the Nation.[2] The man once known as Malcolm Little had risen and fallen in this vibrant context: from dodging the draft in order to evade fighting Japanese forces to becoming a resonant symbol and organizer for the group that became the Nation of Islam, fixing the group's identification firmly with a rising Africa, then—in a sense—coming full circle: slain at the behest of erstwhile NOI comrades while being cradled in his final moments by a woman of Japanese origin.

After being abandoned by a prostrate Tokyo, Black Nationalists in Malcolm's old faith continued to refer to themselves as "Asiatic" officially and in inner sanctums, but it was Malcolm who had led the way to nationalists' renewed identification with Africa, where they remain to this very day. Indeed, now—tellingly—they often see themselves as "blacker than thou," more resolute and uncompromising in their asserted alignment with the "motherland."

Beginning with the Scottsboro case in the 1930s and for the next few decades, left-led organizations like the Civil Rights Congress had led monumental struggles against Jim Crow, but by 1956 the CRC had been compelled to liquidate.[3] In contrast, the group with which Malcolm X had been associated in his heyday, the Nation of Islam, had survived and flourished in the postwar era, despite the imprisonment of its leader, Elijah Muhammad.

In 1957 members of the Nation of Islam marched for seven hours in Harlem protesting a police beating of one of their members and impressing onlookers with their discipline and fortitude. A journalist noted that "they believe that in the days of antiquity, all Negroes were Moslems."[4] By 1958 the Nation was meeting in what was called a "monster convention," deemed to be a "strategic development" and a "turning point."[5] In 1960 Elijah Muhammad returned to his native Georgia, where a journalist without exaggeration described the diminutive leader as "America's Most Powerful Black Man."[6] Just before that, it was estimated that the Nation had "250,000 followers but other sources credit him with only 70,000." Both figures may have been high in retrospect, but were indicative of the weight of the group in public consciousness.[7] As those, notably pro-Moscow Negroes, who had stood with Washington during the war and excoriated pro-Tokyo Negroes in turn, were sidelined, harassed, and jailed, the ideological balance among African Americans was influenced significantly to the benefit of the Nation of Islam.

The Nation of Islam continued to be plagued with questions about its supposed Pacific origins, however. Elijah Muhammad offered a $100,000 reward to detractors who could prove that his faith was founded, as a commentator put it, by "Wallace Dodd, a white, New Zealand born ex-convict . . . who posed as a Negro"; Dodd allegedly had a "white English father and a Polynesian [mother]."[8] Defying those who characterized his faith as racist, Elijah Muhammad asserted in 1963 that, yes, there were no "whites" allowed in its gatherings, but, he insisted, "this does not include the Turkish people, Chinese, Japanese, Filipinos, those of Pakistan, Arabs, Latin Americans, Egyptians and those of other Asiatic Muslim and non-Muslim nations."[9] In other words, he and his comrades were focused on those defined as "white" U.S. nationals, those perceived as being responsible for slavery, Jim Crow, and other horrors, a point often lost and obscured.

Nevertheless, from the moment the Pacific War ended on the deck of the battleship *Missouri*, a readjustment was necessary in the United States. Japan's pre-1945 racial crusade had exposed a serious flaw in the fabric of U.S. national security. If a substantial group of U.S. Negroes were eagerly expecting an invasion on 24 November 1942 in which they planned to join—on the side of the invaders—it was apparent that racial policies needed to be reformed. This was easier proclaimed than implemented, however.

* * *

The nation in which the erstwhile Malcolm Little resided had evolved similarly: from "race war" with Tokyo to "Cold War" with Moscow. The dilemma was epitomized by the postwar musings of Robert Browne, later a distinguished economist, who wrote in 1945 that he "genuinely participated both emotionally and intellectually in the upsurge of anti-Japanese feeling which my patriotism demanded," though "it was not without an undercurrent of satisfaction that a non-white people had at long last slapped the face of the arrogant whites." Like many Negroes, he found it easier to get along with Euro-Americans overseas than at home, a testament to the warped racial atmosphere in the United States. But now with the defeat of Japan, he sensed that "the Soviet Union is the only western power to indicate that it may have grasped this racial aspect of international politics," which was to bring Moscow a kind of grief that Tokyo had experienced. He thought that the United States and its allies owed "a debt of gratitude to the Soviet Union for having provided . . . an impetus to realistic thinking as regards the colored world." That was not the dominant perception in Washington, obviously, though it carried weight with intellectuals like Robeson and Du Bois, once ballyhooed and now besieged.[10]

Browne's words about Moscow—though perceptive—were not necessarily indicative of the temper of the times: ironically, Tokyo's defeat served as a predicate for the rise of once reviled pro-Tokyo Negroes. Suggestive of the importance of Malcolm X to the fortunes of the Nation of Islam was that the Moorish Science Temple did not flourish the way the NOI did. Still, a member, Robert Bey of Newark, captured headlines in 1953 when he successfully flouted Jim Crow practices in Raleigh. "I am not a Negro," he proclaimed. "I am a Moorish-American, and a human being."[11]

Hence, the remnants of "race war" did not perish in the ashes of Nagasaki, not least because the colonialism that had helped to propel war in the first instance had not disappeared in the postwar environment. Thus, when there was a concretizing of Afro-Asian solidarity in a historic gathering in Bandung, Indonesia, in April 1955, Du Bois and Robeson—deprived of passports—were unable to attend. Though Japan sent a sizeable delegation of thirty-four notables, Tokyo's emerging role as U.S. ally prevented it from reaping the full benefits of Bandung. Arguably, however, Japan's historic role was a major factor in bringing this solidarity into being in the first place. "Bandung was at least five hundred years in the making," said one commentator at the time, a reference to the now fading era of European colonialism and the still resonant era of settler colonialism that created the United States; left unsaid was that Tokyo was then being viewed not as an avatar or harbinger of the emerging era of Afro-Asian solidarity that was soon to take flight in the Non-Aligned Movement and the United Nations, but as an ally of those now being targeted by this new epoch of militant solidarity.[12]

Though this profound gathering was held just as the U.S. war in Korea was winding down from its hottest phase and just as the concomitant war in Vietnam was heating up, African American investment in Afro-Asian solidarity was not necessarily accelerating. Washington had learned a painful lesson during the Pacific War and had chosen to make agonizingly halting steps away from the more horrendous aspects of Jim Crow. As a consequence, U.S. Negroes had less cause and reason to seek allies abroad for domestic leverage, though it would be an error to suggest that this solidarity had disappeared altogether, given the impact of India on events in Dixie.[13]

After he had left office, former secretary of state Dean Acheson conceded the obvious when he told Claude Barnett that "the existence of discrimination against minority groups in the United States is a handicap in our relations with other countries."[14] The problem was that this praxis was so deeply ingrained in U.S. culture—as a candid Tokyo could have attested—that gutting it was easier said than done. Yet an attempt to gut it had to be considered.

A Rip Van Winkle awakening after being asleep for two decades might have expected that African Americans—like the younger Malcolm Little and his soon-to-be coreligionists years earlier—would continue their close relationship with Tokyo. Generally, this was not the case. The atomic bombing, combined with painful defeat and U.S. occupation, had transformed Japan and profoundly eroded Tokyo's historic role as "champion of the darker races." In fact, in 1963 a Negro reporter registered his disappointment with the "condescending attitude" taken by Tokyo to racism in the United States. There was a "playing down of the racial implications" of violent unrest in Mississippi and Alabama, and "scenes depicting the Birmingham riots were not published," though the Japanese also "suffered discrimination in the U.S." The conclusion was a turnabout from the pre-Hiroshima history: "Japanese don't feel any emotional ties with the American Negro."[15]

This may not have been true of Japanese visitors to the United States during this time, for those in Chicago were said to be familiar with the lyrics of Negro spirituals, especially those rendered by Paul Robeson. Yet the point could not be evaded that as the anti–Jim Crow movement surged, Tokyo—once keen to capitalize on U.S. racial difficulties—was no longer in the frontlines. The Associated Negro Press, the most comprehensive chronicler of Tokyo's incursion into Black America before the war, was struck by the postwar pell-mell retreat.[16]

* * *

Even before the war concluded, Senator Theodore Bilbo of Mississippi predicted—perhaps promised—that the "relationships between the white and black races are going to get worse especially when the war is over and those Negroes who are trained to shoot come back home."[17] After the war ended, he assured true believers in apartheid, "I shall continue my fight for white supremacy and for the preservation of the American way of life as long as God gives me the strength to do so."[18] Holding aloft the still fluttering banner of white supremacy, Bilbo took time to tutor J. B. Stoner, who was to emerge after the war as his most bloodthirsty pupil.[19] Stoner asked his mentor to "help me deliver a severe blow to the evil Jewish race," whom he called the "Jew-devils" and who were supposedly proven "*by the Bible*" to be "the children of Satan."[20] Fortunately, Stoner and Bilbo were to find that the postwar climate for their vituperation had been changed, not least because of the continuing reverberations from the "race war" in the Pacific basin.

The opponents of Bilbo and Stoner were able to capitalize on this changing climate only in part. Unfortunately, just as Negro-Nisei tension rose as the internment unfolded in Los Angeles, a similarly riddled process unwound when the internees returned home. Days after the

United States and its allies triumphed in Europe, the *Washington Post* reported on "recent outbreaks in California against Japanese American citizens," including "about 15 terrorist attacks on returned Nisei" and "four cases of attempted arson." There was "only one instance," in rural Placer County, where the "terrorists [were] brought to justice," though at trial the defense argued passionately that this was a "white man's country" and should be kept so. The jury freed the defendants.[21]

Just before this disturbing report, Senator Bilbo, whose vitriolic racism tended to attract the like-minded, even when not in Dixie, was informed that "California is being overcrowded with Negroes and it will not be long, not many years, until there will be a race war here." Bilbo's correspondent, J. A. Watkins, believed that "the Negroes must be sent back to Africa, their homeland, or America is doomed to be populated by a yellow or brown race in four hundred years from the Declaration of Independence," the outcome of a "Jewish plot against America"; already in the Golden State there were "more than fifty thousand white women" who were "living with Negroes or Negroids—Philipinos [sic], Chinese," and the like.[22]

Likewise, Mike Masoaka of the Japanese American Citizens League reported that "arson, intimidation and shooting" greeted the return of Nisei and their compatriots to their erstwhile neighborhoods.[23] This hostility was found in Dixie particularly, for when Hawaii-born Yukiko Tomashiro applied for a seventh-grade teaching post in the Washington suburb of Falls Church, Virginia, she was rejected on racist grounds.[24] A few years earlier, a Japanese national was barred from attending the historically Black Langston University in Oklahoma, which determined that these Asians were somehow defined as "white."[25] Ironically, this decision may have been an aspect of the postwar thrust to redefine Japanese Americans as a "model minority"—so as to undermine and complicate their previous ties to U.S. Negroes.

California, the site of returning Nisei and continuously arriving Negroes, was notably combustible. As early as June 1945, Charles Krause of Los Angeles was lamenting the arrival of Negroes who were "poisoned by the virus of Communism or were under the influence of NAACP propaganda." He wondered nervously what would occur "when the war against Japan is over, when the war industries close down, when veterans return in ever increasing numbers." The "outlook is dark and menacing," he declared gloomily, as he encouraged Senator Bilbo to redouble his efforts to oust African Americans altogether from the United States.[26] Bilbo did not have to be reminded; even before D-Day he was telling a constituent with asperity that "we are going to have so many race riots after [the war] is over and [as] these Negro soldiers get back home that they will all be glad to go after the battle is over."[27]

By December 1945 Senator Bilbo was irate about the "awful crimes that are being committed by these Negroes who seem to have gone wild when they reached the Pacific Coast." After the bombing of Pearl Harbor, he had "had to stop my [repatriation] campaign" of dispatching U.S. nationals back to Africa; "but now that the war is over," he contended, he planned to "introduce the bill and make a great drive" for it; for "if the Negro is permitted to stay in this country some have said that in less than 300 years we will all be yellow." He did not mean Asian, but it was unclear whether he meant intimidated or mulatto.[28] What the senator had neglected to note was that those Black Nationalists who had provided grassroots energy for his resettlement campaign in the prewar era were either languishing in prison or ideologically undermined by Tokyo's defeat and the coming rise in anti–Jim Crow measures.

However, Bilbo's supporters proceeded as if nothing had changed. "This government recently deported some Japanese back to their home island," wrote Luscious Casey to Bilbo that same month, which was a possible precedent, he thought, for the resettlement of U.S. Negroes in Africa.[29] In December 1945 Grover Brewer in Oregon reported that "since the war started" more Negroes had been "imported" to "work in war plants"; angrily, he asserted, "you would have no idea of the crime that has been committed up and down this Pacific Coast such as murder, rape, robbery" as a direct result of this migration. "Sending the Negroes back to Africa" was a keen idea, he thought. This self-confessed "Southerner" and "descendant from Scotch and Irish" also detested the arrival of another "race of people here in our country" whom he perceived as "parasites" who "live off one sort of graft or that never produce anything"—"that is the Jew."[30]

Meanwhile, in Chicago the city's population of Japanese origin, which was less than four hundred in the prewar years, was up to twenty thousand by 1948, as a goodly number from the Pacific coast fled eastward. "Is this a threat to Negroes?" asked a Negro reporter, given their efficiency and industry as workers.[31] The answer was likely no, though the question itself exposed a radically transformed landscape.[32] The afore-mentioned "condescending attitude" now seemingly adopted by Japa-nese toward racial matters was all the more jarring since Tokyo was all too aware of the realities of the United States' halting retreat from the excesses of Jim Crow.

* * *

Ironically, with maximum chutzpah and minimal self-awareness, Washington—the pioneer in crafting Jim Crow and articulating white supremacy—was breathing rhetorical fire in the International Military Criminal Tribunal for the Far East, which tried Japanese leaders. Those in the dock, the prosecutors asserted, "systematically poisoned . . . the mind of the Japanese people . . . with harmful ideas of the alleged racial superiority of Japan over other peoples of Asia and even of the whole world." It was as if the implicit gravamen of the indictment was that ideas of racial superiority were the unique province of the North Atlan-tic nations. Some in Tokyo and India and in certain precincts of Black America where the idea of Afro-Asian solidarity continued to illumi-nate, saw this proceeding as illegitimate, a kangaroo court, the justice of victors.[33]

This viewpoint presumably was not shared by another prominent Negro intellectual and educator, Charles Johnson, who made a con-spicuous arrival in Tokyo in 1946, though the circumstances were not what was envisioned in East St. Louis in 1942. Johnson, given the rank of brigadier general, was tasked with the responsibility of helping to co-ordinate the "re-education" of Japan away from militarism.[34] Remaking this proud nation's "cultural" system was also part of his task.[35] In other words—with irony manifest—he was executing an important task that Tokyo thought it would be executing in Black America if the war had ended differently.

Johnson's ministrations might have been better applied to his compa-triots in Japan rather than the Japanese themselves. Writing from Yoko-hama in 1946, Edwin Gregory, a member in good standing of the U.S. elite, informed Senator Bilbo that "many Jews were sent to the training center" there and "they invariably proved poor soldiers and dangerous for other soldiers" besides, since "if sent to the point at the front, they had the attitude of 'let the best of the Gentiles get killed off and [we] will be more powerful after the war.'" African Americans were far worse, he thought; surprisingly, he found "the Northern [white] men hate the Negro more than the Southern ones"; in fact, "all soldiers have to despise the Negro" and acted accordingly. This minority group was responsible for having "stolen millions of dollars from the government. They are the ones who do the stealing," he insisted, and thus "Negro troops [should] be sent home" immediately.[36] By 1949 there were at least fifty-five Negro units assigned to duty in Japan, which provided plenty of opportunity for clashes.[37]

Keeping an eye peeled on the Philippines was one purpose of these bases in Japan, as the collaboration of these two archipelagos against Washington before 1945 had yet to be forgotten. Thus, despite the recent harrowing experience with Japan and the widespread acknowledgment that bigotry had helped to fuel the war, old habits continued to die hard. Robert Bennett was stationed with U.S. forces in Manila after the war. "The type of people who surround us daily," he spluttered furiously, were "clannish, primitive heathens"; they were "friendly yet schemish [sic], you never know what their primitive minds are thinking of next." He was irate with the thought of "missing valuables" of his: "I'd like to get my hands on the little brown-skinned devil who took it," he exclaimed, using expressions that would have not been out of place in his native Athens, Georgia.[38] Subsequently, he worried about an FBI investigation of the Ku Klux Klan in his home state, and inquired whether there were "any discoveries" that would be worrisome to those of his ilk.[39] Whatever the answer to that query, the wider point was that the aftermath of the Pacific War, in which Bennett was now enmeshed, had led to a renewed emphasis on eroding the conditions that caused some in East St. Louis, a few years earlier, to await eagerly an expected Japanese invasion.

By 1946 in Manila considerable anti-Negro propaganda persisted. African Americans were accused by certain Philippine elites of joining in a radical rebellion against the regime, along with "Russians and Chinese."[40] An attempt by the U.S. secretary of war to calm the worried failed, as "vicious white elements" were blamed for the questioning of Negroes' mettle. Apparently some were upset at the leading roles played in Manila by the likes of the U.S. Negro Calvin Parrish, a Manila resident for years and a leading radio personality.[41] Finally, the U.S. military felt compelled to deny that "250 American soldiers deserted the army to become members of the Huks,"[42] the militant anti-colonial resistance. Somehow these charges of Negro sedition persisted, despite the presence in the Philippines of those like Millie Sanders, an African American who had been a highly regarded businesswoman before the war in Manila but wound up interned at the notorious Santo Tomas camp.[43]

The problem for Washington was that the more perceptive Negro leaders realized—even when they did not act upon the idea—that global leverage was mandatory if the United States was to retreat from its racial recalcitrance. Even Lester Granger of the normally staid National Urban League admitted in 1947 that the "hope of Negroes rests on U.S. desire for world respect."[44] Such sentiment helped to unleash a titanic struggle, for the United States was being compelled to retreat from ossified policies that had mass support. This would not have been a simple task in the best of times, but this was an era when a significant percentage of Negro intellectuals, including Robeson and Du Bois, were attracted in various ways to the new foe and former ally, Moscow. One Australian visiting the United States in 1947 found that "Negro vets," who had sacrificed so much so recently, "expressed deep disappointment with the shape of the post-war world" and "wonder[ed] whether their sacrifices in the war have produced commensurate [gain]."[45]

Shortly after this report, President Truman moved to terminate the Jim Crow policies of the military.[46] The war had unleashed anti-colonial forces that were difficult to contain and that even the powerful United States could not resist. As Truman was moving to desegregate the armed forces, a group of Negro intellectuals and administrators departed for a tour of India, which only recently had shed its involuntary title as the jewel in the British crown. T. Thomas Fortune Fletcher, who made this journey, was pleased upon arriving in Bombay: "I received every courtesy," he enthused, at a deluxe hotel akin to Manhattan's Waldorf-Astoria. He glimpsed a sign, "Dogs and South Africans not admitted," a reference to the architects of the recently proclaimed apartheid, which was headed in the opposite direction of global trends. Before independence, he recalled, "non-Europeans" were barred, but times had changed.[47] Fletcher's experience reflected the rise of India, one of the salient and most important aspects of the post-1945 dispensation: New Delhi's ascension to the front ranks of diplomacy ultimately guaranteed that the promise of "Afro-Asian solidarity" signaled by the rise of Japan in the first few decades of the twentieth century would be at least partially fulfilled.

The ongoing maltreatment of African Americans stood as testament to the contradictory nature of "war crime" indictments exclusively of Japanese leadership. Moreover, the ongoing racial abuse dictated that U.S. Negroes would adopt stances contrary to U.S. foreign policy, as had just been exposed during the Pacific War, notably in the U.S. colony that was the Philippines. How many—and whether—Negroes fought alongside the anti-imperialist Huks in the Philippines is unclear, though like those who expressed solidarity with Ethiopia in the 1930s, or like David Fagen, who threw in his lot with the precursors of the Huks decades earlier, this kind of solidarity continued after the Pacific War ended. Inevitably, this global wanderlust took intriguing directions. By May 1948 it was reported that "numerous Negroes here [in the United States] have attempted to volunteer to fight for Israel," including John Harris, who "was reared in a Jewish home. He was confirmed when he was 12."[48]

The postwar hysteria about the African American presence in the Philippines was a throwback to the era decades earlier when numerous Negro soldiers were accused of joining the rebels in the wake of the ouster of Spain in 1898 and the squashing of the archipelago's independence. This accusation notwithstanding, the blistering nature of the war had helped to convince Brigadier General Carlos Romulo in Manila to assert that "the next war will be a race war" unless the world—notably the colonizing powers—were able to "face frankly the problem of the darker peoples of the Pacific."[49]

* * *

Walter White of the NAACP detected the growing importance of Afro-Asian solidarity in 1949 when he traveled to Africa and Asia, where he found much disparagement of the United States because of maltreatment of the Negro. In India, where sympathy for Japan during the war had been strong, "Nehru told [White] personally that it was a hard job to keep his people from sympathizing with the Russians." Indian youth often opted for higher education in Russia since "they fear ill-treatment in America due to their skin [being] dark."[50]

When war erupted on the Korean peninsula, Japan became a staging ground for U.S. and United Nations offensives, which led White's colleague Roy Wilkins to demand a "probe of army bias in Japan," which was "as flagrant as it is in Georgia" and belied the U.S. attempt to portray the Korean conflict as being something other than a "racial war."[51] Negro troops railed against the typical designation "U.N. Forces and Negro Troops," which implied that the latter were otherworldly or that Africans were not part of the human family. Another U.S. observer in Japan found that Negro troops "have always been accepted by the Japanese, since most of them are kind and lack the arrogance of whites which many Japanese find irksome."[52] Evidently, this was reflected in the escalating number of Negro military men filing requests "to marry their Oriental 'flames of passion.'"[53] Ironically, Edith Sampson, who had aided a key figure in the pro-Tokyo Negro movement in Chicago, was appointed to a post at the United Nations, supposedly to provide "an answer to Communist propaganda about the position of Negroes" in the United States.[54]

But the most expert counter-propaganda was hardly effective when the NAACP's Thurgood Marshall verified unjust treatment of Negro soldiers rotating from Japan to Korea, whose rate of court-martial exceeded that of white soldiers by a ratio of sixteen to one.[55] As late as 1952, Negro soldiers slain on the battlefields of Korea could not be buried in cemeteries designated back home for the "white dead."[56] As late as 1953, as the war was stumbling toward a truce, there were credible reports that blood continued to be racially segregated, contrary to directives.[57]

Reportedly, 90 percent of the U.S. prisoners-of-war freed in the immediate aftermath of the 1953 truce were Negroes, as those who had fought Japan and gained legitimacy as a result—North Korean and Chinese Communists—took a page from Tokyo's playbook by seeking to manipulate race relations within the republic. A freed prisoner asserted that "the Reds rated racial bias in the United States as the weak spot in the American armor of democracy. They felt that it would be easier to turn Negroes into Communists than other Americans." Thus, these wily antagonists mimicked Jim Crow by separating Black and white soldiers, as to better influence the former.[58] Reportedly, resistance to collaboration with the stated foe was spearheaded by a group named the Ku Klux Klan, which, it was said, tended to "associate treason with color."[59]

The former prisoner noted above may have had Louis Wheaton in mind. Hailing from New York City, this former Air Force officer defected to China and began broadcasting from there, where he accused his former homeland of engaging in germ warfare and burning Korean women and children alive. From 1942 to 1948 he had been an aviation instructor at Tuskegee. With a law degree from Fordham University, Wheaton was seemingly poised to take advantage of the new era of desegregation then emerging. However, unlike the Black Nationalists who predominated in pro-Tokyo formations before 1945, Wheaton was rumored to be a Communist, suggesting that as long as stains of Jim Crow persisted, the United States would face a continuing national security problem.[60]

Hence, those described as "Tan Yanks" chose not to sing "sad songs" when Douglas MacArthur, the U.S. proconsul in Japan and then commander in Korea, was sacked. According to James Hicks, it was "common knowledge" that "the existence of segregation in the army [persisted] in spite of" Truman's executive order mandating otherwise. MacArthur was fingered as the culprit. "Tokyo today looks like Mississippi," Hicks asserted in 1951, "so far as racial signs are concerned." In MacArthur's own headquarters signs marked the toilets and water fountains as "For Japanese Only" and "Allied Personnel Only"; there were "'white' and 'colored' swimming pools," while in other areas "whites" were allowed to use the pools one day and "colored" the next. Hicks did not comment on the paradoxical fact that Tokyo's self-proclaimed "race war" could end with a Jim Crow result, at least in the short term.[61] Hicks's observations were substantiated by contemporaneous words of Walter White, who lamented, "When I was in Japan, . . . I saw little evidence of any compliance with the integration order," while "Thurgood Marshall found the same to be true in Tokyo and Korea in 1951."[62]

Hicks also commented on the situation in Australia. In one area in Brisbane, MacArthur had demarcated a six-block area where Negro soldiers could go for recreation—and no other area; military police were stationed strategically to enforce this directive and arrested any "colored" soldiers who dared veer beyond their apartheid zone and seek to partake of the Army's modern PX. This, said Hicks, was done at MacArthur's behest for the purpose of keeping Negroes away from Euro-Australian women.[63]

Despite the bitter lesson in Korea, which helped to derail victory, old customs perished uneasily in the United States. Five years after the truce, those defined as "Mongoloid," in addition to "Negroid" and "Caucasian," were directed by the state senate of Georgia to have their blood segregated, running the risk of alienating Japanese, Koreans, Chinese, and Asians generally.[64]

* * *

By 1952, the ANP reported that Japanese expected to face bigotry at the hands of occupation forces yet were still staggered by what was termed the "two Army structure—one white, one black."[65] That same year the leading African American intellectual Hugh Smythe was to be found teaching in Japan. He was struck by the paradox of the U.S. occupation, which created conditions facilitating the rise of Japanese nationalists and extreme right-wing groups who had helped to instigate and aided the prosecution of the last war, while—consistent with the ongoing Red Scare and Cold War—Washington's policy tended to smother the Socialists and Communists who were the opponents of these chauvinists. He was keen to report to the NAACP readership that he espied a "Little Black Sambo" image in Japan uncomfortably close to a picture of Ralph Bunche, then a rising official within the United Nations but previously a professor at Howard University. Smythe and his spouse, Mabel Murphy Smythe, also a Negro intellectual of some note, found this placement not to be coincidental. After all, as war in Korea raged, the Asian antagonists of Washington were routinely referred to as "gooks," a replay of Pacific War verbiage, and perceived as the functional equivalent of "nigger."

Unsurprisingly Japan had not been purged altogether of its sour view of U.S. relations. When a prominent Harlem pastor toured Japan, he was asked by students whether there were still Negro slaves in the republic. Japan, the Smythes concluded, was "historically racially conscious" and islanders wondered why there was "no colored delegate who occupied a commanding or key position" at the San Francisco Peace Conference. "In this colored nation once a world power," they added gravely, "the international significance of racialism is recognized."[66]

The labor movement in Japan was more robust—and more influenced by Communists—than its U.S. counterpart, which became evident when the Negro labor leader A. Philip Randolph arrived in Tokyo in 1952, accompanied by the Socialist leader Norman Thomas. The two barely escaped intact when seeking to address 300,000 in Meiji Park. They were not stoned, as reported, but did escape hurriedly with the expert aid of the U.S. military and Japanese police. The riot, considered the worst in the nation's postwar history, was ascribed to Communists who did not appreciate the two leaders' strident anticommunism. U.S. property was destroyed in the melee and 1,100 were injured.[67]

Two years later seven labor leaders from this Asian nation were received in more genteel fashion when they made a lengthy tour of the United States. They took a keen interest in the problems of Negroes, and raised questions that had not occurred to some in the United States itself—for example, what was to befall Negro teachers if desegregation were to take hold?[68]

U.S.-Japan relations remained complicated, in other words. The fraught occupation was even more complicated, Hugh Smythe noted, since a "considerable percentage of Occupation troops among the non-Negroes are individuals from the South and they have brought with them southern mores and racial patterns." Their presence may have facilitated the wonderment they found among Japanese as to why atomic weapons were dropped on their nation and not in the European theater.[69]

Unsurprisingly given such attitudes, by 1953 reports of Black and white soldiers rioting at Yamanaka, southwest of Tokyo, seemed to be old news; the most newsworthy item was that it took place on the Fourth of July.[70] These confrontations apparently did not leave locals unaffected. Subsequently, Congressman Adam Clayton Powell of Harlem denounced what was termed "Japanese bias to Negroes [by] a Japanese bar in Tokyo."[71]

But even Powell's démarche does not capture wholly the point that the effect of decades of racial proselytizing could not disappear instantaneously. In the spring of 1954, as the U.S. Supreme Court was about to rule in *Brown v. Board of Education* that Jim Crow was no longer legal, the fabled Negro chanteuse Josephine Baker addressed an assemblage in Japan with a speech entitled "Why I Fight Racism." Approximately a century after Commodore Perry opened Japan to foreign influence, she instructed those assembled pointedly that "it is important that one knows what to adopt" from abroad, "and what to leave aside," for example, anti-Black racism. "For all my life," she rhapsodized, "I have dreamt about your country," and her imaginings were fulfilled. She recalled how in 1952 she was beseeched by Japanese Americans in San Francisco to lobby the mayor to return "their tea-garden" that was "confiscated during the war"—a request she granted promptly. She recalled a meeting in Los Angeles during that same period with a "coloured man" married to a Japanese American woman and how they and their children were compelled to abandon their home and reside in a camp because of the presumed wartime sin of possessing "Japanese blood." Her mandate, as she saw it, was to ensure that in the future such racism would no longer obtain.[72]

Baker's presence in Japan was emblematic of the fact that artistic endeavor continued to unite Japanese and African Americans. In 1953 the leading Negro musicians Louis Armstrong and Oscar Petersen toured Japan and there discovered Toshiko Akiyoshi, a twenty-six-year-old piano wizard. She played in the same style—in a homage that echoed the pre-1945 era—as the legendary Negro pianist Bud Powell and went on to establish a protean career in the United States.[73] The artistic favor was reciprocated that same year when Japan began buzzing about the acting and singing ability of the tenor Danny Williams, co-star of the Japanese movie *Yassa Mossa*. This talented thirty-year-old Negro sailor formerly had warbled at the famed St. Louis nightspot the Riviera Lounge.[74]

The fruits of Afro-Asian solidarity, especially in the arts, were not perceived by all, and herein rests an essential contradiction. As the jazz critic Leonard Feather noted, the Japanese American intellectual S. I. Hayakawa was a jazz aficionado. "Visiting Japan in 1935," Hayakawa acknowledged, "I heard American jazz being played constantly on the bathing-beaches between Osaka and Kobe."[75] But decades later, Hayakawa was catapulted into prominence when he vigorously attacked African American students at San Francisco State University, which he then headed, when they fought strenuously for the establishment of a Black studies program.[76] His enhanced notoriety helped him win election as a U.S. senator. By November 1976, the arch segregationist senator James Eastland of Mississippi extended "warm congratulations" to his new colleague,[77] who soon toured war-torn Rhodesia and declared this notorious white supremacist land to be an "open and free society."[78] Unsurprisingly, Hayakawa created an uproar when he declared that it was "perfectly understandable" that Japanese Americans were interned during the war.[79]

* * *

Trans-Pacific kinship, which had been a fixture for decades, had frayed to an extent, but had not disappeared altogether. In 1957, for example, Makaru Sakamoto, an official from Kobe, came to the United States to study Negro life in Chicago.[80] The next year, Harry Levette spoke of "the great Japanese middleweight boxer," the "Tokyo-born 'Young Togo,'" who taught him "the self defense tricks" that had served him well.[81]

These maneuvers may have come in handy when Black and white troops in Japan were engaged in what seemed to be a favorite pastime: brawling. Negro soldiers had been protesting racial discrimination on military bases, but matters deteriorated rapidly.[82] This was not an unusual occurrence, as there had been a turnabout of Japan's prewar policy of displaying preferential treatment to Negroes; apparently, some in Japan were led to believe that accommodating the U.S. occupation also meant bowing to Jim Crow. A refusal to bend the knee to Jim Crow was an apt characterization of the six Negro marines who beat to death a white counterpart and injured another as Congressman Powell was carping.[83]

Though the Japanese and Ethiopian royal families did not merge through marriage, U.S. Negroes sought to compensate. As early as 1952 it was reported that "hundreds of Negro GIs are defying military red tape to marry Japanese [women]."[84] Silas Mosley was among them. This Negro marine taught English in Japan, then married a Japanese woman.[85] He was part of a larger trend suggesting bonds of peculiar intimacy that did not perish in the flames of Hiroshima-Nagasaki. In 1963 a reported three hundred Negro soldiers married Korean women, a figure comparable to that in neighboring Japan.[86] These close bonds were also underscored when a few years earlier, a Negro couple driving in Japan—he was a soldier—spotted an abandoned child roadside and chose to adopt her.[87]

Unfortunately, interactions between Japan and the occupying power were not always so uplifting. Writing from the archipelago in early 1946, Robert Bennett, a U.S. military man from Georgia, reported excitedly that "you can buy a wife for about $65." "She's every bit a wife," he continued exultantly, "yet no divorce is necessary, when a soldier gets ready to leave," he simply departs.[88]

Nevertheless, the incident involving an adoptee may have been further reflection of a still poignant Negro-Japanese alliance. The Black-led anti–Jim Crow movement was both a beneficiary and engineer of the re-worked race relations that this alliance had helped to foment—and this movement would knock down barriers for Asians too, leading by 1965 to a restructuring of the exclusivist U.S. immigration laws that had so infu-riated Tokyo in the 1920s.[89] The Asian American population increased dramatically, opening up opportunities for countless individuals and, in a sense, affirming the mutually beneficial relations that had developed decades earlier between U.S. Negroes and Tokyo.

* * *

After the war, the territory whose bombardment had driven the conflict—Hawaii—was entangled in a battle for statehood, which raised some of the racial issues brought by Pearl Harbor. The colony had a plurality of Japanese Americans, who were thought to be opposed to Jim Crow. This meant that Dixie was hostile to the movement for Hawaiian statehood, which emerged in 1959 precisely when the anti–Jim Crow movement had begun to percolate.[90]

A good deal of this focus on Japan and Hawaii was driven by Frank Marshall Davis, who was formerly employed by Claude Barnett in Chi-cago but moved to Honolulu in 1948. There he sought to continue the prewar bond between Negroes and Japanese—Okinawans in Honolulu, in this case—whom he analogized to African Americans. "Close your eyes," he wrote in 1949, "listen to the thoughts expressed in serious dis-cussion by Okinawa Japanese and you can imagine you're in Harlem." They "occupy the same inferior status as the Negro in America" and "several told me privately they felt a strong bond of kinship with me as a Negro."[91]

This mutuality between Negroes and Asians, which was much more pronounced in the fiftieth state than on the mainland, continued even as ordinary Japanese were protesting in great numbers the arrival of President Eisenhower in Japan and the despised bilateral security treaty he epitomized. The esteemed Negro attorney Raymond Pace Alexander found the Japanese people to be "so gracious that it is almost unbeliev-able that the recent demonstrations against the United States . . . could have occurred."[92]

Alexander may have misjudged the depth of true concord between a predominantly "white" United States and Japan. Recently the *Wall Street*

Journal columnist Peggy Noonan wrote about asking a prominent poll-ster whether he ever found "things in polls that he wasn't looking for and that surprised him." His answer was "yes. . . . The American people don't like the Japanese."[93] Perhaps if she had written "Euro-American" instead, this comment would have been more precise. Remarkably, this opinion persists despite the fact that Japan is today seen as an anchor of U.S. strategy in Asia designed to contain China, ruled by a Communist Party, an entity that was thought to be Public Enemy Number 1.[94]

Hugh and Mabel Smythe, the Negro couple residing in postwar Japan and teaching respectively at Yamaguchi National University and Shiga University, were convinced that the road ahead would not be smooth for the Pacific rivals only recently at war. Hugh Smythe thought that the "type of racialism common in the United States is unknown in Japan,"[95] and as a consequence, Japan had "never forgotten the racial slights she suffered" at the hands of the United States over the decades. "This feeling necessarily had to be repressed during military occupation," the couple wrote. "Doubtless it will figure in her future plans once she has again become a strong and independent nation." After all, as they cautioned during the early stage of the postwar occupation, "time is on her side and the Japanese have had 2600 years of learning how to be patient."[96]

NOTES

INTRODUCTION

1 Malcolm X, *The Autobiography of Malcolm X* (New York: Grove, 1965), 106, 108. For one of the most recent explorations of the tie between Islam and Black America, see, e.g., Sally Howell, *Old Islam in Detroit: Rediscovering the Muslim American Past* (New York: Oxford University Press, 2014). Readers should note that I often cite sources of that era that use racist epithets, including "Jap."

2 George Q. Flynn, "Selective Service and American Blacks during World War II," *Journal of Negro History* 69 (Winter 1984): 14–25; Robin D. G. Kelly, *Theolonius Monk: The Life and Times of an American Original* (New York: Free Press, 2009), 82.

3 Walter White to Walter Karig, 14 August 1941, Box II, A432, NAACP Papers, Library of Congress, Washington, D.C.

4 Fumiko Sakashita, "Lynching across the Pacific: Japanese Views and African American Responses in the Wartime Antilynching Campaign," in *Swift to Wrath: Lynching in Global Historical Perspective*, ed. William D. Carrigan and Christopher Waldrep (Charlottesville: University of Virginia Press, 2013), 192–93.

5 Ibid.; Gerald Horne, "Tokyo Bound: African Americans and Japan Confront White Supremacy," *Souls: A Critical Journal of Black Politics, Culture and Society* 3, no. 3 (Summer 2001): 22.

6 Walter Karig to Walter White, 2 September 1941, Box II, A432, NAACP Papers.

7 Dempsey Travis, *An Autobiography of Black Chicago* (Chicago: Urban Research Institute, 1981), 93, 94. See also Roi Ottley, *New World A-Coming* (New York: Arno, 1968), 342. A "reporter . . . told Mrs. [Eleanor] Roosevelt . . . that he had attended Negro meetings 'where Japanese victories were slyly praised and American defeats at Bataan and Corregidor brought amused and knowing smiles.'"

8 Gerald Horne, *Race War! White Supremacy and the Japanese Attack on the British Empire* (New York: New York University Press, 2005), 105.

9 "Japanese Racial Agitation among American Negroes," n.d., 145.81.84–91, 1942–Apr. 1943, Air Force Historical Research Agency, Maxwell Air Force Base, Montgomery, AL.

10 Randy Weston, *African Rhythms: The Autobiography of Randy Weston* (Durham: Duke University Press, 2010), 15, 34.

11 Release, Associated Negro Press (ANP), April 1942, Reel 24, #69, Part I, Series A, Claude A. Barnett Papers/Associated Negro Press, North Carolina State University, Raleigh (hereafter Barnett Papers). Subsequent citations of ANP press

releases are all from the Barnett Papers. Materials from this microfilm collection can also be found at the Chicago History Museum, along with the original hard copies.

12 Release, ANP, December 1942, Reel 25, #122, Part I, Series A.

13 Ibid.

14 See the many letters to this effect in Box 300, William Colmer Papers, University of Southern Mississippi, Hattiesburg. See also Joe Grant Masaoka to Carey McWilliams, 20 October 1943, Box 7, Carey McWilliams Collection of War Relocation Authority Materials, Claremont Colleges Library, Claremont, CA (hereafter McWilliams Collection): "In the Selective Service registrations, separate files are allegedly kept of Negroes and Whites. A Negro selectee has started a lawsuit because he was called out of turn. By reason of these distinct files he was inducted earlier than he would have been. . . . Negro officers are conspicuous by their scarcity, . . . [also] certain bias to the Jew."

15 Horne, "Tokyo Bound." See also Gerald Horne, "The Revenge of the Black Pacific?," *Callaloo: A Journal of African Diaspora Arts and Letters* 24, no. 1 (2001): 94–96. The literature on Afro-Asian solidarity includes, e.g., Reginald Kearney, *African American Views of the Japanese: Solidarity or Sedition?* (Albany: State University of New York Press, 1998); Fred Ho and Bill Mullen, eds., *Afro Asia: Revolutionary Political and Cultural Connections between African Americans and Asian Americans* (Durham: Duke University Press, 2006); Ernest Allen Jr., "When Japan Was Champion of the 'Darker Races': Satokata Takahashi and the Flowering of Black Messianic Nationalism," *Black Scholar* 24 (1994): 23–46; Ernest Allen Jr., "'Waiting for Tojo': The Pro-Japan Vigil of Black Missourians, 1932–1943," *Gateway Heritage*, 1995, 38–55; Helen Heran Jun, *Race for Citizenship: Black Orientalism and Asian Uplift from Pre-Emancipation to Neoliberal America* (New York: New York University Press, 2011); Marc Gallichio, *The African American Encounter with Japan and China: Black Internationalism in Asia, 1895–1945* (Chapel Hill: University of North Carolina Press, 2000); Shana Redmond, "Extending Diaspora: The NAACP and Up-'Lift' Cultures in the Interwar Black Pacific," in *Traveling Texts and the Work of Afro-Japanese Cultural Production*, ed. William H. Bridges IV and Nina Cornyetz (Lanham, MD: Lexington, 2015). See also Greg Robinson, *After Camp: Portraits in Midcentury Japanese American Life and Politics* (Berkeley: University of California Press, 2012). This book offers an insightful analysis of relations between Japan, Japanese Americans, and African Americans before, during, and after the war. The roots of Afro-Asian solidarity extend deep into the history of the advent of European colonialism. See, e.g., Note in *The Indonesia Reader: History, Culture and Politics*, ed. Tineke Hellwig et al. (Durham: Duke University Press, 2009), 158: in the mid-eighteenth century the planting of cloves in Mauritius was facilitated when seedlings were smuggled from what is now Indonesia. See also Gerald Horne, *The End of Empires: African Americans and India* (Philadelphia: Temple University Press, 2009). On the other hand, as early as the 1890s certain Euro-Americans worried about an adverse Japanese reaction to lynching of African Americans in

Dixie, which aided in the retreat of this macabre phenomenon. See, e.g., Sarah L. Silkey, *Black Woman Reformer: Ida B. Wells, Lynching, and Trans-Atlantic Activism* (Athens: University of Georgia Press, 2015), 125.

16 W. E. B. Du Bois, "The Color Line Belts the World," in *Writings by W. E. B. Du Bois in Periodicals Edited by Others*, ed. Herbert Aptheker (Millwood, NY: Kraus-Thomason, 1982), 330 (from *Collier's Weekly*, 20 December 1906).

17 Arnold Shankman, "'Asiatic Ogre' or 'Desirable Citizen'? The Image of Japanese Americans in the Afro-American Press, 1867–1933," *Pacific Historical Review* 46 (1977): 567–87, 587.

18 Booker T. Washington to Naoichi Masaoka, 5 December 1912, in *Booker T. Washington Papers*, vol. 12, *1912–1914*, ed. Louis Harlan and Raymond W. Smock (Urbana: University of Illinois Press, 1983), 84. Alert African Americans may have noticed that it was in the early twentieth century that a Japanese entrepreneur developed cultured pearls, which served to undermine the deployment of enslaved Africans as deep-sea divers who retrieved pearls from oysters in the Arabian Gulf. See Matthew S. Hopper, *Slaves of One Master: Globalization and Slavery in Arabia in the Age of Empire* (New Haven: Yale University Press, 2015), 10; and Robert Eunson, *The Pearl King: The Story of the Fabulous Mikimoto* (Tokyo: Tuttle, 1964).

19 Charles Lumpkins, *American Pogrom: The East St. Louis Race Riot and Black Politics* (Athens: Ohio University Press, 2008).

20 Adam Fairclough, *Better Day Coming: Blacks and Equality, 1890–2000* (New York: Viking, 2000), 94.

21 Elliott M. Rudwick, *Race Riot at East St. Louis: July 2, 1917* (Carbondale: Southern Illinois University Press, 1964), 261, 121. Perhaps coincidentally, an iconic photograph of racist violence targeting African Americans in Chicago in 1919 during one of the bloodiest massacres of that conflicted era was snapped by Jun Fujita, born in Hiroshima, who migrated to the United States in 1915 and then worked for the *Chicago Evening Post* as a photographer. See David F. Krugler, *1919, The Year of Racial Violence: How African Americans Fought Back* (New York: Cambridge University Press, 2015), 111.

22 Release, ANP, n.d., Reel 8, #593, Part III, Subject Files on Black Americans, Series I: Race Relations, Barnett Papers.

23 Horne, *Race War!*, vii. For a fuller exploration of these issues, the volume in hand should be read in conjunction with this earlier book. See also Buck Clayton, *Buck Clayton's Jazz World* (New York: Oxford University Press, 1986), 66–67. Ernest Clarke, another Negro musician, spent eight years in China, Japan, India, and the nation then known as Malaya. He was interned by Japanese forces in Hong Kong, where he claimed that he was not maltreated, a claim many Europeans and Euro-American prisoners there would find difficult to make. See clipping, uncertain provenance, n.d., circa 1943, Box 8, McWilliams Collection.

24 Memorandum from Portland Field Division, circa 1942, in *The FBI's RACON: Racial Conditions in the United States during World War II*, ed. Robert A. Hill (Boston: Northeastern University Press, 1995), 382.

25 Article by Lucius Harper, n.d., Reel 12, #36, Part II, Organizational Files, Barnett Papers.

26 William "Billy" Mitchell, "The Pacific Problem: Strategical [*sic*] Aspects," 1924, Box 46, William Mitchell Papers, Library of Congress.

27 John Dower, *Japan in War and Peace: Essays on History, Culture and Race* (London: Fontanta, 1996), 258–59.

28 Release, ANP, May 1942, Reel 24, #93, Part I, Releases, Barnett Papers. For more on the Associated Negro Press, whose archive may be the richest in the entire field of African American studies, see, e.g., Lawrence D. Hogan, *A Black National News Service: The Associated Negro Press and Claude Barnett, 1919–1945* (Rutherford: Fairleigh Dickinson University Press, 1984); and Gerald Horne, *The Rise and Fall of the Associated Negro Press: Claude Barnett's Pan-African News and the Jim Crow Paradox* (Urbana: University of Illinois Press, 2017). The ANP was a consortium incorporating scores of writers and analysts in virtually every nook and cranny of Black America and numerous sites abroad. It also employed at various times such luminaries as Richard Wright and Zora Neale Hurston.

29 A. J. Maphike, letter to the editor, *Guardian* (Cape Town), 25 July 1940, 4.

30 "True Democracy the Only Safeguard: Pro-Jap Sympathy Danger," *Guardian* (Cape Town), 12 March 1942, 5.

31 Ahmed Kathrada, *Memoirs* (Cape Town: New Holland, 2004), 35.

32 I. O. Horvitch, letter to the editor, *Guardian* (Cape Town), 26 March 1942, 6.

33 See the pamphlet by Moses Kotane, General Secretary of the Communist Party of South Africa, "Japan—Friend or Foe?," April 1942, Box 1, Communist Party of South Africa Collection, Hoover Institution, Stanford University: "So many non-Europeans (leaders and ordinary people) seriously believe that if the Japanese were to come here, the worst that they (the Japanese) could do to us Africans, Coloured and Indians, would be to treat us as England treats the Afrikaners and other white races in her Dominions and Colonies." The African American intellectual and future Nobel laureate Ralph Bunche found striking parallels with his homeland during a visit in 1937 to South Africa. See Robert Edgar, ed., *An African American in South Africa: The Travel Notes of Ralph J. Bunche, 28 September 1937–1 January 1938* (Athens: Ohio University Press, 1992), 89–90. Just as U.S. Negroes who were pro-Tokyo tended to be dismissive of the suffering of China under Tokyo's lash, on 24 October of that fateful year Bunche encountered in South Africa "a young Garveyite (formerly an African National Congress member) preaching race chauvinism to another small group. All of the Garveyite speeches I've heard there, including this one, were praising Japan's rape of China on color chauvinism grounds." Unfortunately, contributing to this often hostile attitude toward China was what the African American officer James B. McMillan discovered while stationed in Calcutta during the war: He was informed curtly that "Madame Chiang Kai-shek didn't want any blacks in China," speaking of U.S. Negro soldiers. See R. T. King and Gary E. Elliott, eds., *Fighting Back: A Life in*

the Struggle for Civil Rights: From Oral History Interviews with James B. McMillan (Reno: University of Nevada Oral History Program, 1997), 60.

34 Luli Callinicos, *Oliver Tambo: Beyond the Engeli Mountains* (Cape Town: David Philip, 2005), 113.

35 A. Lerumo, *Fifty Fighting Years: The Communist Party of South Africa, 1921–1971* (London: Inkululeko, 1987), 121. After the fall of Singapore, Washington contemplated utilizing Durban as a base from which to attack Japan since it was "the only port in the Indian Ocean which has facilities for supplying a large fleet," making the South African metropolis a "distant base for Pacific operations." The restiveness of the African majority complicated this plan. See Lincoln MacVeigh, Consul General, Pretoria, to Secretary of State, 2 November 1943, RG 59, Decimal File, 1940–1944, From: 848A.00 P.R./118 To: 848A.22/10–1944, Box 5122, General Records of the State Department, National Archives and Records Administration, College Park, MD.

36 U.S. v. Pacific Movement of the Eastern World, 27 January 1943, U.S. District Court, Eastern District of Illinois, Record Group 21, Criminal Case File, Case No. 15840, Box 1, Folder 1, National Archives and Records Administration, Chicago (hereafter PMEW File).

37 U.S. v. PMEW, grand jury transcript, 22 September 1942, Box 3, PMEW file.

38 Release, ANP, August 1936, Reel 13, #634, Part I, Series A.

39 Release, ANP, October 1942, Reel 24, #1008, Part I, Series A.

40 Release, ANP, July 1943, Reel 26, #239, Part I, Series A.

41 Release, ANP, July 1943, Reel 26, #301, Part I, Series A.

42 "Defendant Heard at Trial of 2 on Sedition Charges," *St. Louis Post-Dispatch*, 14 May 1943, 3A.

43 John W. Dower, *War without Mercy: Race and Power in the Pacific War* (New York: Pantheon, 1986), 173–74. See also Kearney, *African American Views of the Japanese*; and Gallichio, *The African American Encounter with Japan and China*.

44 Lt. Commander K. D. Ringle, U.S. Navy, to Chief of Naval Operations, 26 January 1942, Branch Intelligence Office, Eleventh Naval District, Los Angeles, Box 125, Herbert Hill Papers, Library of Congress. See also Ross Coen, *Fu-Go: The Curious History of Japan's Balloon Bomb Attack on America* (Lincoln: University of Nebraska Press, 2014).

45 Release, ANP, February 1944, Reel 26, #848, Part I, Series A.

46 Neil R. McMillen, *Dark Journey: Black Mississippians in the Age of Jim Crow* (Urbana: University of Illinois Press, 1989); Neil R. McMillen, ed., *Remaking Dixie: The Impact of World War II on the American South* (Jackson: University Press of Mississippi, 1997). See also Guy Lancaster, *Racial Cleansing in Arkansas, 1883–1924: Politics, Land, Labor and Criminality* (Lanham, MD: Lexington, 2014).

47 See, e.g., Akinyele Umoja, *We Will Shoot Back: Armed Resistance in the Mississippi Freedom Movement* (New York: New York University Press, 2013); and Krugler, *1919, The Year of Racial Violence*.

48 Manny Lawson, "Some Survived," manuscript, Box 2, Manny Lawson Papers, Clemson University, Clemson, SC.

49 See "Constitution of the Peace Movement of Ethiopia," 1941, University of Virginia, Charlottesville. This paradigmatic organization exemplified many of the principles of its peers:

> We freely coincide with Nationalistic principles laid down by the Hon. Marcus Garvey. We do not oppose any Nationalist Movement that stands for the betterment of its people. We believe in the GOD of our forefathers, the history, language & ISLAM Religion. . . . Mrs. M. M. L. Gordon, founder, . . . was designated to be Executive President permanently by an election held on February 24, 1933. . . . The Peace Movement of Ethiopia was founded December 7, 1932. . . . On the 15th day of November 1933 our signatories had grown to 400,000 . . . to move Congress to action to repatriate all of those who sign our petition to Liberia. . . . When our President was called to Washington by Senator [Theodore] Bilbo to arrange for the presentation of the bill [for repatriation] she carried with her 1,952,000 signatures. . . . On May 24th, 1933 representatives from Angola, Africa appeared in Senator Bilbo's office and filed a membership of 250,000 that live in Africa to lobby for our coming.

> The PME saw repatriation as a way for the United States to combat the Great Depression, in that "the removal of a half million of the poorest from a competitive labor market . . . would tend to relieve to that extent the condition and opportunities of the remainder." See also Earnest Sevier Cox, *Lincoln's Negro Policy* (Richmond: Byrd, 1938). This noted white supremacist termed this petition "the most extraordinary Negro racial document in the history of the nation." As for "M. M. L. Gordon," she was an "indomitable spirit."

50 Sheldon Avery, *Up from Washington: William Pickens and the Negro Struggle for Equality, 1900–1954* (Newark: University of Delaware Press, 1989).

51 William Pickens to "My Dear Prattis," 24 April 1934, Reel 6, #735, Part III, Subject Files on Black Americans, Series I: Race Relations, Barnett Papers.

52 Release, ANP, March 1939, Reel 18, Part I, Press Releases.

53 William Pickens, column, June 1940, Reel 20, #1136, Part I, Press Releases, Barnett Papers.

54 See, e.g., Yukiko Koshiro, *Trans-Pacific Racisms and the U.S. Occupation of Japan* (New York: Columbia University Press, 1999); and Yuichiro Onishi, *Transpacific Antiracism: Afro-Asian Solidarity in 20th-Century Black America, Japan, and Okinawa* (New York: New York University Press, 2013). There is a substantial literature on the persecution of those of European descent by Japanese forces, a reality that unavoidably influenced African Americans who had come to resent all those defined as "white." See, e.g., Yuki Tanaka, *Hidden Horrors: Japanese War Crimes in World War II* (Boulder: Westview, 1996), xv. In his foreword to the Tanaka volume, the scholar John Dower writes of "Japanese brutality against 'white' prisoners," which illuminates "the racial hatreds of World War II in Asia

in their starkest form." Allan Ryan, *Yamashita's Ghost: War Crimes, MacArthur's Justice, and Command Accountability* (Lawrence: University Press of Kansas, 2012); Darlene Deibler Rose, *Evidence Not Seen: A Woman's Miraculous Faith in a Japanese Prison Camp during WWII* (San Francisco: Harper and Row, 1988); John A. Glusman, *Conduct under Fire: Four American Doctors and Their Fight for Life as Prisoners of the Japanese, 1941–1945* (New York: Viking, 2005); Agnes Newton Keith, *Three Came Home* (New York: Time-Life Books, 1965); Margaret Sams, *Forbidden Family: A Wartime Memoir of the Philippines, 1941–1945* (Madison: University of Wisconsin Press, 1989).

55 Vijay Prashad, *Everybody Was Kung Fu Fighting: Afro-Asian Connections and the Myth of Cultural Purity* (Boston: Beacon, 2001).

56 See, e.g., Gerald Horne, *The Counter-Revolution of 1776: Slave Resistance and the Origins of the United States of America* (New York: New York University Press, 2014); and Gerald Horne, *Black Revolutionary: William Patterson and the Globalization of the African American Freedom Struggle* (Urbana: University of Illinois Press, 2013).

57 Horne, *The End of Empires*.

58 Robert G. Parkinson, *The Common Cause: Creating Race and Nation in the American Revolution* (Chapel Hill: University of North Carolina Press, 2016), 325.

59 John Cheng, *Astounding Wonder: Imagining Science and Science Fiction in Interwar America* (Philadelphia: University of Pennsylvania Press, 2012), 138.

60 Christopher Frayling, *The Yellow Peril: Dr. Fu Manchu and the Rise of Chinaphobia* (New York: Thames and Hudson, 2014), 32, 265, 266. See also Cay Van Ash, *Master of Villainy: A Biography of Sax Rohmer* (Bowling Green: Bowling Green University Popular Press, 1972), 253. There was also a Negro angle in that one of the most popular of the Fu Manchu series was grounded in the author's trips to Haiti.

61 Mittie Maude Lena Gordon to U.S. Senate, 27 July 1942, Box 1091, Theodore Bilbo Papers, University of Southern Mississippi, Hattiesburg (hereafter Bilbo Papers). The "movement" to resettle U.S. Negroes in Africa, she claimed, embraced "upward of 4 million people."

62 Gerald Horne, *Black Liberation/Red Scare: Ben Davis and the Communist Party* (Newark: University of Delaware Press, 1994); Gerald Horne, *Red Seas: Ferdinand Smith and Radical Black Sailors in the United States and Jamaica* (New York: New York University Press, 2009); Horne, *Black Revolutionary*.

63 J. Edgar Hoover to Special Agent, 8 December 1942, Roll 2, FBI File on Moorish Science Temple of America (Noble Drew Ali), Duke University.

64 "Confidential" Report, 28 May 1943, Roll 2, FBI File on Moorish Science Temple.

65 "Domestic Intelligence Memorandum No. 5," 9 March 1944, Roll 2, FBI File on Moorish Science Temple.

66 Joseph Hanlon, "Fifth Column Propaganda among Negroes in St. Louis Area Traced to Japanese . . . Subversive Teaching . . . Alarm," *St. Louis Post-Dispatch*, 5 March 1942, 7A.

67 Arthur Smith and Norma Abrams, "D.C. Filipino Held as Head of Jap Ring," *Washington Times-Herald*, 1 August 1942, 1.

68 Release, ANP, November 1942, Reel 24, #1117, Part I, Series A, Barnett Papers.

69 U.S. v. PMEW, opinion by Judge Fred Wham, 15 June 1943, Box 1, Folder 2, PMEW File.

70 Release, ANP, October 1943, Reel 26, #1168, Part I, Series A.

71 Reports, 28 November 1933, circa 1930s and 1940s, 1460–1–3, Ministry of Foreign Affairs, Tokyo.

72 Robert Jordan to Hachiro Arita, 18 November 1936, A461, ET/11, Ministry of Foreign Affairs, Tokyo. This letter can also be found at the Japan Center for Asian Historical Records, National Archives of Japan, Tokyo, #B0203121600. At the same site, see also Robert Jordan to Foreign Ministry, 12 May 1936, #B02031221000; and "Nationalist Negro Movement," 9 August 1935, #B02031218800.

73 Memorandum on Ethiopia Pacific Movement, circa 1943, in Hill, *The FBI's RA-CON*, 530–35, 532, 533.

74 "Confidential" Report, 13 August 1943, State Council of Defense, SG19872, GS-7–29, 28, 53, Alabama Department of Archives and History, Montgomery.

75 Wesley Phillips Newton, *Montgomery in the Good War: Portrait of a Southern City, 1939–1946* (Tuscaloosa: University of Alabama Press, 2000), 136.

76 Langston Hughes, "Here to Yonder," *Chicago Defender*, 16 October 1943, 14.

77 Richard Wright recalled that during his childhood in Dixie his grandmother at times would make the family kneel and say a prayer for the Africans, the Chinese—and the Japanese. Hazel Rowley, *Richard Wright: The Life and Times* (New York: Holt, 2001), 17.

78 Langston Hughes, "Simple and the Atomic Bomb," *Chicago Defender*, 18 August 1945, 12. An observer in Cape Town, doubtlessly well aware of the danger of racism that Hiroshima portended, argued with emphasis that unless this new weapon of war was controlled, "THIS MEANS THE END OF OUR SPECIES." "Atomic Bomb 'Dynamite to Chimpanzees,'" *Guardian* (Cape Town), 9 August 1945, 1. A South Africa–born writer of Ethiopian descent recalled at the time that in the desolate aftermath of the bombing, "a number of people, writers and artists, one or two of whom I knew, were so overwhelmed by the horror that they committed suicide." See Peter Abrahams, *The Black Experience in the 20th Century: An Autobiography and Meditation* (Bloomington: Indiana University Press, 2000), 49–50.

79 Sakashita, "Lynching across the Pacific," 181–214, 188.

80 Release, ANP, April 1942, Reel 23, #1216, Part I, Series A, Barnett Papers.

81 Release, ANP, December 1944, Reel 3, #461, Part III, Subject Files on Black Americans, Series F: Military, Barnett Papers.

82 Robey Paeks, "Rare Human Sacrifices of Jap Directed Spy Ring," *Chicago Herald American*, 23 September 1942, 7.

83 Tony Matthews, *Shadow Dancing: Japanese Espionage Agents against the West, 1939–1945* (London: Robert Hale, 1993), 27. J. Parnell Thomas of the notorious

House Un-American Activities Committee claimed during the war that Tokyo actually had "a division of the Japanese army" on U.S. soil prior to the war in the form of a "Japanese American Veterans Association." See "Supplementary Comments by the War Relocation Authority on Newspaper Statements Allegedly Made by Representatives of the House Committee on Un-American Activities," n.d., Box 1, McWilliams Collection. The following items cited are also in the McWilliams Collection. "Weekly Press Review, Week Ending June 1943," Box 3: HUAC claims that "10,000 Japanese Americans have received training in an espionage school operated by the Imperialistic Black Dragon Society of Japan." "Weekly Press Review, Week Ending July 4, 1943," Box 3: HUAC charges that "7000 Japanese in Hawaii belong to secret military society, Butoku-Kai." John R. Lechner, "Playing with Dynamite: The Inside Story of Our Domestic Japanese American Problem," n.d., prepared during wartime by American Legion, Box 4: "In 1936 one of Japan's shrewdest organizers was directed to Hawaii to prepare the overseas structure for the war against the United States. . . . His task was to orga-nize and consolidate Japanese subversive groups within America, so that Japan might have the assistance of powerful Trojan Horses." T. S. Van Vleet, "Once a Jap, Always a Jap," sponsored by California Veterans of Foreign Wars, circa 1944, Box 6: "There are about one hundred Butoko-Kai [*sic*] societies in the United States and Hawaii, including the fifty located in California." "Report and Minority Views of the Special Committee on Un-American Activities on Japanese War Relocation Centers," 78th Congress, 1st Session, U.S. House of Representatives, Report No. 717, circa 1943, Box 6: Listed here are scores of branches of the Butoku-Kai, mostly on the West Coast and in Hawaii. Clipping, uncertain provenance, n.d., circa 1943, Box 8: Book purportedly found in school in Japanese American neighborhood in Los Angeles, published in 1938, urging youth there to become "guerillas" at onset of war targeting "American military and naval installations" in the region. "Jap Farmer 'Militia' Here before War, Inquiry Told," *Los Angeles Times*, 21 October 1943, 1, Box 8: "Thousands of Japanese farmers in the Southland were members of a thoroughly organized 'partisan militia.'" (Of course, when reading these stories one must bear in mind the mass hysteria in the wartime United States, generated by the real fear that white supremacy had backfired spectacularly.)

84 Leon Taylor, "Japanese Propaganda among American Negroes," *Kansas City Plain Dealer*, 18 June 1943, 7.

85 "Negro Woman's Tip Leads to Roundup by G-Men," *Kansas City Plain Dealer*, 19 June 1942, 1.

86 Horace Boyer, ed., *Lift Every Voice and Sing: An African American Hymnal* (New York: Church Hymnal Corporation, 1993); James Weldon Johnson, *Along This Way: The Autobiography of James Weldon Johnson* (New York: Da Capo, 2000). There was a concerted effort to translate the "Negro National Anthem" into Japanese: see, e.g., Shana L. Redmond, *Anthem: Social Movements and the Sound of Solidarity in the African Diaspora* (New York: New York University Press, 2014), 81–98.

87 Quoted in Etsuko Taketani, *The Black Pacific Narrative: Geographic Imaginings of Race and Empire between the World Wars* (Hanover: Dartmouth College Press, 2014), 36.

88 Asa T. Spaulding, "Facing the Rising Sun: A Report to Policyholders," n.d., Reel 6, Series C, Economic Conditions, Part III, Subject Files on Black Americans, Barnett Papers.

89 Frederick P. Close, *Tokyo Rose/An American Patriot: A Dual Biography* (Lanham, MD: Rowman and Littlefield, 2014), 28.

90 See also Report by Theodore Smith of Headquarters, Western Defense Command, 29 June 1943, Box 125, Herbert Hill Papers: "I certify that this date I witnessed the destruction by burning of the galley proofs, galley pages, drafts and memorandums of the original report of the Japanese evacuation." See also "Evacuation of the Japanese from the West Coast, Final Report and Paper of the Adjutant General's Office," circa 1945, Reels 3 and 4, Louis Nichols Official and Confidential Files and Clyde Tolson Personal File, FBI Confidential Files, Library of Congress.

91 Gerald Horne, *Black and Red: W. E. B. Du Bois and the Afro-American Response to the Cold War, 1944–1963* (Albany: State University of New York Press, 1986); Mary L. Dudziak, *Cold War Civil Rights: Race and the Image of American Democracy* (Princeton: Princeton University Press, 2000).

92 Darlene Clark Hine, *Black Victory: The Rise and Fall of the White Primary in Texas* (Columbia: University of Missouri Press, 2003).

93 See, e.g., Kevin M. Kruse and Stephen Tuck, eds., *Fog of War: The Second World War and the Civil Rights Movement* (New York: Oxford University Press, 2012).

94 Michael W. Myers, *The Pacific War and Contingent Victory: Why Japanese Defeat Was Not Inevitable* (Lawrence: University Press of Kansas, 2015), 1.

95 Carl Murphy to Claude Barnett, 1 April 1942, Reel 17, #242, Part II, Organizational Files, Barnett Papers.

96 Claude A. Barnett to P. B. Young, 2 April 1942, Reel 1, #375, Part II, Organizational Files, Barnett Papers.

97 In 1941 the U.S. authorities intercepted a message from the Japanese embassy in Washington that spoke bluntly of "using a Negro literary critic" whom they helped to "open a news service for Negro newspapers." There was an "advantage," it was said, in "using Negroes in procuring intelligence." The author conceded that he had "not yet used the Negro spies directly," though he was now "instructing" an unnamed "official" of the "National Youth Administration, and a graduate of Amherst and Columbia to be a spy." See "Nomura" to Tokyo, 4 July 1941, Box 2, Frank A. Schuler Jr. Papers, Franklin D. Roosevelt Presidential Library and Museum, Hyde Park, NY. See also David D. Lowman, *Magic: The Untold Story of U.S. Intelligence and the Evacuation of Japanese Residents from the West Coast during World War II* (N.p.: Athena, 2001), 252: "Japanese authorities are watching closely the Negroes who are employed in defense production plants, naval stations and other military establishments."

98 Claude Barnett to Attorney General Biddle, 16 June 1943, Reel 1, #414, Part 2, Organizational Files, Barnett Papers.

99 Gerald Horne, *Negro Comrades of the Crown: African Americans and the British Empire Fight the U.S. before Emancipation* (New York: New York University Press, 2013); Gerald Horne, *Race to Revolution: The United States and Cuba during Slavery and Jim Crow* (New York: Monthly Review Press, 2014).

100 See, e.g., "Petition of American Negroes to Support Bilbo's Bill for Securing a Country in Africa for Those Negroes Who May Desire to Return," UNIA, circa 1939, Box 1073, Bilbo Papers. A version of the preceding can also be found in Box 1128 of the same collection. In Box 1092 can be found a similar petition from the Peace Movement of Ethiopia with signatures affixed from Detroit, Pittsburgh, and Cleveland; however, all signatures seem to be from the same writer. In Boxes 1186 and 1187 there are more signed petitions, numbering in the thousands, all in the same handwriting. In the same collection, Box 1090, see also Senator Bilbo to W. F. Duncan, 17 June 1940: "I have close to three million Negroes all signed up ready to go. The number is increasing daily." Interestingly, during the racial unrest that swept Detroit in 1943, the U.S. authorities claimed that agents of Tokyo played a role in whipping up this devastating conflict. See, e.g., War Relocation Authority, "Weekly Press Review, Week Ending July 4, 1943," Box 3, McWilliams Collection.

101 C. C. Edwards, President of Division #301 of UNIA in Kinston, North Carolina, to Senator Bilbo, 10 December 1938, Box 1091, Bilbo Papers.

102 Senator Bilbo to W. F. Duncan, 17 June 1940, Box 1090, Bilbo Papers.

103 G. E. Harris to Senator Bilbo, 5 June 1941, Box 1091, Bilbo Papers.

104 Mittie Maude Lena Gordon to Senator Bilbo, 29 August 1938, Box 1091, Bilbo Papers. See also Keisha Blain, "'Confraternity among All Dark Races': Mittie Maude Lena Gordon and the Practice of Black (Inter)nationalism in Chicago, 1932–1942," *Palimpsest: A Journal on Women, Gender and the Black International* 5, no. 2 (2016): 151–81.

105 Amy Jacques Garvey, of "Garvey's African Communities League," to Senator Bilbo, 26 March 1944, Box 1090, Bilbo Papers. A parallel movement at the time declared, "Judea for the Jews, Africa for the Africans." See Literature, n.d., Box 1090. In the same box, see J. R. Stewart, UNIA–Cleveland, to Senator Bilbo, 9 October 1939: We "received the 350 copies of your speech and Bill. . . . The demand greatly exceeds the supply. . . . The people of Ohio therefore are anxious to sacrifice now to form a pilgrimage numbering thousands to lend weight to the ultimate passage of this bill." See also Mrs. R. L. Coleman to Senator Bilbo, 11 January 1939, Box 1091: A proposal in the *Christian Century* of 28 December 1938 argued that "we settle *the Jews in Africa* or in a segregated portion of this country. Why not repatriate the Negro or resettle them in a segregated area of this country, as is suggested for the Jews?" She continued, "Why should the South be dominated by them as will be the case in comparatively few years under present trends."

106 J. R. Stewart, State Commissioner of UNIA–Cleveland, to Senator Bilbo, n.d., Box 1091, Bilbo Papers.

107 Marcus Garvey to Senator Bilbo, 12 August 1938, Box 1091, Bilbo Papers.

108 Marcus Garvey to Senator Bilbo, 13 August 1938, Box 1091, Bilbo Papers.

109 Mittie Maude Lena Gordon to Senator Bilbo, 15 October 1939, Box 1090, Bilbo Papers. See also Mittie Maude Lena Gordon to Senator Bilbo, 2 December 1938, Box 1090: She requested more copies of the legislation, "as I have many calls for them."

110 Mittie Maude Lena Gordon to Senator Bilbo, 19 October 1939, Box 1090, Bilbo Papers.

111 Carlos Cooks to Senator Bilbo, 9 November 1939, Box 1090, Bilbo Papers.

112 Clipping of Rogers's column, n.d., Box 1090, Bilbo Papers.

113 Carlos Cooks to Senator Bilbo, 18 July 1941, Box 1091, Bilbo Papers. Tellingly, when Angel Evanah, one of the many "followers of Father Divine," the holy man, made a "demand" to Senator Bilbo that he back "passage of the anti-lynching bill," Bilbo was uncharacteristically reticent: letter, 8 August 1939, Box 1090. On the other hand, Archie Whitehead of the Afro-American Navigating Association of New York was "100 percent in favor" of the resettlement bill since he had "personally spent 12 months in Liberia," along with many of his group who served "as sailors, navigators, shipbuilders and seamen." They saw a route to profit by handling this massive job of transporting Negroes overseas. Letter, 6 August 1939, Box 1090, Bilbo Papers.

114 Theodor Van der Lyn to Senator Bilbo, 16 November 1938, Box 1091, Bilbo Papers. Interestingly, it was Garvey himself who put this London correspondent in touch with Bilbo: Theodor van der Lyn to Senator Bilbo, 18 October 1938, Box 1091. Correspondingly, Bilbo put his comrades in touch with Gordon. See Senator Bilbo to Theodore Jervy, n.d., circa October 1940, Box 1091.

115 F. L. Scofield to Senator Bilbo, 20 November 1939, Box 1090, Bilbo Papers.

116 Wyatt Dougherty to Senator Bilbo, 1 January 1939, Box 1091, Bilbo Papers.

117 "Mr. Bilbo's Afflatus," *Time*, 8 May 1939, 16, Box 1091, Bilbo Papers.

118 Joseph Alsop and Robert Kintner, "Germany's Race Consciousness Lauded by Bilbo in Harangue to Senate on Liberian Bill," *Washington Evening Star*, 28 May 1938, A-9.

119 Speech by Senator Bilbo, 22 March 1944, Box 1084, Bilbo Papers.

120 Senator Bilbo to "Captain James Thornhill," 6 April 1940, Box 1091, Bilbo Papers.

121 Joseph Edgar to Senator Bilbo, 31 January 1941, Box 1091, Bilbo Papers. Tellingly, even Berlin thought it could outflank Washington on the bedrock issue of white supremacy. See, e.g., Roi Ottley, *No Green Pastures* (New York: Scribner's, 1951), 153, 160, 162:

> Under the Nazis, few Negroes were victims of day-to-day brutality, as meted out to the Jews. The savage Nuremberg racial laws, which in theory embraced blacks, never were widely applied to Negroes. . . . Adolf Hitler was an ardent admirer of American racial know-how. There is fine irony in the fact that he sent a mission to the U.S. to study Jim Crow to enable him more ef-

ficiently to discriminate against Jews. . . . He invited Dr. S. J. Wright, a Negro professor doing a special study at Heidelberg, to have dinner with him and his Nazi Friends [in 1932] and revealed a surprising knowledge of the negative aspects of American racialism.

Still, concludes the author, Berlin "wanted both to win over and eventually to enslave the black millions."

122 Ben Davis Jr., "Sen. Bilbo Perpetrates a Vicious Slander," 27 December 1938, 3, Box 1091, Bilbo Papers. In the same box, see also the editorial in Harlem's *New York Age* of 9 August 1941, denouncing Bilbo's proposed speech in Harlem.

123 Gerald Horne, "The Haitian Revolution and the Central Question of African American History," *Journal of African American History* 100 (2015).

124 Charles Eagles, *The Price of Defiance: James Meredith and the Integration of Ole Miss* (Chapel Hill: University of North Carolina Press, 2009).

125 James Meredith, *Japan: As Seen through the Eyes of an American Black Man* (Jackson: Meredith, 1995), i, available at University of Mississippi, Oxford.

CHAPTER 1. JAPAN RISES/NEGROES CHEER

1 Edwina S. Campbell, *Citizen of a Wider Commonwealth: Ulysses S. Grant's Postpresidential Diplomacy* (Carbondale: Southern Illinois University Press, 2016), 153–70.

2 Eunsun Celeste Han, "Making a Black Pacific: African Americans and the Formation of Transpacific Community Networks, 1865–1872," *Journal of African American History* 101, nos. 1–2 (Winter–Spring 2016): 23–48.

3 Report, 14 July 1853, in *The Personal Journal of Commodore Matthew C. Perry: The Japan Expedition, 1852–1854*, ed. Roger Pineau (Washington, D.C.: Smithsonian, 1968), 98.

4 Michael R. Auslin, *Pacific Cosmopolitans: A Cultural History of U.S.-Japan Relations* (Cambridge: Harvard University Press, 2011), 74. See also Eric Gardner, *Black Print Unbound: The "Christian Recorder," African American Literature, and Periodical Culture* (New York: Oxford University Press, 2015).

5 Bayard Taylor, *A Visit to India, China and Japan in the Year 1853* (New York: Putnam, 1855), 429, 434, 440. See also James D. Johnston, *China and Japan: Being a Narrative of the U.S. Steam-Frigate* Powhatan *in the Years 1857, '58, '59 and '60, Including an Account of the Japanese Embassy to the United States* (Philadelphia: Desilver, 1861). The author, a Kentuckian, reflects the sectional and racial biases of that tormented era.

6 Entry, 20 February 1856, in *The Complete Journal of Townsend Harris: First American Consul General and Minister to Japan*, ed. Mario Emilio Cosenza (Garden City: Doubleday, 1930), 64.

7 E. P. Smith to Dear Sir, 19 November 1865, Box 18, Folder 3, Edward Carey Collection, Historical Society of Pennsylvania. See also Ikukuo Asaka, "'Colored Men of the East': African Americans and the Instability of Race in U.S.-Japan Relations," *American Quarterly* 66, no. 4 (December 2014): 971–97.

8 "An Act Supplementary to the Acts in Relation to Immigration . . . March 3, 1875,"
in *The Columbia Documentary History of the Asian American Experience*, ed.
Franklin Odo (New York: Columbia University Press, 2002), 38–40, 38.

9 Nishimura Ekie v. U.S., 18 January 1892, in Odo, *The Columbia Documentary History*, 91–92.

10 In re Saito, 27 June 1894, in Odo, *The Columbia Documentary History*, 101–3.

11 Gerald Horne, *The White Pacific: U.S. Imperialism and Black Slavery in the South
Seas after the Civil War* (Honolulu: University of Hawaii Press, 2005).

12 Christopher W. A. Szpilman, "Miyazaki Toten's Pan-Asianism, 1915–1919," in *Pan-
Asianism: A Documentary History*, vol. 1, *1850–1920*, ed. Sven Saaler and Christopher W. A. Szpilman (Lanham, MD: Rowman and Littlefield, 2011), 133–37, 134.

13 Introduction to *Pan-Asianism: A Documentary History*, vol. 2, *1920–Present*, ed.
Sven Saaler and Christopher W. A. Szpilman (Lanham, MD: Rowman and Littlefield, 2011), 1–41, 24.

14 Theresa Runstedtler, "The New Negro's Brown Brother: African American and
Filipino Boxers and the 'Rising Tide of Color,'" in *Escape from New York: The New
Negro Renaissance beyond Harlem*, ed. Davarian Baldwin and Minkah Makalani
(Minneapolis: University of Minnesota Press, 2013), 104–27, 110.

15 Edward A. Johnson, *History of the Negro Soldiers in the Spanish-American War*
(Raleigh: Capital, 1899), 131.

16 "Philippines for Negro," *Washington Post*, 16 December 1902, 3. See also Joseph A.
Fry, *John Tyler Morgan and the Search for Southern Autonomy* (Knoxville: University of Tennessee Press, 1992).

17 Emma Thornbrough, *T. Thomas Fortune: Militant Journalist* (Chicago: University
of Chicago Press, 1972), 235. See also Shawn Leigh Alexander, ed., *T. Thomas Fortune, The Afro-American Agitator: A Collection of Writings, 1880–1928* (Gaines-
ville: University Press of Florida, 2008).

18 Gerald Horne, *The Deepest South: The United States, Brazil, and the African Slave
Trade* (New York: New York University Press, 2007).

19 Larry Arxen Lawcock, "Philippine Students in the United States and the Independence Movement, 1900–1935" (Ph.D. diss., University of California, Berkeley,
1975), 641.

20 See, e.g., Donald Pease and Amy Kaplan, eds., *Cultures of U.S. Imperialism* (Durham: Duke University Press, 1993).

21 Nerissa S. Balce, "Filipino Bodies, Lynching and the Language of Empire," in
Positively No Filipinos Allowed: Building Communities and Discourse, ed. Antonio
T. Tiongson Jr., Edgardo V. Gutierrez, and Ricardo V. Gutierrez (Philadelphia:
Temple University Press, 2006), 43–60. See also Scot Brown, "The Dilemma of
the African American Solider in the Philippine-American War, 1899–1902" (M.A.
thesis, Cornell University, 1993); Matthew Frye Jacobson, *Barbarian Virtues: The
United States Encounters Foreign People at Home and Abroad, 1876–1917* (New
York: Hill and Wang, 2001), 252; and Willard B. Gatewood, *"Smoked Yankees" and*

the Struggle for Empire: Letters from Negro Soldiers, 1898–1902 (Urbana: University of Illinois Press, 1971).

22 Michael C. Robinson and Frank N. Schubert, "David Fagen: An Afro-American Rebel in the Philippines, 1899–1901," *Pacific Historical Review* 44 (February 1975): 68–83.

23 See, e.g., Rene Ontal, "Fagen and Other Ghosts: African Americans and the Philippine-American War," in *Vestiges of War: The Philippine-American War and the Aftermath of an Imperial Dream, 1899–1999*, ed. Angel Velasco Shaw and Luis H. Francia (New York: New York University Press, 2002), 118–33; Cynthia L. Marasigan, "'Between the Devil and the Deep Sea': Ambivalence, Violence and African American Soldiers in the Philippine-American War and Its Aftermath" (Ph.D. diss., University of Michigan, Ann Arbor, 2010), 1, 12, 33, 34, 133, 186, 187, 223; Hazel M. McFerson, "'Part Black Americans' in the South Pacific," *Phylon* 43, no. 2 (1982): 177–80; and Hazel M. McFerson, ed., *Blacks and Asians: Crossings, Conflict and Commonality* (Durham: Carolina Academic Press, 2006).

24 Marasigan, "'Between the Devil and the Deep Sea,'" 106.

25 Susan K. Harris, *God's Arbiters: Americans and the Philippines, 1898–1902* (New York: Oxford University Press, 2011), 64–65, 66.

26 Winslow Warren, "The White Man's Burden," *Boston Evening Transcript*, 18 February 1899, Massachusetts Historical Society, Boston. See also Willard Gatewood, *Black Americans and the White Man's Burden, 1898–1903* (Urbana: University of Illinois Press, 1975), 307.

27 Frank Erb comment, 27 February 1899, in "Soldiers' Letters; Being Materials for the History of a War of Criminal Aggression," Boston: Anti-Imperialist League, 1899, Massachusetts Historical Society.

28 Entry, 14 March 1905, in *Journal of W. Cameron Forbes*, vol. 1, *Philippines*, Massachusetts Historical Society.

29 Article, 18 January 1906, Box 21, Illinois Writers Project: "Negro in Illinois" Papers, Vivian G. Harsh Research Collection of Afro-American History and Literature, Carter G. Woodson Regional Library, Chicago Public Library.

30 Editorial, *So Chaep'il*, 8 November 1899, in Saaler and Szpilman, *Pan-Asianism: A Documentary History*, vol. 1, 175–76.

31 See, e.g., Colleen C. O'Brien, "'Blacks in All Quarters of the Globe': Anti-Imperialism, Insurgent Cosmopolitanism, and International Labor in Pauline Hopkins' Literary Journalism," *American Quarterly* 61, no. 2 (June 2009): 245–70.

32 Horne, *Race War!*, 45.

33 James Taylor, "Free Thought Africa," *Broad Axe* (Chicago), 22 April 1905, 1.

34 "If the Negro Paid . . . ," *Topeka Plain Dealer*, 5 August 1904, 1.

35 R. W. Thompson, "Short Flights," *Freeman* (Indianapolis), 19 May 1906. Those I quote at times use the derogatory and racist term "Jap" in describing those of Japanese ancestry.

36 "Colored Girl and Japanese Marry," *Freeman* (Indianapolis), 25 February 1911, 4.

37 "Comes to Japs Call," *Topeka Plain Dealer*, 9 November 1906, 1.

38 "Thompson's Weekly Review: Japanese and the States' Rights," *Freeman* (Indianapolis), 10 November 1906, 1.

39 David Hellwig, "Afro-American Reactions to the Japanese and the Anti-Japanese Movement, 1906–1924," *Phylon* 38 (March 1977): 93–104, 94, 96.

40 Oliver Cromwell Cox, "The Nature of the Anti-Asiatic Movement on the Pacific Coast," *Journal of Negro Education* 15 (Fall 1946): 603–64, 609.

41 "What May Result if the Persecution of the Negroes Continues," *Broad Axe* (Chicago), 19 January 1907, 1. Masaharu Homma, a Japanese military officer subjected to a war crimes tribunal in 1946, was born in 1888 and in the early twentieth century spent eight years in England. He told the tribunal that there were two factions in the military of Japan: "the pro-German group" and "the pro-British force," which was "in the great minority. I was considered as the head of the latter group." Hideki Tojo, the premier military figure in Tokyo, was "head of the pro-German group," he said. Despite the self-serving nature of his testimony, the fact remains that London did see Tokyo as its watchdog in Asia—at least until 7 December 1941. See Transcript, 5 February 1946, Masaharu Homma Tribunal Records, University of Georgia, Athens.

42 Sven Saaler, "Pan-Asianism during and after World War I: Kodera Kenkichi (1916), Sawayanagi Masataro (1919) and Teichi Sugita (1920)," in Saaler and Szpilman, *Pan-Asianism: A Documentary History*, vol. 1, 255–60, 259. Even at this early stage, African Americans were making distinctions between Japanese and Chinese migrants. The Negro journalist T. Thomas Fortune, for example, was willing to entertain the idea of restriction of Chinese immigration. See "Fortunes and the Homesteads," *Hawaiian Star*, 30 December 1902, 5.

43 "Jap or Negro Labor?," *Freeman* (Indianapolis), 9 March 1907, 3.

44 "Japanese Colony in Texas?," *Washington Bee*, 29 February 1908.

45 R. W. Thompson, "Short Flight," *Freeman* (Indianapolis), 24 July 1909, 6.

46 "Jap Waiters Succeed Negroes," *Kansas Baptist Herald*, 11 November 1911, 3.

47 John T. Campbell, "Justice to the Negro," *Freeman* (Indianapolis), 13 July 1907, 1.

48 "Patriotism," *Freeman* (Indianapolis), 29 April 1911, 3.

49 "The Week in Society," *Washington Bee*, 24 October 1908, 5.

50 "In the Musical Circles," *Freeman* (Indianapolis), 23 May 1908, 1.

51 "Dr. B. T. Washington," *Washington Bee*, 29 March 1913, 1.

52 "Japanese Honor Dr. Washington," *Freeman* (Indianapolis), 26 April 1913, 3.

53 *Japan-American Diplomatic Relations in the Meiji-Taisho Era* (Tokyo: Pan-Pacific Press, 1958), trans. Michiko Kimura, 295, 299, 209, 211, 265, 266, 267. In 1898 Mary Crawford Fraser, then visiting Japan, reported "a new treaty" between Mexico City and Tokyo that had just been signed. Mrs. Hugh Fraser, *Letters from Japan: A Record of Modern Life in the Island Empire* (London: Macmillan, 1899), 42, 72–173. In a presentiment of the Pacific War, she was stunned to encounter "anti-foreign feeling" during her journey there. "We are occasionally met by scowling faces in

the streets. . . . Once or twice stones have been thrown at the carriage." She was born in Rome to parents who were U.S. nationals and married a British diplomat.

54 Inazo Nitobe, *The Japanese Nation: Its Land, Its People and Its Life* (New York: Putnam's, 1912), 90, 289. See also William Allan Reed, *Negritos of Zambales,* Department of the Interior, vol. 2, part 1, Ethnological Survey Publications (Manila: Bureau of Public Printing, 1904).

55 John de Forest, *The Truth about Japan* (Boston: World Peace Foundation, 1912), Massachusetts Historical Society.

56 Ryutaro Nagai, "The White Peril," 1913, in Saaler and Szpilman, *Pan-Asianism: A Documentary History*, vol. 1, 164–68, 165, 166.

57 Nick Chiles, "Benjamin Tillman," *Washington Bee*, 24 May 1913, 2.

58 Benjamin Tillman, "The Race Issue and the Annexation of the Philippines," Speech in U.S. Senate, 29 January 1900, University of South Carolina, Columbia.

59 Introduction to Saaler and Szpilman, *Pan-Asianism: A Documentary History*, vol. 1, 1–41, 24.

60 "Doings of the Race," *Cleveland Gazette*, 31 May 1913, 2.

61 "Are We a Race of Cowards?," *Broad Axe* (Chicago), 28 November 1914, 4.

62 Owen M. Waller, "Waller against 'Negro,'" *St. Paul (MN) Appeal*, 22 September 1917.

63 Gerald Horne, *Black and Brown: African Americans and the Mexican Revolution, 1910–1920* (New York: New York University Press, 2005). Cf. Horst Von Der Goltz, *My Adventures as a German Secret Agent* (New York: McBride, 1917); Thomas J. Tunney, *Throttled! The Detection of the German and Anarchist Bomb Plotters* (Boston: Small, Maynard, 1919); Franz von Rintelen, *The Dark Invader: War-time Reminiscences of a German Naval Intelligence Officer* (London: Cass, 1998); and Henry Landau, *The Enemy Within: The Inside Story of German Sabotage in America* (New York: Putnam's, 1937).

64 Howard Blum, *Dark Invasion, 1915: Germany's Secret War and the Hunt for the First Terrorist Cell in America* (New York: HarperCollins, 2014), 383, 417; *Washington Post*, 1 March 1917; Thomas Boghardt, *The Zimmerman Telegram: Intelligence, Diplomacy and America's Entry into World War I* (Annapolis: Naval Institute Press, 2012). For more on the notorious "Plan de San Diego," see, e.g., Charles H. Harris III and Louis S. Sadler, *The Plan de San Diego: Tejano Rebellion, Mexican Intrigue* (Lincoln: University of Nebraska Press, 2013).

65 Senator Williams to Ambassador Aimaro Asto, 27 August 1917, Box 2, John Sharp Williams Papers, University of Mississippi, Oxford.

66 Congressional Debate, 15 July 1919, Box 5, John Sharp Williams Papers.

67 Lytle Brown to Chief of Staff, 5 July 1918, 168.7061-30 to 168.7061-71, Air Force Historical Research Agency.

68 M. Churchill, Colonel, General Staff of War Department, to Chief of Staff, 2 July 1918, 168.7061-30, Air Force Historical Research Agency.

69 Horne, *Race War!*, 35–37.

70 Takao Ozawa v. U.S., 13 November 1922, in Odo, *The Columbia Documentary History*, 181–84.

71 "The United States Supreme Court Bars the Japanese from American Citizenship," *Negro World*, 25 November 1922, 3. See also Adam Ewing, *The Age of Garvey: How a Jamaican Activist Created a Mass Movement and Changed Global Black Politics* (Princeton: Princeton University Press, 2014).

72 Eleanor Tupper, *Japan in American Public Opinion* (New York: Macmillan, 1937), 209.

73 Eric Hotta, "Konoe Fumimaro: 'A Call to Reject the Anglo-American Centered Peace,'" 1918, in Saaler and Szpilman, *Pan-Asianism: A Documentary History*, vol. 1, 311–14, 313.

74 E. Taylor Atkins, *Authenticating Jazz in Japan* (Durham: Duke University Press, 2001), 12, 50.

75 W. M. Reicke, "'Now Ain't This Awful,'" *Savannah Tribune*, 9 October 1920, 3.

76 William Pickens, "Japs United Because of Their Thrift," *Savannah Tribune*, 27 November 1920, 1.

77 "Negroes and Japanese Brought into Comparison," *Savannah Tribune*, 15 January 1921, 3.

78 "Japan on American Lynching," *Topeka Plain Dealer*, 4 November 1921, 1.

79 "Japan Holds Mass Meeting of Protest against Injustices to Negroes in America," *Negro World*, 3 June 1922, 7.

CHAPTER 2. HARLEM, ADDIS ABABA—AND TOKYO

1 Chicago Commission on Race Relations, *The Negro in Chicago: A Study of Race Relations and a Race Riot* (Chicago: University of Chicago Press, 1922), 59, 61. See also Reto Hofmann, *The Fascist Effect: Japan and Italy, 1915–1952* (Ithaca: Cornell University Press, 2015).

2 ". . . Says Japan May Attack America in 1922," *Negro World*, 27 August 1921, 7.

3 "Greetings from Yokohama, Japan," *Negro World*, 5 November 1921, 4.

4 "Greetings from the Orient," *Negro World*, 12 November 1921, 4.

5 "Race War Threatens World," *Negro World*, 5 November 1921, 9.

6 "Disarmament Conference," *Negro World*, 12 November 1921, 4.

7 "Darker Races . . . Want Equality," *Savannah Tribune*, 12 January 1922, 4.

8 Andrew David Field, *Shanghai's Dancing World: Cabaret Culture and Urban Politics, 1919–1954* (Hong Kong: Chinese University Press, 2010), 37, 93.

9 "Japan and the Darker Races," *Negro World*, 12 November 1921, 4.

10 Robert Poston, "The Little Brown Democrats," *Negro World*, 19 November 1921, 4.

11 "Harrison on 'Disarmament and the Negro,'" *Negro World*, 4 February 1922, 5.

12 "Japanese Statesman Squashes Race Inferiority Complex," *Negro World*, 29 April 1922, 3.

13 "A Request to Discard the Propaganda of Alien Races," *Negro World*, 3 November 1923, 1.

14 "Though Not Liked, Japanese Are Respected, Says Hon. Marcus Garvey," *Negro World*, 13 May 1922, 9.
15 "Japan Scores American Morals," *Negro World*, 17 June 1922, 5.
16 F. Scott Fitzgerald, *The Great Gatsby* (New York: Scribner's, 1925), 15–16.
17 "Japanese Problem More Threatening Than Negro Problem, Declares Attorney General," *Negro World*, 26 May 1923, 5.
18 "Jap Birth Rate Trebles That of Whites in State," *Los Angeles Examiner*, 21 January 1923, 4.
19 "Negroes Show Their Sympathy for the Japanese," *Negro World*, 22 September 1923, 2.
20 "Japanese Journalists Rebuffed and Insulted in South Africa," *Negro World*, 10 July 1926, 2.
21 "Japanese People Greatly Offended by the Exclusion Act," *Negro World*, 7 June 1924, 4.
22 "Japanese Diet Condemns U.S. Exclusion Law," *Negro World*, 12 July 1924, 14.
23 "Japanese Lining Up Asia for Coming Race Conflict," *Negro World*, 5 July 1924, 15.
24 "Jingoes and Japanese," *Negro World*, 3 January 1925, 4.
25 Jonathan Peter Spiro, *Defending the Master Race: Conservation, Eugenics and the Legacy of Madison Grant* (Lebanon, NH: University Press of New England, 2009), 224, 232, 233, 141, 338.
26 Sugita Teiichi, "An Argument for Uniting Greater Asia," 1924, in Saaler and Szpilman, *Pan-Asianism: A Documentary History*, vol. 1, 265–69, 267.
27 T. Thomas Fortune, "Some Dream Hours in Glorious Japan," *Negro World*, 14 June 1924, 4.
28 "Asiatics Meet in Convention to End Domination by Aliens," *Negro World*, 14 August 1926, 2.
29 Haruji Tawara, "Japanese Journalist's Message to U.S. Negroes," *Negro World*, 30 July 1927, 1.
30 Sakashita, "Lynching across the Pacific," 184, 187, 190, 191.
31 Yukiko Koshiro, *Imperial Eclipse: Japan's Strategic Thinking about Continental Asia before August 1945* (New York: Columbia University Press, 2013), 27–28.
32 Alex Lubin, *Geographies of Liberation: The Making of an Afro-Arab Political Imaginary* (Chapel Hill: University of North Carolina Press, 2014), 61, 74, 75. See also Ian Duffield, "Duse Mohammed Ali and the Development of Pan-Africanism, 1866–1945" (Ph.D. diss., Edinburgh University, 1971).
33 Ewing, *The Age of Garvey*, 129, 134; *Negro World*, 26 March 1927.
34 J. Lawson to B. D. Amis, 5 April 1932, Reel 234, Delo 3038, Papers of the Communist Party-USA, Library of Congress.
35 Seth McMeekin, *The Berlin-Baghdad Express: The Ottoman Empire and Germany's Bid for World Power* (Cambridge: Harvard University Press, 2010).
36 Mikiya Koyagi, "The Hajj by Japanese Muslims in the Interwar Period: Japan's Pan-Asianism and Economic Interests," *Journal of World History* 24, no. 4 (December 2012): 849–76.

37 Selcuk Esenbel, "Abdurresid Ibrahim: The World of Islam and the Spread of Islam in Japan," 1910, in Saaler and Szpilman, *Pan-Asianism: A Documentary History*, vol. 1, 195–201, 197.

38 Renee Worringer, "Hatano Uho: 'Asia in Danger,'" 1912, in Saaler and Szpilman, *Pan-Asianism: A Documentary History*, vol. 1, 149–53, 149.

39 Nakano Seigo, "The Mountains and Rivers of a Fallen State," in Saaler and Szpilman, *Pan-Asianism: A Documentary History*, vol. 2, 52–53, 52.

40 Hosoi Hajime, "Japan's Resolve," 1932, in Saaler and Szpilman, *Pan Asianism: A Documentary History*, vol. 2, 120.

41 See, e.g., Horne, *The End of Empires*, 79.

42 Release, ANP, July 1930, Reel 3, #30, Part I, Series A, Barnett Papers. See also Release, ANP, February 1935, Reel 10, #217, Part I, Series A: "Delegation of Negroes from the southern part of the United States . . . failed in its request for a land grant from the Polish government. . . . [They] said they represented 500 families ready to immigrate into southern Poland from the United States if they are granted homesteads. . . . The delegates left Poland for Romania." See also Release, ANP, November 1938, Reel 17, #1084, Part I, Series A: In Crimea there was reputedly a Negro colony comprising "dissatisfied elements of the United States, French and English colonies," as well as "South Africa, . . . Belgian Congo," and so on. Many were artists and physicians.

43 Claude Andrew Clegg, *An Original Man: The Life and Times of Elijah Muhammad* (New York: St. Martin's, 1997), 65, 82, 89.

44 Revilo Oliver, "The Black Muslims," 1963, Vertical File, University of Southern Mississippi, Hattiesburg.

45 U.S. v. Elijah Mohamed, alias Elijah Poole, alias Gulan Bogans, alias Mohammed Rassoull, October term 1942, U.S. District Court, Northern District of Illinois, Eastern Division of Chicago, Record Group 21, Criminal Case Files, Case no. 33647, Box 1152, National Archives and Records Administration, Chicago.

46 See, e.g., Allen, "When Japan Was Champion of the 'Darker Races'"; and Allen, "'Waiting for Tojo.'" Allen also makes the point that many of these pro-Tokyo organizations formed among Negroes had a view reflecting "millennialism" that stretched back to the days of slavery.

47 Memorandum, 1939, in Hill, *The FBI's RACON*, 515.

48 William Pickens, "Stimson and Japan—Communists and Congress," *Topeka Plaindealer*, 11 December 1931, 2.

49 William Pickens, "Japan in Manchuria Takes Leaf from Book of 'Occupation' in Haiti," *Topeka Plaindealer*, 25 December 1931, 1. See also Etusuko Taketani, "The Cartography of the Black Pacific: James Weldon Johnson's 'Along This Way,'" *American Quarterly* 59, no. 1 (March 2007): 79–106.

50 William Pickens, "'White Supremacy' Is Dead," *Kansas City (KS) Wyandotte Echo*, 11 March 1932, 1.

51 "The Case for Japan," *Baltimore Afro-American*, 15 January 1938, 4. Particularly in the 1960s, many Black Nationalists and some on the left began to view China the

way Japan was viewed decades earlier, as a kind of "champion of the darker races," with little reference to how China had been viewed previously by African Americans. See, e.g., Robeson Taj Frazier, *The East Is Black: Cold War China in the Black Radical Imagination* (Durham: Duke University Press, 2015). One scholar has observed that "from 1880–1935 almost every time those of Chinese origin were mentioned in the black press, it was in connection with intrigue, prostitution, murder, the sale of opium or children for money," not to mention "superstitious practices, shootings or tong wars." See Arnold Shankman, "Black on Yellow: Afro-Americans View Chinese-Americans, 1850–1935," *Phylon* 39, no. 1 (Spring 1978): 1–17, 7. On the other hand, note that the anti-Chinese initiatives in Washington, such as the Chinese Exclusion Act in 1882 and other proposals to bar Chinese immigration, were greeted with "almost unanimous opposition" in the "black press." See Jun, *Race for Citizenship*. See also Edlie L. Wong, *Racial Reconstruction: Black Inclusion, Chinese Exclusion, and the Fictions of Citizenship* (New York: New York University Press, 2015).

52 Release, ANP, May 1936, Reel 12, #867, Part I, Series A, ANP News Releases, Barnett Papers.

53 Release, ANP, August 1936, Reel 13, #640, Part I, Series A.

54 *Kansas City Plaindealer*, 17 March 1933.

55 William R. Scott, *The Sons of Sheba's Race: African Americans and the Ethiopian War, 1935–1941* (Bloomington: Indiana University Press, 1993); Joseph Harris, *African American Reactions to War in Ethiopia, 1936–1941* (Baton Rouge: Louisiana State University Press, 1994).

56 Horne, *Race War!*, 231–32. See also Richard Bradshaw, "Japan and European Colonialism in Africa, 1800–1937" (Ph.D. diss., Ohio University, 1992), 337, 343.

57 U.S. v. Leonard Robert Jordan, alias Robert Gordon, Lester Holness, alias Lester Casey, Joseph Hartrey, alias Joseph Ashley, Ralph Green Best, alias Ralph Thomas Best, and James Thornhill, 1942–1943, U.S. District Court, Southern District of New York, C113–40 and C-113–264, National Archives and Records Administration, New York (this record, however, was retrieved from storage at the National Archives and Records Administration facility in Kansas City, MO).

58 U.S. v. Mittie Maude Lena Gordon et al., U.S. Circuit Court of Appeals, Seventh Circuit, Brief and Argument for the Appellants, 8 June 1943, #8256, National Archives and Records Administration, Chicago.

59 Release, ANP, May 1936, Reel 12, #854, Part I, Series A, ANP News Releases, 1928–1944, Barnett Papers.

60 Release, ANP, October 1935, Reel 11, #658, Part I, Series A.

61 Release, ANP, November 1930, Reel 3, #475, Part I, Series A.

62 Letters from Emperor Haile Selassie, Dr. W. Martin, and Dr. Tecle Hawariate, in "The Friends of Ethiopia in America," New York, 1935, University of Virginia, Charlottesville.

63 Release, ANP, August 1935, Reel 11, #43, Part I, ANP News Releases, Series A, 1928–1944, Barnett Papers.

64 Release, ANP, May 1936, Reel 12, #1043, Part I, Series A.
65 Release, ANP, August 1935, Reel 11, #67, Part I, Series A.
66 Release, ANP, August 1935, Reel 11, #118, Part I, Series A.
67 Release, ANP, August 1934, Reel 11, #126, Part I, Series A.
68 Release, ANP, August 1934, Reel 11, #143, Part I, Series A.
69 Release, ANP, November 1935, Reel 11, #874, Part I, Series A.
70 Release, ANP, October 1935, Reel 11, #666, Part I, Series A.
71 Release, ANP, April 1936, Reel 12, #712, Part I, Series A.
72 Release, ANP, December 1935, Reel 11, #992, Part I, Series A.
73 Release, ANP, June 1936, Reel 13, #193, Part I, Series A.
74 Release, ANP, May 1936, Reel 12, #1056, Part I, Series A.
75 Release, ANP, September 1935, Reel 11, #294, Part I, Series A.
76 Release, ANP, December 1933, Reel 8, #232, Part I, Series A.
77 Release, ANP, September 1935, Reel 11, #295, Part I, Series A.
78 Release, ANP, December 1935, Reel 11, #1072, Part I, Series A.
79 Release, ANP, March 1936, Reel 12, #469, Part I, Series A.
80 Release, ANP, January 1936, Reel 11, #146, Part I, Series A.
81 Release, ANP, January 1936, Reel 11, #170, Part I, Series A.
82 Release, ANP, May 1936, Reel 12, #1090, Part I, Series A.
83 Release, ANP, October 1935, Reel 11, #602, Part I, Series A.
84 Release, ANP, December 1935, Reel 11, #1034, Part I, Series A.
85 Release, ANP, May 1936, Reel 12, #1098, Part I, Series A.
86 Release, ANP, June 1936, Reel 13, #66, Part I, Series A.
87 Release, ANP, May 1936, Reel 12, #1077, Part I, Series A.
88 Release, ANP, April 1936, Reel 12, #809, Part I, Series A.
89 Release, ANP, March 1936, Reel 12, #953, Part I, Series A.
90 Release, ANP, September 1936, Reel 13, #694, Part I, Series A.
91 Release, ANP, January 1936, Reel 11, #1124, Part I, Series A.
92 Release, ANP, August 1936, Reel 13, #630, Part I, Series A.
93 Release, ANP, September 1936, Reel 13, #746, Part I, Series A.

CHAPTER 3. JAPAN ESTABLISHES A FOOTHOLD IN BLACK AMERICA
1 Testimony of George Young, grand jury, September 1942, Box 3, Folder 2, PMEW File.
2 U.S. v. PMEW, transcript, n.d., circa May 1943, Box 2, Folder 1, PMEW File.
3 PMEW to Claude A. Barnett, 17 August 1932, Reel 1, #23, Part III, Subject Files on Black Americans, Series I: Race Relations, Barnett Papers.
4 Claude Barnett to "Dear Dean," 31 August 1932, Reel 1, #24, Part III, Series I, Barnett Papers.
5 "Pacific Topics," 22 April 1933, U.S. District Court, Eastern District of Illinois, Record Group 21, Criminal Case Files, Case No. 15840, Box 1, Folder 4, National Archives and Records Administration, Chicago. See also Gerald Horne, *Powell v.*

Alabama: The Scottsboro Boys and American Justice (New York: Franklin Watts, 1997).

6 "Constitution and By-Laws" of PMEW, Box 1, Folder 4, PMEW File.

7 On the "one-drop rule," see Gerald Horne, *The Color of Fascism: Lawrence Dennis, Racial Passing, and the Rise of Right-Wing Extremism in the United States* (New York: New York University Press, 2006).

8 Statement by General Lee Butler, 15 September 1942, Box 1, Folder 4, PMEW File. On the pogrom in Butler's new hometown, see, e.g., Rudwick, *Race Riot at East St. Louis*.

9 Testimony of Henry Hall, grand jury, September 1942, Box 3, Folder 4, PMEW File.

10 Testimony of William Baker, circa 1943, Box 2, Folder 2, PMEW File.

11 Testimony of Lula Livingston, circa 1943, Box 2, Folder 2, PMEW File.

12 Testimony of Charles T. Nash, circa 1943, Box 3, Folder 2, PMEW File.

13 Testimony of Thomas Albert Watkins, circa 1943, Box 3, Folder 1, PMEW File. See also Grif Stockley, *Blood in Their Eyes: The Elaine Race Massacres of 1919* (Fayetteville: University of Arkansas Press, 2001). The authorities in the Razorback State were energetic in persecuting the small population of Japanese origin residing there. See, e.g., War Relocation Authority, "Weekly Press Review, Week Ending January 18, 1943," Box 3, McWilliams Collection: "Land ownership in Arkansas by Japanese—whether citizens or aliens—would be barred by Bill introduced in Arkansas legislature by State Senator D. Frank Williams." In the same collection, Box 9, see Clipping, Uncertain provenance, circa 27 February 1943: In neighboring Oklahoma, a U.S. congressman proposes that all of Japanese ancestry in the United States be subjected to "sterilizing," thus preventing future births in this community.

14 Krugler, *1919, The Year of Racial Violence*, 178, 180.

15 Testimony of Lula Livingston, September 1942, Box 3, Folder 1, PMEW File.

16 Testimony of Artie Mays, grand jury, September 1942, Box 3, Folder 1, PMEW File.

17 Release, ANP, August 1937, Reel 15, #456, Part I, Series A.

18 Testimony of Frank Mart, circa 1943, Box 3, Folder 3, PMEW File.

19 Testimony of E. M. Johnson, circa 1943, Box 2, Folder 2, PMEW File.

20 Testimony of E. M. Johnson, circa 1943, Box 3, Folder 4, PMEW File.

21 Testimony of Pink Brown, circa 1943, Box 2, Folder 2, PMEW File.

22 Testimony of Eugene Moore, circa 1943, Box 3, Folder 3, PMEW File.

23 Release, ANP, September 1934, Reel 9, #523, Part I, Series A.

24 See, e.g., "Sikeston among Towns Organized by Negro 'Benevolent' Order," *Sikeston (MO) Standard*, 14 September 1934, 1. See also Kenneth Barnes, "Inspiration from the East: Black Arkansans Look to Japan," *Arkansas Historical Quarterly* 69, no. 3 (Autumn 2010): 201–19. See also Clipping, uncertain provenance, n.d., circa 1943, Box 8, McWilliams Collection: Tokyo radio reports lecture in Japan by

"Ken Nakazawa described as a former lecturer of the University of Southern California"; accompanying his remarks were "40 pictures . . . 'unmasking lynchings and many atrocities perpetrated by bloodthirsty Yankee mobs.'" His "stepson is in the U.S. Navy."

25 Newsletter, n.d., *Pacific*, vol. 6, no. 9, Box 1, Folder 4, PMEW File.

26 Postcard from David D. Erwin, 28 July 1935, Box 1, Folder 5, PMEW File.

27 Note from David D. Erwin, 26 November 1935, Box 1, Folder 5, PMEW File.

28 Report, n.d., circa 1935, Box 1, Folder 4, PMEW File.

29 Report, 11 September 1938, Box 1, Folder 5, PMEW File.

30 General Lee Butler to Reverend F. R. Baker, 13 September 1939, Box 1, Folder 5, PMEW File.

31 Testimony of General Lee Butler, circa 1943, Box 2, Folder 4, PMEW File.

32 U.S. v. PMEW, transcript, circa 1943, Box 2, Folder 1, PMEW File.

33 Testimony of Mimo De Guzman, September 1942, Box 3, Folder 5, PMEW File.

34 Testimony of William M. Officer, circa 1943, Box 3, Folder 2, PMEW File.

35 Testimony of George Floore, grand jury, September 1942, Box 3, Folder 2, PMEW File.

36 Release, ANP, April 1939, Reel 18, #743, Part I, Series A, Barnett Papers. See also Michael Fitzgerald, "'We Have Found a Moses': Theodore Bilbo, Black Nationalism and the Greater Liberia Bill of 1939," *Journal of Southern History* 63, no. 2 (May 1997): 293–320.

37 Material on Mittie Gordon, 1931, Box 25, Earnest Sevier Cox Papers, Duke University, Durham, NC.

38 Release, ANP, August 1939, Reel 19, #299, Part I, Series A: EWF just completed a five-day convention in New York City with delegates arriving from Africa, South America, the Caribbean, and the United States. "Negroes only" were present.

39 "Brief History of the Petition of the Peace Movement of Ethiopia to President Roosevelt," circa 1938, Box 1090, Bilbo Papers.

40 Release, ANP, July 1938, Reel 17, #743, Part I, Series A.

41 Release, ANP, August 1941, Reel 22, #1047, Part I, Series A.

42 Claude Barnett to A. J. Siggins, 8 July 1939, Box 200, Folder 4, Barnett Papers.

43 Release, ANP, March 1937, Reel 14, #552, Part I, Series A.

44 Release, ANP, September 1937, Reel 15, #600, Part I, Series A.

45 Malaku E. Bayen to Claude Barnett, 31 March 1935, Box 170, Folder 9, Barnett Papers.

46 Malaku E. Bayen to Claude Barnett, 30 January 1935, Box 170, Folder 9, Barnett Papers.

47 Claude Barnett to E. G. Roberts, Department of Mechanical Industries, Tuskegee, 17 July 1935, Box 170, Folder 9, Barnett Papers.

48 Laurie F. Leach, *Langston Hughes: A Biography* (Westport: Greenwood, 2004), 82–83; Arnold Rampersad, *The Life of Langston Hughes*, vol. 2, *1941–1967, I Dream a World* (New York: Oxford University Press, 1988), 50.

49 Release, ANP, October 1937, Reel 15, #818, Part I, Series A. See also Gerald Horne, *Paul Robeson: The Artist as Revolutionary* (London: Pluto, 2016).

50 W. E. B. Du Bois, "As the Crow Flies," *Crisis* 39, no. 4 (April 1932): 116. Cf. *New York Amsterdam News*, 21 October 1931. See also W. E. B. Du Bois, "No Chance," *Pittsburgh Courier*, 29 February 1936, A2: "The thing that must impress us as colored people is that the chances for economic reform [in China] under Japanese imperialism are infinitely greater than any chances which colored people would have under the most advanced white leaders of Western reform, except in Russia."

51 Robert Fikes Jr., "Japan," in *W. E. B. Du Bois: An Encyclopedia*, ed. Gerald Horne and Mary Young (Westport: Greenwood, 2001), 111–13, 112.

52 Patrick S. Washburn, *A Question of Sedition: The Federal Government's Investigation of the Black Press during World War II* (New York: Oxford University Press, 1986), 261.

53 Claude A. Barnett to Horino Uchi, 12 February 1934, Reel 6, #720, Part III, Subject Files on Black Americans, Series I: Race Relations, Barnett Papers.

54 Release, ANP, October 1938, Reel 17, #903, Part I, Series A.

55 Release, ANP, August 1932, Reel 6, #49, Part I, Series A.

56 Releases, ANP, October 1934, Reel 9, #634 and #693, Part I, Series A.

57 Release, ANP, October 1932, Reel 6, #403, Part I, Series A.

58 *Kansas City Plaindealer*, 6 September 1935.

59 Release, ANP, August 1935, Reel 11, #292, Part I, Series A.

60 Release, ANP, August 1932, Reel 6, #120, Part I, Series A.

61 Release, ANP, October 1938, Reel 17, #976, Part I, Series A.

62 LaShawn Harris, *Sex Workers, Psychics, and Numbers Runners: Black Women in New York City's Underground Economy* (Urbana: University of Illinois Press, 2016), 98–99.

63 See, e.g., Heike Raphael-Hernandez and Shannon Steen, eds., *AfroAsian Encounters: Culture, History, Politics* (New York: New York University Press, 2006).

64 Release, ANP, August 1932, Reel 6, #122, Part I, Series A.

65 Release, ANP, March 1934, Reel 6, #607, Part I, Series A.

66 Release, ANP, April 1937, Reel 14, #608, Part I, Series A.

67 Release, ANP, April 1937, Reel 14, #706, Part I, Series A.

68 Release, ANP, May 1935, Reel 10, #863, Part I, Series A.

69 Release, ANP, May 1937, Reel 14, #937, Part I, Series A.

70 Release, ANP, October 1937, Reel 15, #766, Part I, Series A.

71 Release, ANP, November 1937, Reel 15, #909, Part I, Series A.

72 Release, ANP, December 1937, Reel 16, #43, Part I, Series A.

73 Release, ANP, August 1938, Reel 17, #452, Part 1, Series A.

74 Raymond Gavins, *The Perils and Prospects of Southern Black Leadership: Gordon Blaine Hancock, 1884–1970* (Durham: Duke University Press, 1993).

75 Release, ANP, October 1938, Reel 17, #920, Part I, Series A.

76 Release, ANP, November 1938, Reel 17, #1126, Part I, Series A.

77 Release, ANP, May 1939, Reel 18, #1053, Part I, Series A.

78 Release, ANP, March 1935, Reel 10, #340, Part I, Series A.

79 Release, ANP, November 1930, Reel 3, #499, Part I, Press Releases.

80 Release, ANP, May 1935, Reel 10, #755, Part I, Series A.

81 Release, ANP, November 1928, Reel 1, #139, Part I, Press Releases.

82 "'Hands off China' Contingent Makes an Appeal to Negroes," *Philadelphia Tribune*, 16 June 1927, 1.

83 Clipping, 12 August 1925, Box II, L249, NAACP Papers: "Racial prejudice and oppression that arise therefrom are doomed; the Chinese with their millions will finally overthrow it just as the Negro will finally overthrow it in America. Of course, it is going to take time and patient toiling but God is against it and hence it must go."

84 Release, ANP, January 1938, Reel 16, #243, Part I, Series A.

85 Release, ANP, June 1935, Reel 10, #967, Part I, Series A.

86 Release, ANP, May 1938, Reel 16, #1127, Part I, Series A.

87 Mittie Maude Lena Gordon to Senator Bilbo, 5 August 1939, Box 1090, Bilbo Papers. Seemingly, relating to Gordon helped to convince some white supremacists to rethink their views of some Negroes. See Letter to Senator Bilbo, 4 July 1938, Box 1091: She was considered to be one of the "mix breeds," along with her spouse, who was viewed as "capable." This correspondent deemed her to be a sound dispenser of good advice when she was said to counsel that an attack on "'intellectuals' of the Negro race who abandon their race and seek white mates" would be a "popular approach," while deriding them as "race traitors." Will R. Rose of Greenville, Mississippi, also thought misery was a good reason for resettlement in that the "U.S.A. has a few Negroes too many for its workers under the condition of the Depression," and, assuredly, things could hardly be worse in Africa: see Letter, 22 August 1939, Box 1091. Strikingly, a number of white Chicagoans tended to agree with Gordon that Negroes must go. "If the Jews are a menace to the German race," said one from this community, "then surely one can see the need of this precaution," meaning resettlement. "At least 2/3 of the colored population here in the Chicago area are on relief" and their departure "would relieve congestion and filth" and "crime" too. It "would give our American [*sic*] youth a higher standard of living, a new Empire" in fact. Instead of compelling Paris and London to "pay war debts honorably," why not compel the two to provide land for Negroes in Africa? Of course, when Jim Crow advocates supported resettlement, it hardly prepared Negroes to be supportive of the U.S. war effort against Japan. See Della Johnson to Senator Bilbo, n.d., Box 1091, Bilbo Papers.

88 Mittie Maude Lena Gordon to Senator Bilbo, 10 August 1938, Box 1091, Bilbo Papers. On the other hand, Bilbo was told that "Firestone interests and the shipping companies," both with close ties to Liberia, were salivating at the prospect of bereft Negroes to pluck. The racist novelist Thomas Dixon inquired as to "what steps we have taken to support the [Bilbo] bill," while "Mary Caperton Bingham, wife of the owner of the *Louisville Courier-Journal* is fully in accord with our repatriation work." As for the poverty-stricken, "many signers of the Negro" petition in favor of resettlement were from Bilbo's own Mississippi: Letter to Senator Bilbo, 16 October 1938, Box 1091, Bilbo Papers.

89 Belle Steiner to Senator Bilbo, 18 September 1939, Box 1090, Bilbo Papers.
90 Kathryn Mitchell to Senator Bilbo, 26 June 1939, Box 1091, Bilbo Papers.
91 Release, ANP, February 1937, Reel 14, #122, Part I, Series A.

CHAPTER 4. WHITE SUPREMACY LOSES "FACE"

1 Release, ANP, December 1941, Reel 23, #496, Part I, Series A. Similarly, during the war Senator Bilbo was asked by a teacher in a class on "Race Relations" what "you feel the American people should do relative to the Negroes and Japanese," who again were conflated. M. L. Jordan to Senator Bilbo, 16 June 1944, Box 1084, Bilbo Papers.

2 Release, ANP, July 1943, Reel 26, #87, Part I, Series A. See also Eduardo O. Pagán, *Murder at the Sleepy Lagoon: Zoot Suits, Race and Riot in Wartime L.A.* (Chapel Hill: University of North Carolina Press, 2003).

3 U.S. v. Gordon et al., Brief and Argument for the Appellants, and Brief for the U.S., 9 July 1943. Quoted material in the following paragraphs is taken from the records of this case.

4 Release, ANP, February 1943, Reel 25, #366, Part I, Series A.

5 Release, ANP, February 1943, Reel 25, #411, Part I, Series A. As with African Americans, it seemed that the revulsion toward U.S.-style white supremacy drove many Filipinos into the arms of Tokyo. See, e.g., Theresa Kaminski, *Angels of the Underground: The American Women Who Resisted the Japanese in the Philippines in World War II* (New York: Oxford University Press, 2016).

6 Affidavit of Keith Brown, Assistant U.S. Attorney, Southern District of New York, U.S. v. Holness, C113–40, C113–264, National Archives and Records Administration, New York (via National Archives and Records Administration, Kansas City).

7 Exhibit 5, Transcript of Testimony of George Buchanan, Direct examination of [John] Sonnett, and Remarks of John Thornhill, circa 1943, C113–40 and C113–264, National Archives and Records Administration, New York (via National Archives and Records Administration, Kansas City).

8 Transcript of Testimony of James Henry Thornhill, circa 1942, C113–40 and C113–264, National Archives and Records Administration, New York (via National Archives and Records Administration, Kansas City).

9 Keith Brown affidavit, circa 1943, C113–40 and C113–264, National Archives and Records Administration, New York (via National Archives and Records Administration, Kansas City).

10 Release, ANP, October 1940, Reel 21, #607, Part I, Series A.

11 Kenneth Robert Janken, *Rayford W. Logan and the Dilemma of the African American Intellectual* (Amherst: University of Massachusetts Press, 1993).

12 Release, ANP, March 1941, Reel 22, #210, Part I, Series A.

13 "Intelligencer," May 1944, HQ, A2, Stout Field, Indianapolis, 250.608, 250.717–1, 12.43–5.44, Air Force Historical Research Agency.

14 Report, 15 December 1943, Roll 2, FBI File on Moorish Science Temple. See also Michael Gomez, *Black Crescent: The Experience and Legacy of African Muslims in*

the Americas (New York: Cambridge University Press, 2005); and Richard Brent Turner, *Islam in the African American Experience* (Bloomington: Indiana University Press, 1997).

15 Report, 30 October 1944, Roll 2, FBI File on Moorish Science Temple.
16 "Confidential" Report, 28 May 1943, Roll 2, FBI File on Moorish Science Temple.
17 Report, 6 April 1940, Roll 2, FBI File on Moorish Science Temple.
18 "Confidential" Report, 10 April 1942, Roll 2, FBI File on Moorish Science Temple.
19 Report, 28 May 1941, Roll 2, FBI File on Moorish Science Temple.
20 Colonel J. T. Bissell, General Staff, to "Lt. Colonel J. Edgar Hoover," 2 March 1943, Roll 2, FBI File on Moorish Science Temple.
21 Report, 26 May 1943, Roll 2, FBI File on Moorish Science Temple.
22 Okakura Tenshin, "The Awakening of the East," in Saaler and Szpilman, *Pan-Asianism: A Documentary History*, vol. 1, 98–99.
23 Colonel Elliot D. Cooks to Inspector General, 25 June 1942, 145.81.84–91, 1942–Apr. 1943, Air Force Historical Research Agency.
24 "Japanese Racial Agitation among American Negroes," n.d., circa 1942, 145.81.84–91, 1942–Apr. 1943, Air Force Historical Research Agency.
25 Ibid.
26 Ibid.
27 "Intelligencer," August 1944, 250.608–717.1, Dec. 1943–May 1944, Air Force Historical Research Agency.
28 "Harlem's Nazi Is Convicted . . . ," *New York Herald Tribune*, 10 March 1942, 38.
29 Clipping, 15 September 1942, Box IF18, National Urban League Papers, Library of Congress.
30 Release, ANP, December 1942, Reel 25, #128, Part I, Series A.
31 Release, ANP, June 1943, Reel 25, #1202, Part I, Series A.
32 Ibid.
33 Alan Hynd, *Betrayal from the East: The Inside Story of Japanese Spies in America* (New York: McBride, 1943), 146–47, 152. See also Alan Hynd, *Passport to Treason: The Inside Story of Spies in America* (New York: McBride, 1943).
34 "Final Report: Japanese Evacuation from the West Coast, 1942," Headquarters Defense Command and Fourth Army, Office of the Commanding General, Presidio of San Francisco, CA, "Exhibit D," Box 125, Herbert Hill Papers.
35 Statement by Martin Dies, 20 September 1941, Reel 4, #1049, Louis Nichols Official and Confidential File and Clyde Tolson Personal Files.
36 Harry Woodring, Secretary of War, and Claude Swanson, Secretary of the Navy, to President Roosevelt, 22 October 1936, Box 167, Harold Ickes Papers, Library of Congress.
37 Judge Advocate General to Secretary of Navy, 18 September 1936, "secret," Box 125, Herbert Hill Papers.
38 Jack Jones to Helen Gandy of Department of Justice, 10 October 1943, Reel 15, #80, J. Edgar Hoover Official and Confidential File, Library of Congress, Washington, D.C.

39 Toru Kiuchi et al., eds., *The Critical Response in Japan to African American Writers* (New York: Peter Lang, 2003), x-xi, x.
40 Release, ANP, January 1942, Reel 23, #639, Part I, Series A.
41 Release, ANP, February 1942, Reel 23, #882, Part I, Series A.
42 Release, ANP, March 1942, Reel 23, #1034, Part I, Series A.
43 Release, ANP, March 1945, Reel 30, #549, Part I, Series A.
44 Release, ANP, March 1942, Reel 23, #1062, Part I, Series A.
45 Release, ANP, November 1943, Reel 27, #109: "Trace Jap ambition to League failure to recognize equality."
46 Release, ANP, March 1942, Reel 23, #1042.
47 Release, ANP, November 1942, Reel 24, #1103.
48 "Halsey 'Yellow Monkey' Interview Is Protested," *Arkansas State Press*, 28 January 1944, 1.
49 Release, ANP, February 1942, Reel 23, #836, Part I, Series A.
50 Release, ANP, September 1943, Reel 24, #822.
51 Release, ANP, January 1943, Reel 25, #221.
52 Gerald Horne, *Fighting in Paradise: Labor Unions, Racism and Communists in the Making of Modern Hawaii* (Honolulu: University of Hawaii Press, 2012).
53 Release, ANP, November 1943, Reel 27, #126.
54 E. H. Pitts to Senator Bilbo, 16 June 1945, Box 1084, Bilbo Papers.
55 Senator Bilbo to E. H. Pitts, 25 June 1948, Box 1084, Bilbo Papers.
56 Clipping, circa 1943, Box 1028, Bilbo Papers.
57 Joseph Edgar to Sporting Editor, 13 March 1940, Box 1073, Bilbo Papers.
58 Senator Bilbo to J. L. Pierce, Secretary of the Brotherhood of Road Trainmen, McComb, MS, 23 June 1943, Box 1067, Bilbo Papers.
59 Senator Bilbo to E. A. Bates, 26 June 1942, Box 1090, Bilbo Papers.
60 Mary Polk to Senator Bilbo, 12 January 1943, Box 1090, Bilbo Papers.
61 Senator Bilbo to Thomas Lane, 20 February 1942, Box 1091, Bilbo Papers.
62 Senator Bilbo to Louie Thomas, 1 February 1944, Box 1091, Bilbo Papers.
63 L. B. Norton, Arizona House of Representatives, to Senator Bilbo, 25 June 1943, Box 1091, Bilbo Papers.
64 *Cleveland (MS) Enterprise*, 24 June 1942, Box 1046, Bilbo Papers.
65 Homer Brett, *Blueprint for Victory* (New York: D. Appleton-Century, 1942), 1, 34, 74, 54, 84.
66 Thorne Lane to Senator Bilbo, 14 February 1942, Box 1091, Bilbo Papers.

CHAPTER 5. PRO-TOKYO NEGROES CONVICTED AND IMPRISONED

1 Frazier, *The East Is Black*. African American intellectuals and activists were far from alone in being seduced by Maoism; see, e.g., Richard Wolin, *The Wind from the East: French Intellectuals, the Cultural Revolution and the Legacy of the 1960s* (Princeton: Princeton University Press, 2010).
2 Gerald Horne, *Race Woman: The Lives of Shirley Graham Du Bois* (New York: New York University Press, 2001); Gerald Horne, *Blows against the Empire: U.S.*

Imperialism in Crisis (New York: International, 2008); Gerald Horne, *From the Barrel of a Gun: The United States and the War against Zimbabwe, 1965–1980* (Chapel Hill: University of North Carolina Press, 2001).

3 Release, ANP, September 1942, Reel 24, #958, Part I.

4 Horne, *Negro Comrades of the Crown.*

5 Release, ANP, 30 December 1942, Reel 25, #158, Part I, Series A.

6 Vernon Williams to NAACP, 17 December 1942, Box II, B12, NAACP Papers.

7 Release, ANP, September 1942, Reel 24, #904.

8 U.S. v. Jordan et al., 1942–1943, U.S. District Court for the Southern District of New York, Record Group 21, Criminal Dockets, 8–27/1942–2/1/1943, HMFY 2013, Box 113, National Archives and Records Administration, New York.

9 Application for Writ of Habeas Corpus of Lester Holness, circa 1942, U.S. District Court, Southern District of New York, C113-40 and C113-364, National Archives and Records Administration, New York (via National Archives and Records Administration, Kansas City).

10 U.S. v. Jordan et al.

11 Release, ANP, January 1943, Reel 25, #197, Part I, Series A.

12 *People's Voice*, 28 February 1942, Roll 3, FBI File on Moorish Science Temple.

13 James Henry Thornhill, Petitioner v. C. J. Shuttlesworth, Defendant, Application for Writ of Habeas Corpus, C: V 4356, U.S. Circuit Court of Appeals for Eastern District of Michigan, Detroit, National Archives and Records Administration, Chicago.

14 Ibid.; U.S. v. Jordan et al., Box 113.

15 "Harlem Orator Sentenced for Praising Hitler," *New York Herald Tribune*, 5 August 1942, 6.

16 J. A. Ruggles, FBI Agent, Savannah, to New York City, 11 February 1943; attached is Clipping, 25 February 1943, Roll 3, FBI File on Moorish Science Temple.

17 "F.B.I. Arrests 7 Cult Members as Foes of Draft," *New York Herald Tribune*, 14 January 1943, 7.

18 Release, ANP, February 1943, Reel 25, #347.

19 Testimony of Daisy Herron, circa 1943, Box 2, Folder 3, PMEW File: "Stretch forth your left arm straight forward, four fingers close together and straight up with the thumb of the hand wide open, place the right hand in like manner but draw it close to your right shoulder; place your left hand across your right elbow in the bend of the arm and bend it twice."

20 Release, ANP, 11 March 1942, Reel 23, #1031, Part I, Series A.

21 Scribbled remarks of Pickens, 1942, Reel 25, #181, Part I, Series A.

22 Testimony of Trammie Polk, circa 1942, Box 2, Folder 2, PMEW File.

23 Release, ANP, May 1943, Reel 25, #1018.

24 Release, ANP, March 1942, Reel 23, #1081, Part I, Series A.

25 Release, ANP, October 1942, Reel 24, #991, Part I, Series A.

26 Release, ANP, April 1944, Reel 1, #673, Part III, Series C, Barnett Papers.

27 Ibid.

28 Earl Brown and George P. Leighton, "The Negro and the War," Public Affairs Pamphlet no. 71, 1942, Chicago History Museum. See also Dominic J. Capeci, *The Lynching of Cleo Wright* (Lexington: University Press of Kentucky, 1998).

29 "Fifth Column Alarms Negro Leaders," *St. Louis Post-Dispatch*, 8 March 1942, 3A.

30 Release, ANP, March 1942, Reel 23, #1081, Part I, Series A.

31 Release, ANP, September 1942, Reel 24, #896.

32 Release, ANP, October 1942, Reel 24, #947, citing *Chicago Sun-Times*.

33 Release, ANP, October 1942, Reel 24, #991.

34 U.S. v. Gordon et al., 23 October 1942, U.S. District Court, Northern District of Illinois, Eastern Division of Chicago, Record Group 21, 33645, Box 1152, National Archives and Records Administration, Chicago.

35 Affidavit of Mittie Maude Lena Gordon, 25 February 1943, for leave to appeal in forma pauperis, Record Group 21, Box 1153, National Archives and Records Administration, Chicago.

36 U.S. v. Gordon et al., October Term 1942, 33646, Box 1152, National Archives and Records Administration, Chicago.

37 Affidavit of Mittie Maude Lena Gordon, 25 February 1943.

38 Seon Jones to Senator Bilbo, n.d., Box 1073, Bilbo Papers.

39 Informant to J. Edgar Hoover, 18 August 1942, Roll 3, FBI File on Moorish Science Temple.

40 Karl Evanzz, *The Messenger: The Rise and Fall of Elijah Muhammad* (New York: Pantheon, 1999), 106, 135, 145.

41 U.S. v. Linn Karriem, October Term 1942, 33648, Box 1152, Record Group 21, National Archives and Records Administration, Chicago.

42 Travis, *An Autobiography of Black Chicago*, 94.

43 *Baltimore Afro-American*, 20 February 1941. See also Washburn, *A Question of Sedition*, 63; and Lee Finkle, *Forum for Protest: The Black Press during World War II* (Rutherford: Fairleigh Dickinson University Press, 1975).

44 U.S. v. Charles Newby, October Term 1942, 33650, Box 1152, National Archives and Records Administration, Chicago.

45 Report, 27 February 1935, Box 942, Record Group 21, National Archives and Records Administration, Chicago.

46 U.S. v. Stokley Delmar Hart, October Term 1942, 33651, Box 1152, National Archives and Records Administration, Chicago.

47 Remarks, 10 August 1942, U.S. v. Stokley Delmar Hart, 33651. In the same file, see Hart's remarks of 11 August 1942: Speaking at Washington Park at a meeting of the "Brotherhood of Liberty for Black Men of America" before a "large number of persons," he asserted that the "American Government is headed for a fall and that he [Hart] would do all in his power to help crush it"; reportedly, "he glories in Hitler."

48 See, e.g., Horne, *Black Revolutionary*; and Horne, *Black Liberation/Red Scare*.

49 U.S. v. Stokley Hart, October Term 1942, 33652, Box 1152: Robb also speaking at the Brotherhood of Liberty for the Black Man meeting at Washington Park was

cited as saying, "The Negroes had better learn the color of the Japanese flag if they wanted to go on living for the next three or four years." It was "necessary for the Negro to eat the right food, drill, exercise and learn how to handle a gun" in order to survive. "There was not a single cross on a black man's grave in France because he had been there himself after the last war." Robb also wrote for the Associated Negro Press. See, e.g., article on Chicago Fair, August 1933, Reel 7, #817, Part I, Series A.

50 ". . . Jap Directed Spy Ring," *Chicago Herald American*, 23 September 1942, 7.

51 U.S. v. Frederick Robb, 33652, Affidavit of Edith Sampson of 310 East 38th Street: "Social Worker" owns in "fee simple" lot at above address with rents and income at $1,890 annually, worth $16,000, bought in 1939 from "Louise F. Lomax." She is worth at least $30,000. On Sampson, see, e.g., Carol Anderson, *Bourgeois Radicals: The NAACP and the Struggle for Colonial Liberation, 1941–1960* (New York: Cambridge University Press, 2014).

52 Horne, *Black and Red*.

53 Release, ANP, April 1943, Reel 25, #789, Part I, Series A.

54 Bench Opinion of Judge William R. Holly, U.S. v. Gordon et al., 15 February 1943, U.S. Circuit Court of Appeals, Seventh Circuit, Brief and Argument for the Appellants, #8256, National Archives and Records Administration, Chicago.

55 "Jap Leader Branded 'Most Disloyal Citizen' Gets Three Years," *Wichita Negro Star*, 7 May 1943, 1.

56 Report, 28 January 1942, Roll 3, FBI File on Moorish Science Temple.

57 Report, 26 March 1942, Roll 3, FBI File on Moorish Science Temple.

58 William Cathey to Senator Bilbo, 19 June 1943, Box 1084, Bilbo Papers.

59 Report, 15 December 1942, Roll 3, FBI File on Moorish Science Temple.

60 Charles W. Wade to Senator Bilbo, 4 June 1943, Box 1084, Bilbo Papers. Subsequently, the Mississippian Carroll Case argued that a "mass killing of black soldiers" had taken place on a "nearby Army base" in Centerville precisely in 1943. "Over a thousand black soldiers from the 364th Infantry were slaughtered. The perpetrators were not local white racists but the United States Army itself." According to Case, "My research revealed a collage of racial violence involving black troops during World War II. There were hundreds of disturbances at military bases across the country," all of which "threatened the war effort" while "Military Intelligence" suspected "outside agitators"—that is, the Japanese. His claims were disparaged, however: see, e.g., Roberto Suro and Michael A. Fletcher, "Mississippi Massacre, or Myth?," *Washington Post*, 23 December 1999. See Carroll Case, *The Slaughter: An American Atrocity*, 1998, University of Southern Mississippi, Hattiesburg.

61 Gerald Horne, *Confronting Black Jacobins: The U.S., the Haitian Revolution, and the Origins of the Dominican Republic* (New York: Monthly Review Press, 2015).

62 Elwood B. Chapman, Chestnut Street Association, Philadelphia, to Theodore Spaulding, 6 October 1944, Box II, 325, NAACP Papers.

63 U.S. v. PMEW, 27 January 1943, Box 1, Folder 1, PMEW File.

64 U.S. v. PMEW, opinion by Judge Wham, Box 1, Folder 2, PMEW File.

65 Krugler, *1919, The Year of Racial Violence*, 305–6.

66 Motion on Exhibits, 1 March 1944, Box 1, Folder 3, PMEW File.

67 Photographs, n.d., Box 1, Folder 5, PMEW File.

68 Testimony of Harrison Fair, circa 1943, Box 2, Folder 2, PMEW File.

69 Brochures, circa 1942, Box 1, Folder 8, PMEW File.

70 Testimony of K. D. Branch, circa 1942, Box 2, Folder 1, PMEW File.

71 Testimony of K. D. Branch, grand jury, September 1942, Box 3, Folder 2, PMEW File.

72 Testimony of Beverly R. Waddell and David O'Brien, circa 1942, Box 2, Folder 1, PMEW File.

73 Testimony of Henry Bishop, circa 1942, Box 2, Folder 1, PMEW File.

74 Testimony of Edgar Sherrod, circa 1942, Box 2, Folder 2, PMEW File.

75 Testimony of Frank P. Townsend, circa 1943, Box 2, Folder 1, PMEW File.

76 Testimony of L. B. Huff, circa 1943, Box 2, Folder 2.

77 Testimony of Sidney Winston, circa 1943, Box 2, Folder 2.

78 Testimony of Sidney Winston, grand jury, September 1942, Box 3, Folder 2, PMEW File.

79 Statement at grand jury, September 1942, Box 3, Folder 5.

CHAPTER 6. JAPANESE AMERICANS INTERNED, U.S. NEGROES NEXT?

1 "Defendant Heard at Trial of 2 on Sedition Charges," *St. Louis Post-Dispatch*, 14 May 1943, 3A.

2 Grand jury transcript, 22 September 1942, Box 3, Folder 1, PMEW File.

3 Testimony of Finis Williams, grand jury, September 1942, Box 3, Folder 1, PMEW File.

4 Testimony of Finis Williams, circa 1943, Box 2, Folder 3, PMEW File.

5 Testimony of General Lee Butler, circa 1943, Box 2, Folder 4, PMEW File.

6 Testimony of David Erwin, circa 1943, Box 2, Folder 4, PMEW File.

7 Release, ANP, April 1931, Reel 4, #28, Part I, Series A. The U.S. authorities thought they had reason to believe that at the time of the bombing of Pearl Harbor, "Fifth Columnists and saboteurs" were "planted at strategic points along the Amazon" in Brazil ready to pounce. Like the United States, Brazil too contained a sizeable population of Japanese origin and the federal prosecutors may have thought that these East St. Louisans' expressed desire to migrate to South America was in aid of this larger scheme. See War Relocation Authority, "Weekly Press Review, Week Ending November, 3, 1943," Box 3, McWilliams Collection.

8 Statements in grand jury, September 1942, Box 3, Folder 5, PMEW File.

9 Testimony of Wolcie Gray, grand jury, September 1942, Box 3, Folder 1, PMEW File.

10 Testimony of Thomas Albert Watkins, grand jury, September 1942, Box 3, Folder 1, PMEW File.

11 Testimony of Pauline Verser, grand jury, September 1942, Box 3, Folder 4, PMEW File.

12 Statement made by prosecutor in context of testimony by Bessie Fair, grand jury, September 1942, Box 3, Folder 4, PMEW File.

13 Testimony of Forest Stancel, grand jury, September 1942, Box 3, Folder 4, PMEW File.

14 Testimony of Beatrice Branch, grand jury, September 1942, Box 3, Folder 4, PMEW File.

15 Testimony of John Bedford, grand jury, September 1942, Box 3, Folder 2, PMEW File.

16 Testimony of Howard R. Bayne, grand jury, September 1942, Box 3, Folder 2, PMEW File. Interestingly, Luther Gilmer, a steelworker in East St. Louis who migrated from Laurel, Mississippi, and joined the PMEW in 1933, said that the password was "Chicana."

17 Testimony of Harrison Fair, grand jury, September 1942, Box 3, Folder 2, PMEW File.

18 Testimony of Roscoe Standifer, grand jury, September 1942, Box 3, Folder 3, PMEW File.

19 Testimony of Cuver Vernon Young, grand jury, September 1942, Box 3, Folder 3, PMEW File.

20 Tony to "Mother and Dad," 17 September 1942, Box II, B294, NAACP Papers.

21 Release, ANP, November 1944, Reel 29, #1052, Part I, Series A.

22 Release, ANP, January 1945, Reel 30, #251.

23 Release, ANP, February 1942, Reel 23, #947, Part I, Series A.

24 Release, ANP, January 1942, Reel 23, #750, Part I, Series A.

25 Release, ANP, February 1942, Reel 23, #791.

26 Release, ANP, January 1942, Reel 23, #841, Part I, Series A.

27 "South Africa Yields a Bit as Natives Riot: Smuts Says He Will Arm Africans Rather Than Permit Japs to Conquer," *Wichita Negro Star*, 22 January 1943, 1.

28 Office of Censorship guidelines, September 1942, Reel 24, #796.

29 Gunnar Myrdal, *An American Dilemma: The Negro Problem and Modern Democracy* (New York: Harper and Row, 1969), 911–12.

30 Hayward Farrar, *The Baltimore Afro-American, 1892–1950* (Westport: Greenwood, 1998), xi, xii, 7, 16, 17.

31 P. L. Prattis, "The Horizon: What Shall We Do When the Japanese American Knocks at the Door?," *Pittsburgh Courier*, 12 August 1944.

32 Wallace Lee, "Should Negroes Discriminate against Japanese?," *Negro Digest* 2, no. 11 (September 1944): 66.

33 Release, ANP, January 1942, Reel 23, #726, Part I, Series A.

34 Release, ANP, February 1942, Reel 23, #862.

35 Release, ANP, December 1944, Reel 29, #1063.

36 Release, ANP, January 1945, Reel 30, #78, Part I, Series A.

37 Release, ANP, January 1945, Reel 30, #146, Part I, Series A.

38 C. L. Dellums to Walter White, 7 July 1942, Box II, A325, NAACP Papers. At the same site, see the files on Korematsu v. U.S., and Ex Parte Endo, Box 116, Wiley

Rutledge Papers, Library of Congress, Washington, D.C.; and in the same collection, Hirabayashi v. U.S., Box 93.

39 Walter White to Attorney General Biddle, 10 July 1942, Box II, A325, NAACP Papers. NAACP leader Roy Wilkins caught the attention of those in charge of the internment when he distinguished what he saw as the slow, methodical rounding up of German spies and the wholesale evacuation of Japanese and Japanese Americans. "Some of the good white people," he was said to have remarked, "say this was not a race war, but their actions deny it." See War Relocation Authority, "Weekly Press Review, Week Ending July 25, 1943," Box 3, McWilliams Collection.

40 Release, ANP, January 1945, Reel 30, #252, Part I, Series A.

41 "Confidential" Memorandum from Headquarters, Western Defense Command, to Commanding General, 3 May 1943, Box 125, Herbert Hill Papers.

42 Ringle to Chief of Naval Operations, 26 January 1942, Box 125, Herbert Hill Papers.

43 George Schuyler, "The World Today," *Pittsburgh Courier*, 29 May 1943, 1; and George Schuyler, "Views and Reviews," *Pittsburgh Courier*, 29 May 1943, 13.

44 See, e.g., Paula Giddings, *Ida: A Sword among Lions; Ida B. Wells and the Campaign against Lynching* (New York: Amistad, 2009).

45 Officers' Reports and Proceedings of the 43rd Annual Convention of the California State Federation of Labor, Long Beach, Resolution No. 64, 21–25 September 1942, Box 167, Herbert Hill Papers.

46 Resolution of Moving Picture Projectionists, 21–25 September 1942, Box 167, Herbert Hill Papers.

47 "Negro Labor Leader Fights Bias[ed] Union Demands to Discharge American-Japanese Workers," *Wichita Negro Star*, 11 August 1944, 1.

48 Amina Hassan, *Loren Miller: Civil Rights Attorney and Journalist* (Norman: University of Oklahoma Press, 2015), 126–27.

49 Gerald Horne, *Fire This Time: The Watts Uprising and the 1960s* (Charlottesville: University Press of Virginia, 1995).

50 Release, ANP, April 1942, Reel 23, #1243, Part I, Series A.

51 Claude A. Barnett to Assemblyman Gus Hawkins, 18 May 1942, Reel 2, #369, Part III, Subject Files on Black Americans, Series A: Agriculture, Barnett Papers.

52 "Artists of West Coast Take War in Stride," *Wichita Negro Star*, 2 January 1942, 1.

53 "Twenty Colored Students per Day Register to Replace Jap Farmhands," *Wichita Negro Star*, 24 April 1942, 4.

54 Release, ANP, July 1944, Reel 28, #1081, Part I, Series A.

55 Release, ANP, July 1944, Reel 28, #1140.

56 Release, ANP, November 1943, Reel 27, #198, Part I, Series A.

57 Release, ANP, April 1942, Reel 23, #1193, Part I, Series A.

58 Release, ANP, April 1942, Reel 24, #16, Part I, Series A.

59 Entry for Charles Williams in *Who's Who in California*, Los Angeles, 1948, Box 7, Betty Gubert Papers, Vivian G. Harsh Research Collection of Afro-American History and Literature, Carter G. Woodson Regional Library, Chicago Public Library.

60 Release, ANP, April 1942, Reel 24, #44, Part I, Series A.

61 Release, ANP, October 1943, Reel 26, #1163, Part I, Series A.

62 Comment, *Bronze* 4, no. 11 (January–February 1945), Southern California Library for Social Studies and Research, Los Angeles.

63 Release, ANP, January 1945, Reel 30, #71, Part I, Series A.

64 John Larremore to Senator Bilbo, 5 October 1944, Box 1073, Bilbo Papers.

65 Charles Wills to Senator Bilbo, 24 November 1939, Box 1073, Bilbo Papers.

66 Release, ANP, August 1942, Reel 24, #743, Part I, Series A.

67 Memorandum for Assistant Chief of Staff, 8 May 1942, 145.81.84, 145.81–91, 1942–Apr. 1943, Air Force Historical Research Agency.

68 Memorandum for Chief of Staff, 14 April 1942, 145.81.84, 145.81–91, Air Force Historical Research Agency.

69 Major General George V. Strong to "Assistant Chief of Staff, G-3," 17 June 1942, 145.81.84, 145.81–91, Air Force Historical Research Agency.

70 Report by Major Bell Wiley, "The Training of Negro Troops, Study No. 36," 172.1–30–172.10701–6, vol. 1, 1946–1947, Air Force Historical Research Agency.

71 John Duff to Major General Walter Weaver, 10 June 1942, 168.7061, 13 July 1945, 26 Apr. 1941–10 June 1942, Gropman, A.L. Col. 42, Air Force Historical Research Agency.

72 Mayor Walter A. Scott to Senator Pat Harrison, 4 March 1941, 145.93–80, 145.93–92, Jan. 1936–Apr. 1936, June 1941–Sept. 1941, Air Force Historical Research Agency.

73 "History of the Second Air Force," 7 December 1941–31 December 1942, vol. 2, 432.01, 7 Dec. 1941–31 Dec. 1942, vol. 1, vol. 3, Air Force Historical Research Agency.

CHAPTER 7. "BROWN AMERICANS" FIGHT "BROWN JAPANESE" IN THE PACIFIC WAR?

1 Statement by Walter White, 9 April 1945, Box II, B12, NAACP Papers.

2 Release, ANP, October 1944, Reel 29, #713, Part I, Series A.

3 Truman Gibson to Claude A. Barnett, 14 November 1942, Reel 2, #1488, Part III, Subject Files on Black Americans, Series F: Military, Barnett Papers.

4 Remarks of L. D. Reddick in New York City, 22 April 1961, Reel 4, #525, Part III, Subject Files on Black Americans, Series I: Race Relations, Barnett Papers.

5 Report, Office of the Commandant, 30 October 1925, 168.7061–30, 168.7061.71, 13 July 1945, 26 Apr. 1941–10 June 1942, Air Force Historical Research Agency.

6 *Kansas City Plain Dealer*, 30 January 1942. Cf. *Manila Tribune*, 12 April 1942: "Baron Kinochi Okura, member of the House of Peers" in Tokyo, denies that "Japan is leading a racial war against the White races. . . . [and] emphasized that complete racial equality should be advocated."

7 "Louis Kayoes Abe Simon in 6th Round," *Manila Tribune*, 30 March 1942, 1.

8 "Vargas, Aquino Urge Full Collaboration," *Manila Tribune*, 23 January 1942, 1.

9 "Rizal as Impressed by Japanese Life, Culture," *Manila Tribune*, 11 February 1942, 3.

10 "Vicious Intolerance of Allies Regretted," *Manila Tribune*, 30 March 1942, 1. In a jujitsu maneuver, the Japanese occupation force in Manila allowed Hollywood's most offensively racist movies to be exhibited, perhaps as a reminder to Filipinos of the insensitivity of the previous occupier. See advertisement for *Birth of the Blues*, featuring Negro comic Eddie "Rochester" Anderson, *Manila Tribune*, 11 February 1942, 4. For more on the Copernican changes that occurred on the racial front, see, e.g., Horne, *Race War!* Of course, the major victims of Japanese aggression were China and Korea. Colonies of the North Atlantic powers, such as the Philippines, were more likely (at least initially) to be thankful to Tokyo for ousting their immediate colonial oppressors.

11 Release, ANP, March 1945, Reel 30, #549, Part I, Series A.

12 Lin Yutang to Walter White, 9 July 1942, Box II, A402, NAACP Papers. See also Walter White, *A Rising Wind* (Garden City: Doubleday, 1945).

13 Release, ANP, September 1945, Reel 31, #901, Part I, Series A.

14 George Watson, *Memorable Memoirs* (New York: Carlton, 1987), 60. On the fraught matter of how German Nazis were at times treated with more humanity and concern than African Americans, even in the United States, see, e.g., Monique Laney, *German Rocketeers in the Heart of Dixie: Making Sense of the Nazi Past during the Civil Rights Era* (New Haven: Yale University Press, 2015).

15 Remarks by Arthur Peterson, Sam Green, et al., in *African American Voices from Iwo Jima: Personal Accounts of the Battle*, ed. Clarence W. Willie (Jefferson, NC: McFarland, 2010), 3, 7, 86, 91, 107. See also Robert F. Jefferson, *Fighting for Hope: African American Troops of the 93rd Infantry Division in World War II and Postwar America* (Baltimore: Johns Hopkins University Press, 2008); and James Campbell, *The Color of War: How One Battle Broke Japan and Another Changed America* (New York: Crown, 2012). As late as July 1945 the Euro-American serviceman Robert Bennett "did hear Tokyo Rose again on our improvised radio. There is a pretty reliable rumor going around," he claimed without providing evidence, "that Tokyo Rose is none other than Amelia Earhart, the woman aviatrix supposedly 'lost at sea'—who knows?" Robert L. Bennett to "My Darlings," 28 July 1945, Robert L. Bennett Letters, University of Georgia, Athens.

16 Hilton P. Goss, "American Experience with Subversive Activities and Their Threat to Target Systems," March 1947, Historical Research Section, Air University, Maxwell Field, Alabama, K239.04–55A, K239.04–64, Sept. 1959–1964, Air Force Historical Research Agency.

17 John D. Silvera, *The Negro in World War II* (New York: Arno, 1969), n.p.

18 Enoch P. Waters, *American Diary: A Personal History of the Black Press* (Chicago: Path Press, 1987), 367, 372.

19 Noah Riseman, *Defending Whose Country? Indigenous Soldiers in the Pacific War* (Lincoln: University of Nebraska Press, 2012), 111.

20 Walter White to "Dear Folks," 23 March 1945, Box II, A611, NAACP Papers.

21 Grand jury transcript, September 1942, Box 3, Folder 4, Record Group 21, PMEW File.

22 Release, ANP, 15 July 1942, Reel 24, #958, Part I, Series A.

23 Release, ANP, October 1942, Reel 24, #1014, Part I, Series A.

24 Release, ANP, November 1943, Reel 25, #02, Part I, Series A.

25 Release, ANP, June 1943, Reel 25, #1160, Part I, Series A.

26 Release, ANP, January 1945, Reel 30, #106, Part I, Series A.

27 Release, ANP, August 1943, Reel 26, #607, Part I, Series A.

28 Thant Myint-U, *Where China Meets India: Burma and the New Crossroads of Asia* (New York: Farrar, Straus and Giroux, 2011), 62.

29 Leon Bryan to Mary Bryan, 12 June 1945, in "A Tour of Duty: Letters from Leon S. Bryan to Mary L. Bryan from the Pacific Theater of World War II, 1944–1946, Transcripts," 2002, University of South Carolina, Columbia.

30 Leon Bryan to Mary Bryan, n.d., in "A Tour of Duty."

31 Release, ANP, May 1945, Reel 30, #1116, Part I, Series A.

32 See, e.g., J. Todd Moye, *Freedom Flyers: The Tuskegee Airmen of World War II* (New York: Oxford University Press, 2010).

33 Aerospace Studies Institute, "Negroes in the AAF," circa 1946, K239.0441–446.9, 1910–1960, 1956, Air Force Historical Research Agency.

34 Release, ANP, January 1944, Reel 28, #580.

35 See Gerald Horne, *Storming the Heavens: African Americans and the Early Fight for the Right to Fly* (Baltimore: Black Classic Press, 2017).

36 Letter to Dr. L. A. Ransom, 9 October 1940, Box II, B194, NAACP Papers.

37 Carl Ransom to President Roosevelt, 28 November 1940, Box II, B194, NAACP Papers.

38 "History of U.S. Army Air Service, 1862–1920," Box 32, William Mitchell Papers.

39 "Japanese Aviation," n.d., Box 42, William Mitchell Papers.

40 Newspaper clipping, unclear provenance, 30 January 1920, Box 28, William Mitchell Papers, Library of Congress.

41 Major General H. H. Arnold, Chief of Air Corps, to General Brett, 16 December 1940, 220.740, 220.765–2, 1940–1945, vol. 2, vol. 3, Air Force Historical Research Agency.

42 Major Ralph F. Stearley to Commanding General, 8 May 1941, 220.740, 220.765–2, 1940–1945, 1942 vol. 2, vol. 3, Air Force Historical Research Agency.

43 Press Release, 14 February 1941, Box II, B194, NAACP Papers.

44 Edward Lawson to Lester Granger, 18 January 1941, Box IF11, National Urban League Papers.

45 Brigadier General G. C. Brant to Chief of Air Corps, 18 November 1940, 145.93–80, 145.93–92, Jan. 1936–Apr. 1936, June 1941–Sept. 1941, Air Force Historical Research Agency.

46 General G. C. Brant to Chief of Air Corps, 19 November 1940, 145.93–80 145.93–92 Jan. 1936–Apr. 1936, June 1941–Sept. 1941, Air Force Historical Research Agency.

47 Lieutenant Colonel Perry C. Ragan to President, Board of Officers, 18 March 1942, 220.765–2, 220.8635.1, 1943, vol. 4, vol. 2, Air Force Historical Research Agency.

48 Memorandum, "Outline of Plans for Colored Training," circa 15 January 1943, 220.765–2, 220.8635.1, 1943, vol. 4, vol. 2, Air Force Historical Research Agency.

49 Major General B. K. Yount to Chief, Training and Operations Division, 5 October 1940, 145.93–80, 145.93–92, Jan. 1936–Apr. 1936, June 1941–Sept. 1941, Air Force Historical Research Agency.

50 "Negroes in AAF," n.d., circa 1956, K239.0441–1, K239.046–9, 1910–1960, 1956, Air Force Historical Research Agency.

51 William Varner to Hons. John Bankhead and Lister Hill, 23 April 1941, 145.93–80, 145.93–92, Jan. 1936–Apr. 1936, June 1941–Sept. 1941, Air Force Historical Research Agency.

52 Petition to Hons. John Bankhead and Lister Hill, 21 April 1941, 145.93–80, 145.93–92, Jan. 1936–Apr. 1936, June 1941–Sept. 1941, Air Force Historical Research Agency.

53 Lieutenant Colonel William Maxwell to Commanding General, 7 April 1941, 145.93–80, 145.93–92, Jan. 1936–Apr. 1936, June 1941–Sept. 1941, Air Force Historical Research Agency.

54 Report by Dr. Lawrence Kubie, 28 September 1943, 141.281–20, 141–0281–37K, 1945, Air Force Historical Research Agency.

55 Oral History, Benjamin O. Davis, January 1973, K239.0512–914, c. 1, 1016304, Air Force Historical Research Agency.

56 Release, ANP, July 1944, Reel 28, #1108, Part I, Series A.

57 Release, ANP, July 1944, Reel 28, #973, Part I, Series A.

58 Release, ANP, July 1944, Reel 28, #1054, Part I, Series A. On the Republic of New Africa, see Robert Sherrill, *We Want Georgia, South Carolina, Mississippi and Alabama Right Now—We Also Want Four Hundred Billion Dollars Back Pay: These Are the Demands of the Republic of New Africa, a Growing Movement to Form a Black Nation within the United States* (Chicago: Esquire, 1968), University of North Carolina, Chapel Hill.

59 Release, ANP, July 1944, Reel 28, #1079, Series I, Part A.

60 Release, ANP, September 1944, Reel 29, #435, Part I, Series A.

61 Oral History, Lee Archer, 13 March 2001, K239.0512–2580, 01156065, Air Force Historical Research Agency.

62 Memorandum from Britain, unclear correspondent, received 21 June 1943, 527.755, 527.7771 A, Dec. 1944–May 1945, 6 July 1943–15 Dec. 1943, Air Force Historical Research Agency.

63 Major General Henry J. F. Miller to Commanding General, 13 July 1943, 519.758–519.77151, Aug. 1942–July 1945, 1943–1945, Air Force Historical Research Agency.

64 Rudolph Dunbar to Claude Barnett, 20 November 1944, Box 200, Folder 1, Barnett Papers, Chicago History Museum.

65 Rudolph Dunbar to Claude Barnett, 28 November 1940, Box 200, Folder 1, Barnett Papers, Chicago History Museum.

66 Rudolph Dunbar to Claude Barnett, 20 November 1945, Box 200, Folder 1, Barnett Papers, Chicago History Museum.

67 Rene McColl, British Press Service, to Claude Barnett, 29 December 1942, Box 201, Folder 4, Barnett Papers.

68 Release, ANP, October 1944, Reel 29, #572, Part I, Series A.

69 R. G. Hersey, Adjutant General's Office, War Department, Washington, D.C., to Commanding General, 14 February 1942, 519.758–519–77151, Aug. 1942–July 1945, 1943–1945, Air Force Historical Research Agency.

70 Cf. Richard Durham, "Negro Scientists Help to Split the Atom," *Chicago Defender*, 18 August 1945, 1: "Many Negro workers get jobs at Tenn. Atom Bomb Plant. . . . A number of Negroes held highly technical positions in the vast plant near Knoxville." In the same issue it was reported that "the highest ranking Japanese soldier captured in this war was taken prisoner . . . by Negro soldiers."

71 "Clergy Calls Atomic Bombing Both Blessing and Curse," *Washington Afro-American*, 18 August 1945, 1. See also Vincent J. Intondi, *African Americans against the Bomb: Nuclear Weapons, Colonialism and the Black Freedom Movement* (Stanford: Stanford University Press, 2014), 1.

72 Hughes, "Simple and the Atomic Bomb."

73 George Schuyler, "Views and Reviews," *Pittsburgh Courier*, 8 August 1945, 7.

74 Dower, *War without Mercy*, 9.

75 Robert L. Bennett to Dear Dad, 26 August 1945, Robert L. Bennett Letters.

76 Release, ANP, October 1949, Reel 41, #814, Part I, Series B.

77 Release, ANP, May 1946, Reel 32, #1214, Part I, Series B.

78 Release, ANP, June 1954, Reel 54, #884, Part I, Series B, Barnett Papers.

79 Claude A. Barnett to Harry V. Richardson, President, Gannon Theological Seminary, Atlanta, 10 August 1954, Reel 1, #90, Subject Files on Black Americans, Series I: Race Relations.

80 Release, ANP, 6 April 1955, Reel 56, #986, Part I, Series B.

81 Release, ANP, 5 December 1956, Reel 61, #599, Part I, Series B.

82 Horne, *The End of Empires*.

CHAPTER 8. AFTERMATH

1 William Yardley, "Rights Activist Who Befriended Malcolm X, Dies at 93," *New York Times*, 5 June 2014, B19; Diane Fujino, *Heartbeat of Struggle: The Revolutionary Life of Yuri Kochiyama* (Minneapolis: University of Minnesota Press, 2005).

2 Revilo Oliver, "The Black Muslims," 1963, Vertical File, University of Southern Mississippi, Hattiesburg; Horne, *Paul Robeson*.

3 Gerald Horne, *Communist Front? The Civil Rights Congress, 1946–1956* (London: Associated University Press, 1988).

4 Release, ANP, May 1957, Reel 62, #767, Part I, Press Releases.

5 Release, ANP, February 1958, Reel 64, #674, Part I, Press Releases.

6 Release, ANP, 21 September 1960, Reel 71, #676, Part I, Series C, Barnett Papers.

7 Release, ANP, August 1959, Reel 68, #397, Part I, Press Releases.

8 Release, ANP, 14 August 1963, Reel 80, #252, Part I, Series C. Interestingly, in New Zealand, bias against the Maoris gave rise to the Ratana Movement in the era of

World War I apparently. It was based on Christianity but was fervently pro-Tokyo. Horne, *Race War!*, 161–62.

9 Release, ANP, 25 November 1963, Reel 81, #66, Part I, Series C.

10 Quoted in Roger Baldwin, *Race Relations in International Affairs* (Washington, D.C.: Public Affairs, 1961), Box 168, Folder 1, Barnett Papers, Chicago History Museum.

11 Release, ANP, January 1953, Reel 51, #752, Part I, Series B.

12 Homer A. Jack, "Bandung: An On-the-Spot Description of the Asian-African Conference, Bandung, Indonesia, April 1955," University of South Carolina, Columbia. See also Brian Russell Roberts and Keith Foulcher, eds., *Indonesian Notebook: A Sourcebook on Richard Wright and the Bandung Conference* (Durham: Duke University Press, 2016); and Kweku Ampiah, *The Political and Moral Imperatives of the Bandung Conference of 1955: The Reactions of the U.S., U.K., and Japan* (Kent, U.K.: Global, 2007).

13 Kimberley L. Phillips, *War! What Is It Good For? Black Freedom Struggles and the U.S. Military from World War II to Iraq* (Chapel Hill: University of North Carolina Press, 2012); Lawrence Allen Eldridge, *Chronicles of a Two-Front War: Civil Rights and Vietnam in the African American Press* (Columbia: University of Missouri Press, 2011).

14 Claude Barnett to General Julius Holmes, 14 February 1955, Box 208, Folder 1, Barnett Papers.

15 Release, ANP, 24 July 1963, Reel 80, #88, Part I, Series C, Barnett Papers. The "victor's justice," as exemplified by the war crimes trials of Japanese leaders, also inevitably altered the sentiment in Tokyo toward African Americans. See, e.g., Yuma Totani, *Justice in Asia and the Pacific Region, 1945–1952: Allied War Crimes Prosecutions* (New York: Cambridge University Press, 2015).

16 Release, ANP, 14 August 1963, Reel 80, #301, Part I, Series C.

17 Senator Bilbo to F. L. Dusenbery of New Orleans, circa 1945, Box 1084, Bilbo Papers.

18 Senator Bilbo to Ensign L. D. Jameson, 18 September 1945, Box 1084, Bilbo Papers.

19 See, e.g., Stuart Wexler and Larry Hancock, *Killer King: The Multi Year Effort to Murder MLK* (Berkeley: Counterpoint, 2013); Clive Webb, *Rabble Rousers: The American Far Right in the Civil Rights Era* (Athens: University of Georgia Press, 2010). See his obituary, *New York Times*, 29 April 2005. See also Stuart Wexler and Larry Hancock, *The Awful Grace of God: Religious Terrorism, and the Unsolved Murder of Martin Luther King, Jr.* (Berkeley: Counterpoint, 2012).

20 J. B. Stoner to Senator Bilbo, 2 February 1944, Box 1084, Bilbo Papers.

21 Marquis Childs, "Washington Calling: West Coast Terror," *Washington Post*, 24 May 1945, 6. See also Newsletter of the U.S. Department of the Interior, War Relocation Authority, Southern California Area Release Number 77, 8 October 1945, Box 1, McWilliams Collection: "A new outbreak of threats, intimidations, prejudice, discrimination and violence has taken place in Northern California Communities against returning Americans of Japanese descent, . . . shootings,

incendiarism and vandalism. . . . These incidents may be the prelude to a program instigated by the residuary legatees of the late Adolph Hitler's followers in the United States." In the same collection, Box 2, see also "Community Analysis Report, No. 13, June 6, 1945. Prejudice in Hood River Valley": "lengthening list of shooting into evacuee homes and destruction of evacuee property. . . . pattern of violence and lawlessness." This was a continuation of the prewar pattern, as "white landowners in the area resented the better economic position and land buying activities of the Japanese." It does appear that fear of falling behind economically was a force driving Euro-American racism targeting Japanese and Japanese Americans. In Box 3 of this collection, see War Relocation Authority, "Weekly Press Review, Week Ending March 23, 1943": Congressman Henry Jackson of the state of Washington claimed that these two discrete Asian groups "controlled much of the hotel and restaurant business although always there was a white manager who would front for them. . . . They forced out their white competitors in the fruit and vegetable business. . . . There was a society within a society and a race within a race." See also in same collection, Box 6: William Swain, "Sneak Attack: On Americans—by Americans," April 1945: "In 1941, the year before Pearl Harbor, Japanese produce dealers in Los Angeles reported a gross business of about $30,000,000. In 1942, the year after Pearl Harbor, Los Angeles people paid about $50,000,000 for 10,000 carloads less of produce. The business in 1942 was wholly in the hands of Caucasian Americans because the Oriental Americans— citizen Japs and alien Japs together—had been [interned]."

22 J. A. Watkins to Senator Bilbo, 6 April 1945, Box 1090, Bilbo Papers.
23 Release, ANP, January 1948, Reel 36, #852, Part I, Press Releases.
24 Release, ANP, August 1959, Reel 68, #230, Part I, Series B.
25 Release, ANP, February 1952, Reel 47, #1139, Part I, Series B.
26 Charles Krause to Senator Bilbo, 3 June 1945, Box 1090, Bilbo Papers.
27 Senator Bilbo to J. N. Wiggo, 10 May 1944, Box 1067, Bilbo Papers.
28 Senator Bilbo to Grover Brewer, 13 December 1945, Box 1067, Bilbo Papers.
29 Luscious Casey to Senator Bilbo, 12 December 1945, Box 1090, Bilbo Papers.
30 Grover Brewer to Senator Bilbo, 5 December 1945, Box 1090, Bilbo Papers.
31 Release, ANP, November 1948, Reel 39, #196, Part I, Series B.
32 For a radical endorsement of the internment, see Michelle Malkin, *In Defense of Internment: The Case for "Racial Profiling" in World War II and the War on Terror* (Washington, D.C.: Regnery, 2004): African Americans should pay close attention to this endorsement. See also Scott Kurashige, *The Shifting Grounds of Race: Black and Japanese Americans in the Making of Multiethnic Los Angeles* (Princeton: Princeton University Press, 2008); and Valerie J. Matsumoto, *City Girls: The Nisei Social World in Los Angeles, 1920–1950* (New York: Oxford University Press, 2014).
33 Indictment, International Military Tribunal for the Far East, *Album: Trial of Major Japanese War Criminals . . . Tokyo, Japan, 1946–47*, University of Georgia, Athens.
34 Release, ANP, March 1946, Reel 32, #764, Part I, Press Releases.

35 Clipping, April 1946, Reel 2, #859, Part III, Subject Files on Black Americans, Barnett Papers.

36 Edwin C. Gregory to "Dear Senator," 4 August 1946, Box 1067, Bilbo Papers.

37 Release, ANP, February 1949, Reel 40, #18, Part I, Series B.

38 Robert L. Bennett to Dearest Family, 6 September 1946, Robert L. Bennett Letters.

39 Robert L. Bennett to Dearest Family, 17 September 1946, Robert L. Bennett Letters.

40 Release, ANP, October 1946, Reel 33, #1156, Part I, Press Releases, Barnett Papers.

41 Release, ANP, September 1946, Reel 33, #966, Part I, Press Releases.

42 Release, ANP, December 1946, Reel 34, Part I, Press Releases.

43 Clipping, circa 1946, Reel 3, #691, Part III, Subject Files on Black Americans, Series F: Military, Barnett Papers.

44 Release, ANP, July 1947, Reel 34, #88, Part 1, Press Releases.

45 Release, ANP, July 1947, Reel 35, #80, Part I, Press Releases.

46 Release, ANP, November 1947, Reel 36, #227, Part I, Press Releases.

47 Release, ANP, August 1948, Reel 38, #753, Part I, Series A.

48 Release, ANP, May 1948, Reel 37, #860, Part I, Press Releases.

49 Release, ANP, January 1946, Reel 32, #382, Part I, Press Releases.

50 Release, ANP, October 1949, Reel 41, #931, Part I, Series B.

51 Release, ANP, July 1950, Reel 43, #959, Part I, Series B.

52 Release, ANP, October 1950, Reel 44, #488, Part I, Series B.

53 Release, ANP, November 1950, Reel 44, #567, Part I, Series B.

54 Release, ANP, August 1950, Reel 43, #1105, Part I, Series B.

55 Release, ANP, February 1951, Reel 45, #306, Part I, Series B. For more on persecution of Negro soldiers in Korea, see Horne, *Communist Front?*

56 Release, ANP, January 1952, Reel 3, #354, Part III, Subject Files on Black Americans, Series C, Barnett Papers.

57 Alex Poinsett, associate editor of *JET*, to American Red Cross, 23 June 1953, Reel 5, #549, Part III, Subject Files on Black Americans, Series E: Medicine, Barnett Papers.

58 Release, ANP, August 1953, Reel 52, #411, Part I, Series B.

59 Charles S. Young, *Name, Rank and Serial Number: Exploiting Korean War POWs at Home and Abroad* (New York: Oxford University Press, 2014), 83.

60 Release, ANP, May 1956, Reel 60, #121, Part I, Series B.

61 Release, ANP, April 1951, Reel 45, #757, Part I, Series B.

62 Release, ANP, June 1951, Reel 45, #1136, Part I, Series B.

63 Release, ANP, April 1951, Reel 45, #757, Part I, Series B.

64 Release, ANP, February 1958, Reel 64, #701, Part I, Press Releases.

65 Release, ANP, March 1952, Part I, Series B.

66 Hugh H. Smythe and Mabel M. Smythe, "Report from Japan: Comments on the Race Question," *Crisis*, March 1952, 159–64, 160, 161, Box 73, Hugh H. Smythe and Mabel M. Smythe Papers, Library of Congress, Washington, D.C.

67 Release, ANP, June 1952, Reel 48, #964, Part I, Series B.

68 Release, ANP, October 1955, Reel 58, #374, Part I, Series B.

69 Hugh H. Smythe, "A Note on Racialism in Japan," *American Sociological Review*, December 1952, 823–24, Box 73, Hugh H. Smythe and Mabel M. Smythe Papers.

70 Release, ANP, July 1953, Reel 52, #157, Part I, Series B.

71 Release, ANP, June 1957, Reel 63, Part I, Series B.

72 Josephine Baker, Official International Delegate of Propaganda against Racism, League of International Cultural Associations, "Why I Fight Racism," Tokyo and Osaka, 1954, University of Georgia, Athens.

73 Release, ANP, January 1956, Reel 59, #109, Part I, Series B.

74 Release, ANP, March 1953, Reel 51, #55, Part I, Series B.

75 S. I. Hayakawa, "35th and State: Reflections on the History of Jazz," *Illinois Tech Engineer and Alumnus*, May 1945, Box 116, John Steiner Collection, University of Chicago.

76 Leonard Feather, "No Hari-Kari for Hayakawa," n.d., Box 8, Leonard Feather Papers, University of Idaho, Moscow. This tie between Japan and jazz merits further exploration. When Art Blakey, a famed drummer of African descent, toured Japan in 1962, he declared that this "was the first time I experienced real freedom. . . . We've played a lot of countries but never has the whole band been in tears when we left. My wife cried all the way to Hawaii." See article, 1962, Box 8, Leonard Feather Papers. The spouse and manager of the jazz giant Charles Mingus echoed this sentiment. "He has a huge following in Japan," said Sue Mingus; the famed bassist and composer "probably sells more records there than anywhere in the world." See Interview with Sue Mingus, in *Mingus Speaks*, ed. John Goodman (Berkeley: University of California Press, 2013), 178. The stubborn popularity of jazz in Japan to this very day is a lingering emblem of a past era of solidarity that united Japanese and African Americans. See also Morroe Berger et al., *Benny Carter: A Life in American Music*, vol. 1 (Lanham, MD: Scarecrow Press, 2002), 379–80: "The Japanese are among the world's most avid record collectors," notably of jazz,

> to such an extent that the Japanese have been blamed for inflating international prices by their high auction bids. . . . 1946 saw the first issue of *Swing Journal*, Japan's leading jazz periodical and, by the 1970s, the most impressive jazz magazine anywhere. . . . Pianist Hampton Hawes [African American] also a soldier was stationed in Japan in 1953–1954 and helped the young Toshiko Akiyoshi, later to become an internationally known pianist and leader of one of the top big bands of the 1970s.

77 Senator Eastland to Senator-elect S. I. Hayakawa, 15 November 1976, File 1, Sub-Series 18, Box 5, James Eastland Papers, University of Mississippi, Oxford.

78 Report by Senator Hayakawa, 1 August 1978, File 1, Sub-Series 18, Box 5, James Eastland Papers.

79 "Linguist, Former Sen. S. I. Hayakawa," *Chicago Tribune*, 28 February 1992, Section 2, 9. This unseemly attitude was something of a turnabout for Hayakawa, who as a regular columnist for the *Chicago Defender*—which catered to Negro

readers—expressed grave reservations about the internment as the war unfolded. See, e.g., S. I. Hayakawa, "Second Thoughts: Negroes and Japanese," *Chicago Defender*, 16 December 1944, 13. He recounted a vignette about how "none of their white fellow-passengers" traveling by train in 1942 alongside Japanese Americans headed to Chicago "knew about this relocation," while "there was hardly a single Negro porter or dining-car waiter who did not know about this enormous mass expulsion. . . . Many Japanese Americans, expelled from their homes, found their first friends in the outside world among Negroes."

80 Release, ANP, November 1957, Reel 64, #125, Part I, Press Releases.

81 Release, ANP, September 1958, Reel 66, #300, Part I, Series B.

82 Release, ANP, Reel 80, #387, Part I, Series C. See also Terese Svoboda, *Black Glasses Like Clark Kent: A GI's Secret from Postwar Japan* (St. Paul, MN: Graywolf, 2008), 12.

83 Release, ANP, October 1957, Reel 63, #950, Part I, Press Releases.

84 Release, ANP, February 1952, Reel 47, #1104, Part I, Series B. See also Almena Lomax, "4 Scions of State's Pioneer Japanese," *San Francisco Chronicle*, 23 August 1970, Section B, 6: "Four Sacramento Negroes and their offspring have been found to be the only known descendants in Northern California, perhaps the country, of the first Japanese settlers in America." The article noted a "tradition of inter-mingling between Negroes and Japanese which has been closer for Negro relations than with any other of America's minorities except the Indian." During the Jim Crow era, those of Japanese ancestry "even joined Negroes in such civil rights actions as the suits to outlaw restrictive covenants in housing. Negroes could always stay in Japanese hotels and eat in Japanese cafes when otherwise barred."

85 Release, ANP, March 1960, Reel 69, #1076, Part I, Press Releases.

86 Release, ANP, May 1964, Reel 82, #500, Part I, Series C.

87 Release, ANP, March 1956, Reel 59, #742, Part I, Series B. On the question of babies fathered in Japan by African American soldiers there, see, e.g., James McGrath Morris, *Eyes on the Struggle: Ethel Payne, the First Lady of the Black Press* (New York: HarperCollins, 2015), 64–66. Of course, white supremacists were far more upset by the fact that Negro soldiers were fathering children in Europe: see "G.I. Joe" to "My Dear Sir," circa 1940s, Box 1067, Bilbo Papers. The correspondent attached a clipping detailing "babies fathered by Negro troops," a reality that tended to "arouse the British." The note added, "watch your blood pressure" when contemplating this. One U.S. national was disgusted to find that "our Negro soldiers are passing themselves off to English and Australian girls as North American Indians and being intimate with them" in a "disgraceful" display: C. Dale Campo to Senator Bilbo, 12 January 1945, Box 1067, Bilbo Papers.

88 Robert L. Bennett to "Dear Folks," 6 January 1946, Robert L. Bennett Letters.

89 "Immigration and Nationality Act, October 3, 1965," in Odo, *The Columbia Documentary History*, 350–54. As Tokyo-Washington relations deteriorated, African Americans were not left unaffected. Thus, by 1991 as a kind of "Ja-panic" de-scended in the United States amidst news items about this Asian nation surpass-

ing the North American behemoth economically, the NAACP chapter in Silver
Spring, Maryland, sought to organize a protest at the Japanese embassy. Branch
leader Leroy W. Warren Jr. charged that "Japanese entities practice unfair trading
and locate their plants away from locations with a substantial number of people
of color." See Leroy W. Warren Jr. to Dr. William F. Gibson, Chair of NAACP
Board of Directors, 6 January 1991, Box 6, Folder 9, Kelly M. Alexander, Jr. Papers,
University of North Carolina, Charlotte. For sixty days the NAACP maintained an
"informational picket line at the Embassy of Japan in Washington, D.C.," in light
of the foregoing charge and a controversy involving "a series of racial insults from
high-ranking Japanese officials." See Benjamin L. Hooks to NAACP Board, 12
February 1991, Box 6, Folder 9, Kelly M. Alexander, Jr. Papers. African Americans' relations with the former whipping boy that was China also fluctuated as
Washington's foreign policy evolved. During the 1975 crisis over the U.S. role in
seeking to circumvent independence for Angola, a number of African Americans
sided with their homeland—and apartheid South Africa—since Maoist China was
their new beacon and the United States opposed the triumphant African faction
because it was supported by Beijing's (and Washington's and Pretoria's) antagonist
in Moscow. See, e.g., *The Facts on Angola* (New York: National Anti-Imperialist
Movement in Solidarity with African Liberation, 1976), Schomburg Center, New
York Public Library. This publication was produced by the author of this book.
However, by the early twenty-first century, as China's economic growth made
headlines, China was being referred to routinely by many African Americans as
the "new colonialist" in Africa. See, e.g., Howard French, *China's Second Continent: How a Million Migrants Are Building a New Empire in Africa* (New York:
Knopf, 2014). The alert reader would not be mistaken in drawing the inference
that a by-product of the kind of citizenship bestowed upon African Americans
in recent decades has been a closer identification of this oft besieged group with
Washington—and opposition to its antagonist du jour. I do not think this trend
will end well. See, e.g., Philip S. Golub, *East Asia's Reemergence* (Malden, MA: Pol-
ity, 2016).

90 Horne, *Fighting in Paradise.*
91 Release, ANP, April 1949, Reel 40, #411, Part I, Series B.
92 Release, ANP, August 1960, Reel 71, #225, Part I, Series C.
93 Peggy Noonan, "A Flawed Report's Important Lessons," *Wall Street Journal*, 12
December 2014.
94 See, e.g., Horne, *Blows against the Empire.* As suggested in this earlier book, I
believe that even if Washington is able to impose upon China the fate endured
by the Soviet Union—ouster of Communists from power accompanied by
destabilization—this could only be done by boosting Tokyo and New Delhi in order to encircle Beijing, guaranteeing that Japan and India, whose ties stretch back
to the founding of Buddhism 2,500 years ago, would emerge as a future duopoly,
to the detriment of the United States.
95 Hugh H. Smythe, "A Note on Racialism in Japan," 823.

96 Smythe and Smythe, "Report from Japan," 161. See also Van Vleet, "Once a Jap, Always a Jap." In this presumed conversation with a Japanese patriot before August 1945, the author claims that his interlocutor said, "Some day" after the war, "mebbe fifty year, mebbe one hundred year—Japanese kill all white man. Then Japanese Emperor make white woman marry Japanese man, make white woman have big family. . . . Japan help Germany lick the United States and then Japan probably hafta lick Germany." Cf. Joanne Miyang Cho, Lee M. Roberts, and Christian W. Spang, eds., *Transnational Encounters between Germany and Japan: Perceptions of Partnership in the Nineteenth and Twentieth Centuries* (New York: Palgrave, 2016).

INDEX

Abyssinia. *See* Ethiopia
Abyssinians, 41–42
Adams, Sherman, 145–46
Addis Ababa, Ethiopia, 41–56, 68
Africa, 29–30, 47, 74–75, 79, 147, 157; China as new colonialist in, 211n89; Great Britain in, 42–43, 55; Moscow assuming moral leadership in, 72; repatriation to, 19–22, 152–53, 172n49; white supremacy strengthened by, 92
African Americans. *See specific topics*
Africans, 6–7, 8, 18–19, 26, 91, 111; Asians conflated with, 30; Asiatic Black Man produced by, 30; Euro-Americans subjugating, 25
Afro-America, 126–27
Afro-Asian solidarity. *See specific topics*
Alabama, 14, 27, 43, 118, 137, 138–39; Tuskegee in, 143
Alejandrino, Jose, 28, 36
Alexander, Raymond Pace, 164–65
Alexandria, Louisiana, 127–29
Ali, Duse Mohammed, 46–47
Allah Temple of Islam, 12, 13, 49–50, 84
American Indians. *See* Native Americans
Americans. *See* Euro-Americans
American South. *See* Southern U.S.
Anglo-American-centered peace, 38–49
ANP. *See* Associated Negro Press
anti-Tokyo movement, 31–32
antiwar activists, 14–15
apartheid, 119–20, 151, 156–57, 159
Arizona, 73, 126–27, 129

Arkansas, 3, 9, 40, 62–63, 133
Army, U.S., 79, 83, 130, 135, 159, 198n60; Air Corps, 118, 136–41; Air Force, 143; Temple of Islam member joining, 102–3; War College, 131
Ashe, Charles, 99, 100
Asia, 9, 42, 47, 72, 75, 165; British in, 6–7, 55, 182n41; White, Walter, in, 157–58; white domination in, 51, 74; WWII in, 172n54
Asians, 9, 26, 29–30, 46, 73–74, 164–65; bias against, 39; California dominated by, 44; labor, 32; racial polarization influencing, 45; Tokyo toughening, 51; as white, 152. *See also* Asiatics; Filipinos; Japanese
Asia-Pacific region, 1, 30, 90–91. *See also* Pacific War
Asiatic Black Man, 36, 81, 84, 94, 102, 147; Africans producing, 30; Asians producing, 30; NOI popularizing, 48–50
Asiatics, 5–6, 9, 17, 18–19, 35, 58; Black Nationalists as, 94, 147; as citizens, 100; Japanese fighting for, 106; race, 49–50
Associated Negro Press (ANP), 55, 72, 74, 85–86, 90–91, 120; in France, 142–43; on Japanese, 160; overview of, 170n28; on pilots, 136; on Selfridge Field, 140; Tokyo striking, 151. *See also* Barnett, Claude A.
Australia, 38, 134–35, 156, 159
Axis propaganda, 122–23

Miller, Henry, 141–42

Mississippi, 3, 8, 9–10, 23, 53, 130; Centerville in, 106–7, 198n60; congressman of, 76; PMEW membership of, 63; senator from, 162. *See also* Bilbo, Theodore; Jackson, Mississippi

Mississippi River, 9–10, 92–93, 95, 109

Missouri, 3, 62, 98, 99–100, 131–32; Sikeston in, 112–13. *See also* St. Louis, Missouri

Mohammed, Elijah, 49, 105–6

Monrovia, Liberia, 67–68

Moore, Arthur J., 71–72

Moorish Science Temple (MST), 12, 78, 79, 81–83, 86, 97; FBI on, 106; NOI compared with, 149

Moors, 2, 81

Moros, 29, 51

Moscow, Russia, 14, 21, 22, 47, 128, 156; alliance with, 104–5; atom bomb acquired by, 144–45; Cold War with, 149; Tokyo clashing with, 72, 149; white supremacy threatened by, 145

Moses, 42, 102

Moten, Etta, 124–25

Mounds, Illinois, 109–11, 115

MST. *See* Moorish Science Temple

Muhammad, Elijah, 102, 105, 147, 148

Muslims, 3, 15, 48–50, 80, 85, 95. *See also* Nation of Islam

NAACP. *See* National Association for the Advancement of Colored People

Nagasaki, Japan, 14, 46, 144–45, 149–50

National Association for the Advancement of Colored People (NAACP), 1–2, 15, 16, 74, 105, 211n89; in Alabama, 118, 137; Boraster information of, 95; Chicago told about to, 107; Halsey berated by, 90; internment influencing, 122–23, 125; on Korea, 158; propaganda, 152–53; segregation protested by, 137; Smythe, H., reporting to, 160. *See also* Pickens, William; White, Walter

National Urban League, 9, 137, 156

Nation of Islam (NOI), 14, 48–50, 81, 84, 94, 105–6; Malcolm X's importance to, 149; MST compared with, 149; Oliver on, 147; overview of, 147–48; whites focused on by, 148. *See also* Malcolm X

Native Americans, 12, 26, 32, 35, 130

Navy, U.S., 117, 130, 189n24

Nazis, 9, 17–18, 90, 119, 178n121, 203n14

Nazism, 89–90

Negro Question, 91, 107

Newby, Charles, 103–4, 106

New Delhi, India, 146, 156–57, 212n94

New Orleans, Louisiana, 3, 6, 95, 98

New York, 20, 52, 85

New York City, New York, 1, 2–3, 19, 20, 53, 55; Bilbo speaking in, 67; De Guzman working in, 58; EPM detained in, 95–97. *See also* Harlem

Nicaraguan bandits, 50–51

NOI. *See* Nation of Islam

non-Europeans, 7, 156–57

North America, 15, 17, 29

North Carolina, 16, 19, 54, 73, 75, 149

North Korea, 158–59

Officer, William, 65–66

Ohio, 119–20; Cleveland in, 16, 19–20, 36, 86

Oliver, Revilo, 49, 147

Pacific Movement of the Eastern World (PMEW), 12–16, 83, 84, 97–99, 112; Blanton on, 113; fire responsibility of, 117; Garvey reminiscence of, 100; military of, 108–11; trial of, 113–19; in *U.S. v. Pacific Movement of the Eastern World*, 7, 57–66

"Pacific Problem," 5

Pacific War, 8–10, 14–23, 100, 120–22; brown Americans fighting, 130–46;

brown Japanese fighting, 130–46; colored races benefiting from, 103–7, 111;
overview of, 130–46; PMEW looking
askance at, 112; racial policies influenced by, 148–57; Washington, D.C.'s,
attention on, 150; white supremacists
seeing, 91–93
Palestine, 19, 67
Pan-Asianism, 27, 32, 45, 48
Paris, France, 72, 90, 127
Peace Movement of Ethiopia (PME), 76–
80, 97, 100, 101–2, 172n49, 177n100. *See
also* Gordon, Mittie Maude Lena
Pearl Harbor, Hawaii, 2–3, 90, 107, 108,
164, 199n7
Pennsylvania, 25, 29
Philippines, 10, 27–29, 32, 35, 51, 131–32;
Euro-Americans ousted from, 75; hys-
teria in, 157; Japanese dominating in,
44, 203n10; Manila in, 155–56, 203n10;
Pan-Oriental Society formed in, 36;
Wade in, 107; Washington, D.C., col-
laborated against by, 155–56, 157; White
visiting, 90
Pickens, William, 11, 19, 50–51, 53–54,
61, 98; Du Bois echoing, 69; on
Ethiopians, 76; Tobias and, 71; Tokyo
defended by, 72
Pitchfork. *See* Tillman, Ben
PME. *See* Peace Movement of Ethiopia
PMEW. *See* Pacific Movement of the
Eastern World
Poole, Elijah, 49, 105–6
Powell, Adam Clayton, Jr., 15, 122, 161, 163
pro-Moscow Negroes, 72–73, 148, 149
pro-Tokyo Negroes: Cairo, Illinois, as
bastion of, 7, 98, 99–100, 106, 117, 138;
conviction of, 94–111; Eads Bridge
blown up by, 8, 109, 112, 114; Hancock
on, 94–95; imprisonment of, 94–111;
Jordan as leader of, 13, 15, 84, 85, 96;
Officer collaborating with, 66; over-
view of, 1–23; PME as, 76–80, 97, 100,

101–2, 172n49, 177n100; pro-Moscow
Negroes excoriating, 148; Sampson
aiding, 158. *See also* East St. Louis,
Illinois; Gordon, Mittie Maude Lena;
Moorish Science Temple
Prudence Crandall Association, 33–34

Randolph, A. Philip, 78, 160–61
Reddick, L. D., 55, 130–31
Ressoull, Mohammed. *See* Mohammed,
Elijah
Rising Sun, 16, 22
Robb, Frederick Harold, 105, 197n49
Robeson, Paul, 69, 147, 149, 150, 151, 156
Rome, Italy, 14, 73
Roosevelt, Franklin Delano, 72, 88, 136
Russia, 4, 30–31, 32, 45, 58, 119; Commu-
nistic ideology of, 145; Du Bois on,
191n50; Indian youth in, 157

Sampson, Edith, 105, 158, 198n51
San Angelo, Texas, 137–38
San Antonio, Texas, 33, 122
San Diego, California, 34–35, 124
San Francisco, California, 31–32, 35, 58,
65, 84, 88; Japanese in, 161–62; Peace
Conference, 160
Satokata Takahashi, 16, 50, 81–82, 86
Schuyler, George, 69, 123, 144
Scottsboro case, 58, 147–48
Seattle, Washington, 33, 34, 87, 101
Selective Service, 1, 168n14
Selfridge Field, 140–41
Shanghai, China, 43, 51, 71
Shantung, China, 42–43
Sherrod, Pearl, 13, 50
Shimjiro Akimota, 67–68
Sikeston, Missouri, 99–100, 112–13
Singapore, 5–7, 93, 96, 108, 119, 143
Smith, Theodore, 176n90
Smuts, Jan, 7, 91, 119–20
Smythe, Hugh, 160–61, 165
Smythe, Mabel Murphy, 160, 165

ABOUT THE AUTHOR

Gerald Horne is Moores Professor of History and African American Studies at the University of Houston and has published three dozen books, including *The Counter-Revolution of 1776: Slave Resistance and the Origins of the United States of America* and *Race War! White Supremacy and the Japanese Attack on the British Empire.*